HERE BE YAKS

Travels in Far West Tibet

INDIA

Ali

Indus

Gar

Gartok

Glungg

I
N
D
I
A

Shipki La

Sutlej

F A R   W E

Tsaparang

Toling

Sutlej

G U G E

Kamet

Kyunglung

Gya

*Kailash
Kora*

Dhiraphuk

Lba cbu

Mount Kailash

Drolma La

Nandi

*Gouri
kund*

Selung cbu

Chuku

Dzong cbu

Tarpoche

sky burial site

Selung

Zutrulphuk

Darchen

Darbenbu

Barkha

*The
Old Tasam Highway
through
FAR WEST TIBET*

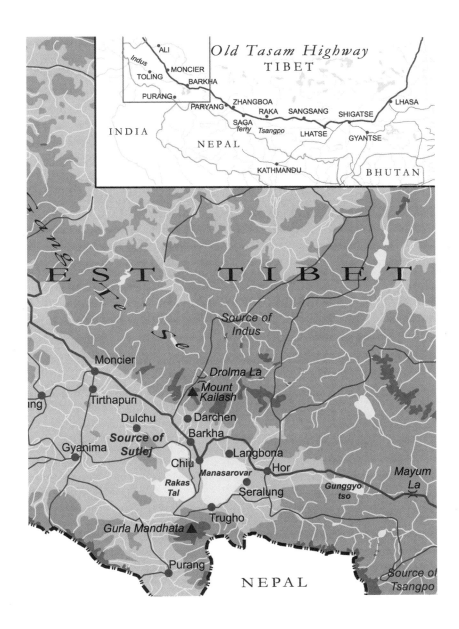

HERE BE YAKS

Travels in Far West Tibet

MANOSI LAHIRI

With a Foreword by
HIS HOLINESS THE DALAI LAMA

First U.S. Edition

Here Be Yaks
Travels in Far West Tibet

Published by
The Intrepid Traveler
P.O. Box 531
Branford, CT 06405
http://www.intrepidtraveler.com

Copyright ©2006, 2007 Stellar Publishers Pvt Ltd.
Originally published in India by Jyoti Sabharwal for Stellar Publishers 2006

First American edition published in 2007 by The Intrepid Traveler
Printed in the U.S.A.
Cover design by Foster & Foster
Interior design by The Intrepid Traveler and Anvi Composers

ISBN: 978-1-887140-72-0
Library of Congress Control Number: 2006939942

Credits: Photographs in this book are from the author's collection. Satellite map on page 235 courtesy of the Indian Space Research Organisation, reproduced with permission. Back cover photo: author. All rights reserved.

10   9   8   7   6   5   4   3   2   1

In early times, when there were vast expanses left unexplored, cartographers marked uncharted lands and seas with the words, *Here Be Dragons.* This was a warning to travellers of the potential dangers.

This book is dedicated to all those who have travelled with me to places which even today could be labelled on maps, *Here Be Dragons.*

CONTENTS

ACKNOWLEDGEMENTS

- All my fellow travellers to Far West Tibet, those who completed the journey and those who attempted it, I thank them for making a dream come true. There were those who did not accompany us, but took care of home and hearth while we were away. But for them, we would not have left for Tibet. And, of course, the silent support of my daughters Pia and Radha travelled with me all along.

- I appreciate the generosity of my companions on this journey in sharing their photographs for all to see and include in this book.

- The Indian Space Research Organisation provided the satellite image that was the key to solving the Sutlej conundrum. Were it not for this image, the world would not know where the source of the Sutlej is today.

- My special thanks to Jyoti Sabharwal, Editorial Director of Stellar Publishers, New Delhi, India, for making this book possible.

THE DALAI LAMA

Mount Kailash has been the focus of inspiring pilgrimage for longer than historical memory. For Tibetans, it was sacred long ago to the Bönpos, practitioners of the indigenous pre-Buddhist religion of Tibet. For Buddhists, it is associated with great practitioners like the famous yogi and poet Milarepa and is regarded as one of the sacred locations of the meditational deity Heruka. For Hindus, it is the abode of the deities Shiva and Parvati, while Jains and Sikhs have their own special associations with it. Besides this, even for those without a specific faith, the mountain's physical form and colour make it a natural symbol of purity. Pilgrims approach it with faith hoping to create virtue and spiritual merit.

In this book, Dr. Manosi Lahiri recounts her and her companions' experiences when they too journeyed to Kailash and performed the sacred *parikrama*, circumambulation of the mountain and Lake Manasarovar nearby, much as pilgrims before them have been doing down the centuries. In addition, the group went on to explore the remains of the ancient Kingdom of Guge in western Tibet, a region crucial to the second propagation of Buddhism in the Land of Snow that took place just a thousand years ago.

Visitors to this remote and challenging part of the world are invariably filled with awe and respect, perhaps because pilgrimage through wild, open lands often provides visions that help shape the proper attitude and inner awareness for spiritual practice. It remains one of my cherished aspirations that such respect be restored to the whole of Tibet, that it becomes a sanctuary, a zone of peace, a place of harmony between people, animals and the environment. Visitors from all over the world could then come to Tibet, as Dr. Lahiri and her friends have done, to share that experience of peace and harmony, which derives in large part from the special and unique character of Tibet's environment.

His Holiness The Dalai Lama

PREFACE: WANDERLUST

Tibet was on my mind. It was an escape to a haven evoked by an indistinct mental image of a faraway hidden land. In my own study, an antique map, frayed at the edges, embossed with strong black Pali characters and framed in a gold border of great artistry, caught my attention. My right forefinger and eyes followed a line across the lower edge of the map to rest at Lhasa, and then moved to Shigatse. The Tasam Highway, running across Tibet, was either lost in the fading colours on the parchment or was never recorded on it. Nondescript shapes in the west marked what I assumed were the twin lakes of Manasarovar and Rakas Tal. Immediately to their north was marked a little inverted V, annotated Kang Rinpoche, with clouds floating around it. I assumed this to be the fabled Mount Kailash, the centre of the Universe. Those were the pools of water and that was the mountain that I planned to visit.

Conveniently dispensing with reason, my mind's eye saw the most ethereal mountain reflected on the sheets of water at its foot. It was an image made even more alluring by references to blue lotuses in the poems of Kalidasa in *Meghdoot*, The Cloud Messenger. That was the picture of beauty and peace that I longed to savour and be a part of, far away from the oppressive reality of my world. A world where I was uncertain of my place, and where everything that I had known for sure, suddenly seemed questionable. My natural response to my circumstances was to undertake a long journey, to flee from what was familiar. For what did Tao say about journeys? That the journey is the reward. And my reward on this journey would be to regain happiness and peace of mind. A journey merits a destination; and mine would be Far West Tibet.

Remote places, and more specifically, landscapes, far from the crowded thoroughfares of modern civilization, hold great attraction for me. As a child, I had developed a deep love for atlases and books about nations. The pride of place on my bookshelf was given to the seven volumes of *Lands and Peoples*. For years, I referred to these volumes as the ultimate, undisputed fountainhead of data on all places on earth and communities that live on it.

As a family, we travelled the length and breadth of the country, wet our feet in sea foam along the shore, climbed mountains and went deep into mica quarries and coal mines. The love of adventure and the seed of inquiry into our world were sown well and early in my life. Many years ago, in school, I had been fascinated by the description of the high plains. I recall my geography teacher explain the difference between plains that were near sea level and the high plains far above sea level. The highest of them all was Tibet, the Roof of the World, the Land of Snow. And not only was it the highest plateau, it was also isolated and hidden from the rest of the world by the still higher Himalayas in the south and the most barren deserts imaginable in the north. That was the precise moment when I first thought of Tibet as a real place to visit, a possible destination for a later journey. I had not yet heard of Mount Kailash, and the lakes, Manasarovar and Rakas Tal. But whatever I gathered from my teacher's lessons, I knew that this land would offer a very different experience from my visits to hill stations in India.

My earliest introduction to Tibet had been via yaks and yeti, *momos* and opera. As children, it was the land of the lugubrious yak and the mysterious, obscure yeti that held our interest. We had heard tales about the shaggy large animals. But it was the yeti that tickled our imagination. It was the unfathomable creature of the snow with large feet, which appeared at night and searched for people to cuddle when it got lonely. So you had to look for it on moonlit nights and one could sometimes see its footprints on the snow in the early morning. These harmless tales had long outlived their purpose of captivating young minds, but my interest in the land of snow and yak remained. It was the remoteness and the altitude that now enticed me.

I have a faint recollection of once watching *lhamo*, a Tibetan folk opera, during my childhood in the 1960s in Calcutta. I cannot recall the story but I remember the impressive masks and many foot-long trumpets. There was colour and romance, war and dance. But today I can mostly remember the music. Every so often the cymbals would clang and the dancers in weighty garments and evocative headdresses, reminiscent of the Kathakali dancers of Kerala, would twirl and move around in circles. It was, all in all, the ultimate exotica, that left you yearning to see more. Recently, on a visit to the Nobrulingka Institute in Lower Dharamsala, Himachal Pradesh, I visited the Losel Dolls Museum. There I saw several well-designed tableaux, in which the dolls seemed to be replicas of the characters in the opera that I had seen as a child.

All through my years in school, my family travelled over the vast expanse of our country. Amongst my earliest memories is that of a journey by train for three days without break. Steam engines dragged along passenger and luggage compartments on parallel bars. The train swayed from side to side and we, the passengers, swayed in tandem. As the train sped through the countryside, I watched with consummate interest the telegraph wires apparently rise and fall. Sometimes the smoke blew in and bits of soot and coal dust went into our eyes. The crunching, thudding, rhythmic sound that the wheels made on the ground changed when it moved over bridges and culverts. So even in the middle of the night, when everyone was asleep and the only light came from a blue night bulb, I knew instinctively when we crossed over rivers. I shut my eyes tight hoping that the bridge below the train would not collapse. When the train went up inclines, it slowed down considerably and when it made unscheduled stops in the country, which was often, the labourers working on the tracks would wave out. At the railway stations, the tea vendors shouted *'chai, cha garam.'*

Everywhere we went, we met fellow Bengalis. The Bengalis are inveterate and the most ubiquitous of travellers. They can be spotted in groups in all tourist destinations in India. The adventurous Bengali favours the hill stations, where he is parodied sporting a 'monkey cap' (a balaclava) and shivering, though well clad. Scenic mountain views are said to remind the sensitive Bengali of Darjeeling and Kalimpong and the poems and music of their great litterateurs.

It was a matter of great sorrow to my mother that we never visited her home in 'East Bengal', as she referred to it, and all others 'East Pakistan'. A refugee in her teens, she had been sent in 1947 to India, to safety and ultimately marriage. She missed her home and parents painfully, but like many others, never had the opportunity to return to her native land. She spoke of the swollen rivers that overflowed their banks every monsoon and of the currents that carried enormous round leaves and flowers of the lotus into their garden. Mother said that this happened every year. She spoke of ponds that were covered with lotus in shades of pink and mauve. When I first heard the all-pervasive Tibetan mani mantra, *Om mani padme hum*, I literally imagined a sparkling brilliant crystal in a half-open lotus flower with dark pinkish-mauve petals that was borne on the crest of a flood wave.

My father was the greatest raconteur that I have ever met. He painted vivid images of foreign lands, people and customs. It was my father's unwritten travelogues that sowed the first seeds of my passion for long journeys. Early in life I began craving to see those places and meet those imagined people he spoke of. They were a varied lot: near-naked Naga warriors with their spears decorated in feathers, Tibetan lamas in flowing red garb, blowing into horns made of human bones, and the 'ching-chong' Chinamen in cone-shaped hats. But the most fascinating of them all were the little blue-eyed English cherubs, who lived in the bamboo forest near his home in Patna and followed him as he cycled to school. As no one else could see them, they played pranks on everyone around. His stories made us want to do heroic things, like he did along with his brothers. They were a family of men who played games, rode horses, fenced and practiced gymnastics. They loved adventure and were not shy of helping others in time of need. I heard stories of the Bihar earthquake of 1934, when they rescued a child from under a collapsed wall. But that was decades ago . . .

Father also wove stories around the most mundane events and transformed them into unprecedented adventures and the most nail-biting suspense. He loved children and they adored him, the magician who delivered fantasy. Old and young would gather around him to hear tales of atom bombs bursting and B-52s zooming into the sky from

Kalaikunda military air base to bomb the Japanese during the Second World War. We never really knew where reality ended and the story began, and we did not care then, for good always triumphed over evil. It was not till after he died that several of those who had listened to him enthralled as wide-eyed children, wondered if there could have been many truths hidden in his tales.

Being in the British Indian Army, in his youth, my father had journeyed over great distances. He had told us of the mosquito-infested Singapore island of 1942. Three days after his arrival, the Japanese bombed it. He was evacuated like the others. But that was only the beginning of their troubles. After reaching the mainland, they walked through the rainforests. The jungle was thick and poisonous fruit and snakes hung from the branches of the trees and tigers' eyes shone through the thickets of bamboo. Many men got sick and died, while some fell prey to the poison arrows of cannibals.

After several weeks of search by his family, my father was given up as lost and dead. His parents forgot him. (Here we wondered at their short memory.) Until one day, many months later, he reached India. I think he kept changing the place of his arrival in India in the interest of variety, but often it was Kohima. When he was strong enough to travel again, he went home. But the *durban* would not let him enter, for the Rai Bahadur, his father, would not meet a vagabond in rags. But my father insisted on meeting the lady of the house, who was inspecting the plants in the garden. That was his mother, but she did not recognise him either. As the altercation between my father and the *durban* became louder, his brother's wife recognised his voice and rushed out to welcome him home. The dead son had come alive.

But now to return to the early days of our interest in a journey to Tibet. The year was 1999. One day, Ray, a friend of many years, expressed a tentative, casual desire to travel to Mongolia. I expressed my longtime interest in the Roof of the World. But the obvious problem was to gather a group of people who would be interested in travelling with us. It would also take several days to reach Mongolia or Tibet, my friends pointed out. 'Experience of a journey is as important as reaching the destination,' I reminded my friends. 'In this case, it's long journeys and unknown destinations!' they countered. All along, similar lighthearted banter led to no conclusive prospects of a journey, but at the back of my mind was the idea that I would one day reach the high plateau. Deep inside me was wanderlust. I grew up knowing that if I were born in another day and age, I would have been a travelling mendicant, or perhaps a wanderer or an explorer.

But often at night I was faced with unhappy thoughts of my recent bereavement and, during the day, was busy making practical adjustments to life without my partner. Sometimes, in my despair, I wanted to simply run away from this place that replayed the past and tried to shut it off behind my closed eyes. Occasionally, I consulted my frayed evocative map of Tibet and wistfully blew the dust that had settled on it. Somehow, life's inconsequential events warranted more attention and time than did a plan to scale the heights of Far West Tibet along the Tasam Highway.

It was a year later that we talked of the possibility of going on an expedition to Tibet, specifically, Lake Manasarovar and Mount Kailash. That would take the spiritually inclined amongst us to Heaven's Door and I would have my few weeks on the Roof of the World, breathe in clean fresh air and marvel at mountains. And who could tell, perhaps reaching the mystical lake and mountain would rid my mind of negative thoughts and awaken the positive vibrations within.

I did not seriously think that it would actually happen, but I encouraged Ray to start working on the blueprint. He was single-minded in his pursuit and calculated the expected level of expense to be incurred. He shared the plan with several others, many of whom evinced interest but were reluctant to take the final plunge. A few surmised it would turn out to be an adventurous holiday. But Ray discouraged them, saying it needed complete awareness and appreciation of the fact that there would be adversities. Being mentally prepared for a tough call was not only essential, but a primary requisite was to have a strong nerve. Ray took on the onus of connecting with travel agents and meticulously reviewed profiles of people to be invited to join the expedition. He read about High Altitude Sickness (HAS), made lists of medicines and other supplies to be carried through the sojourn.

HAS became the leitmotif of our mission to Tibet. On one occasion, I asked Ray how would I know that I had HAS. He instantly answered, 'Breathing would become laboured.' Later, he sent me a series of emails stating I could feel disoriented, or suffer from lack of sleep or lose appetite. He also informed duly that he had read one could have headaches and, for that matter, even hallucinations were known to occur at high altitude. And the final ominous warning was that one could be constipated if assailed by HAS. Well, I thought, that certainly was a strange disorder, with such a wide spectrum of non-specific symptoms.

We learnt that HAS could affect anyone, at any time, at so high an altitude. Some are affected at lower altitude than the rest, while others could be affected on one trip but not another, and the same person could show different symptoms at different times. There was no certified, foolproof method of combating HAS, though, for an affected person, the responses were sure: relief lay in moving to lower altitude and death awaited at higher elevation.

One day, while Ray was busy making arrangements for this exciting trip, on an impulse, I drove along the Ring Road that encloses inner Delhi and leads to the Tibetan refugee settlement by the banks of the Yamuna. I had visited this place several years ago as a student, while still at Delhi University. This little cluster of huts had been my first introduction to Tibetans. And now a modern several-lane flyover passed by the settlement and the arched entrance that could once be seen from the road was hidden away by the network of pavements. I could imagine that the *momos* and *chhang* that we eagerly sought then would still be as delicious, but I did not venture further after I overshot the access, while rush hour traffic built up.

Many young Tibetans who were born and raised here were perhaps as unfamiliar with Tibet as I was. But all along they have stayed closely associated with the Tibetan way of life. This fleeting thought warmed my heart, for it was the preservation of their culture and religion, and the right to live their own way, that led the refugees to seek shelter in India.

To begin with, my interest in Tibet had little to do with either Buddhism or the Chinese occupation. I had travelled to some of Buddhism's most sacred places, Sanchi, Nalanda and Bodh Gaya some twenty years back and was struck by the fact that except for the monuments, there was little that was Buddhist in practice in those places. Incidentally, in 1999, I accompanied my friends to hear His Holiness the Dalai Lama, address a gathering of about three hundred people at the India International Centre in Delhi. This was ten years after he had been conferred the Nobel Peace Prize. It was not so much what he said but the aura of serenity and peace he emanated that impressed me. Here was a king sans any crown or kingdom and yet he had followers all over the world. I was really moved to see his disciples wait patiently for long hours to seek his blessings.

For the first time, I wondered if this moot quality of compassion that defines Buddhism could possibly be found in Tibet today, although their religious leader was far away in a foreign land. After all, they had imbibed a religious ethos for so many centuries. It could not possibly be that every vestige of their cultural identity had been erased in half a century, notwithstanding such strident suppression of the same. Given the militancy of the occupation forces from May 1951 onwards, enforcing Communist ideology on Buddhist minds, I was interested to know how much had changed. After several decades of restrictions on foreigners travelling to the Tibet Autonomous Region, the Chinese government had relented somewhat, giving group visas to tourists. It was time to plan a visit and explore the fascinating region that had not ceased to enchant me.

In my earnest endeavour to brush up my reading on Buddhism, I found most of the literature was aimed at those who had a certain level of awareness about the religion and the many associated deities and teachers. All this was well above my level of knowledge. As I persisted with my efforts, I stumbled upon a short note written by His Holiness the Fourteenth Dalai Lama. It was the simplest, most lucid explanation on Buddhism, and just adequate for my understanding. I was indeed surprised to note the parallels between Hindu and Buddhist philosophies and was fairly impressed by the rational focus. Paradoxically, I was equally attracted by the complex litany of rituals, ancient chants and artifacts used for prayer services in both the religions.

I was particularly interested in His view that to achieve the state of a concentrated mind, which is free from even subtle mental agitation, we must first gain control over our activities of body and speech. When body and speech are controlled, the higher faculties of mind could easily be cultivated. The purpose of training to achieve this ability (to abide effortlessly on an object of meditation for as long as one desires), was to gain mental stability and thus generate a more effective mind. The idea appealed to me; a technique I could follow to bring peace to my then turbulent mind and grieving heart.

We were now well geared and prepared for our first-ever journey to Tibet, to appease our wanderlust and undertake the ultimate of pilgrimages to Lake Manasarovar (Mapam Tso) and Mount Kailash (Kang Rinpoche). In the final count, we were a group of five. The only one among us who could claim respectable knowledge of trekking at high altitude was Ayone. Years earlier, I had done my share of scrambling up the slopes of the Jutogh Hills, for there was no other way to reach home. Home was at about 5,000 feet, on a hill slope that was a meadow of cosmos swaying and heaving to gusts of breeze in October and motionless dry grass the rest of the year. Anita had been to school in Shimla, a hill station, so she had some practical experience of walking on high heels on valley slopes and ridge tops. Medha and Ray had all the right gear, but were novices to the mountains. For most of us travelling to Tibet that year was our opportunity to do or die. Baffled, a friend asked, 'Why? For what?' The rationalist would rightly say, 'For the couch potatoes to stir and plod around a high mountain.' My friend prophesied, 'It would certainly be the most uncomfortable holiday ever.'

In the months leading up to the journey, we met several times and discussed one another's state of preparedness. Other concerned friends created unexpected psychological pressure. In general conversation, they would often enquire, 'Would it be safe?' My extended family was worried, 'Who would take care of the children should something happen to you?' We learned over time to manage our own and others' anxieties, many of which were well founded.

It seemed like everyone, except I, was well-equipped with suitable clothes and boots. Some had even read books as esoteric as *The Way of the White Clouds* by Lama Govinda. Ray had himself outfitted in Germany, while Anita and Medha went to the same fashionable travel store in New York. Ayone had his kit from the past, including the sure mark of a pro: beeswax. In the end, the thick pair of tracksuits and a down jacket borrowed from my daughter seemed to suffice for me to be attired in the fashion of a backpacking tourist. A pair of comfortable waterproof boots were bought, but when it came to the test, they failed miserably in protecting my feet from being wet. What was widely known, but not bargained for, was the high level of ultraviolet (UV) that filters through the clear thin atmosphere at high altitude, and their disastrous effect on the eyes.

I also read *India and Tibet*, a captivating account of Francis Young-husband's military expedition to Tibet in 1904, including the siege of Gyantse. But my daughters pointed out that a century had passed since and reading a guidebook would have better prepared me for the journey. With hindsight, I think a contemporary view, as in Dawa Norbu's *Tibet: The Road Ahead*, would have prepared us well to understand the existing realities of the country.

Of that first sojourn to Tibet, I won't say much here, except that it left a deep impression on my mind. Tibet offers a romantic dip into history and an incomparable space in geography. My enduring image of Tibet is that of a vast land of extremes. Tibet is a land of extreme height, extreme expanse, extreme climate and extreme isolation. The journey was hard and at times perilous, but ultimately fulfilling and gratifying. Since my reading and research on Tibet before embarking on that journey was inadequate, surprises aplenty were in store and many an unexpected situation was encountered.

While in Tibet, I noticed that each of my friends had a special interest. It seemed to me that Ayone knew all about the early travellers to Tibet. He spoke with equal eloquence about the Russian Prejalvsky, who climbed up from the north, and the Indian *pandits* who slipped in from the south. Ray was well-versed with the works of the Italian writer Guiseppe Tucci and the history of Sino-Tibetan relations. Anita spoke of the environmental aspects of Chang Tung and the human rights abuses in the country, while Medha was our authority on Tibetan Buddhism and culture. I was the one who knew but little about the country's rich and varied past and present, and keenly observed the landscape, which honed my instinct for serendipity. In the end, each of us agreed that the journey was a test of mental strength and physical stamina. And in most ways, the dangers associated with trekking were very different from those in many other remote places. There were no criminals to guard against, infectious diseases to protect oneself from or heavy backpacks to carry. We found our greatest challenge was to survive at high altitude.

During the sojourn, a cursory scan of a map picked up from the Thamel shopping district of Kathmandu showed the two high-altitude lakes: Manasarovar and Rakas Tal. It was perplexing to see the words, Lanchen Khambab, written at two different places. These words translate into 'the river from the elephant's head,' or, the source of the Elephant River. This refers to the Sutlej, one of the four great rivers that have their origin in the region near Mount Kailash and the two large freshwater lakes. This was intriguing, because on the west, the map noted Source of the Sutlej and on the east, approximately fifty kilometres away, it read Alternate Source of the Sutlej. For the other three rivers, Tsangpo (Brahmaputra), Indus and Karnali, with their source in the same general area, one definite origin for each was recorded on the map.

'See the alternate sources of the Sutlej marked on the map? Is this perhaps a misprint?' I asked aloud.

'Not quite', said a knowledgeable companion, bending over my shoulder and pointing to the map. 'That one's a traditional source, and the other's a scientific source.'

'But which is the principal source? How come the RGS could not decide on this one? After all, the RGS took great pains to pronounce its verdict on sources of Asian rivers in the last two centuries'. The Royal Geographic Society was very active in matters geographica, as we all knew. It had observed that the legendary explorer Sven Hedin's contribution was in 'determining' and not 'discovering' the source of the Tsangpo-Brahmaputra.

Once my curiosity was aroused, I inquisitively examined the general topography of the area and documented my observations, which pointed to the apparent incorrectness of the supposition that the Sutlej had two sources. However, in the summer of that year, 2000, in the days spent on the shores of Mapam Tso (Manasarovar) and Rakas Tal, I was convinced that the Ganga *chu* was no longer a conduit for water flowing from the former to the latter. But, being unprepared, I was not able to collect evidence in an organised manner to support my views. But everywhere I looked, I saw that there was little to support the 'two-sources' point of view. The time had come to rethink on the matter of the two alternate sources of the Sutlej. By the time we ended our journey, the idea of solving the mystery of the alternate sources of the Sutlej had completely besotted me.

On our return from Tibet, I undertook some serious research on the alternate sources of the Sutlej. I read accounts of famous explorers, checked maps and satellite images. Several new and only partly formulated ideas on the source of the Sutlej kept me awake late into nights. My studies and earlier observations had revealed that changing morphology had affected the traditional and known headwaters of the Sutlej. With a few pieces of evidence in hand, I was trying to assemble all the pieces of the jigsaw together to make sense. But as all geographers know, there is a time when you must pack your bags and be off to the laboratory to collect empirical evidence to test ideas and theories. And so it was with me. It was time to set off once more to my laboratory: the magnificent, mysterious world of pirated streams, gurgling springs and placid lakes.

To reach this isolated and poorly connected corner of the world requires ample time and funds in equal proportion. I approached a few organisations that I believed to be interested in scientific discovery, but understandably, I failed to attract any financial or other support. The age for exploring the origin of a river is long since over. The sources of all major rivers on earth have been found and documented decades ago. After the discovery of the Tsangpo gorges and the headwaters of the Nile, it seemed like there was nothing left to discover about rivers, their courses and sources; even those hidden away in dense rain forests or a maze of high mountain ranges.

Then, a second opportunity arose to make another journey in 2002, when Ray once more organised an elaborate expedition to western Tibet to coincide with the Year of the Horse.

Tibetans have a sixty-year calendar cycle, the *Rabyung*. This sixty-year cycle is subdivided into smaller cycles of twelve years each. Each year of the twelve-year cycle is associated with an animal and the seventh year is the Year of the Horse or *Ta-lo*. Tibetans consider circling Kailash or Manasarovar during the Year of the Horse particularly meritorious.

Somewhere along the way, our group began putting much faith in this belief and every effort was made to ensure that our next visit to Tibet should coincide with the *Ta-lo* of 2002. This time, the added bonus was a tour of Chung Tung to the north of the Gang Te Se range, a land as desolate as the surface of the moon. It is the home of the wild yak, a different beast from the much smaller and tamer domesticated version that is ubiquitous in Tibet. My mind's eye conjured cinematic images of large herds roaming over the high plain, just as the wildebeest do in the African savannah. Although I had outlived my childhood fantasy of being cuddled by the yeti on a moonlit night, the heady mix of the unknown, uninhabited and possibly dangerous, was a cocktail that no self-respecting explorer could possibly resist.

With a sense of *déjà vu*, I gathered my field book and bought a smart 'point and shoot' Nikon camera to record my evidence. Into the bag went Polaroid dark glasses to ward off harsh light reflection and UV protection cream for the skin. Preparation for the expedition was largely focused on building up reserves of energy by walking several kilometres a day and taking yoga lessons from a master who made every conceivable contortion of the body appear easier than it actually was. Walking around carrying weights was the best practice, which none of us cared to do. This was so because even the basic essentials that are carried in a rucksack on a day's trek can be substantially heavier than what we normally carry for long hours at a stretch. A trekker's rucksack could include a camera, a notebook and pen, a waterproof poncho, a fleece jacket, four bottles of water, a hands-free torch, a bottle of UV cream, some strips of medicines, small packets of snacks and a can of oxygen. I made a serious effort to discipline my mind to begin thinking of heights in the metric system. For some inexplicable reason, my mind understands and responds to horizontal distances in kilometre but vertical distances in feet. In this matter, I have failed miserably in bringing consistency to bear.

I feel fortunate to have been able to undertake this journey and document the discernible natural changes taking place today in this geologically active area. I would like to believe that my finding was a 'discovery' and the journey, an 'exploration'. One night, I dreamt that I was writing a narrative of our journey to Tibet. My fountain pen leaked and large blobs of royal blue ink splattered on the page. I crumpled the sheet and dropped it on the floor. I looked up from my writing and saw Kingsley Amis, an illustrious author of yesteryears. He remarked, 'One more featureless, flavourless lump of cultural lumber.' I cringed at his words and said pompously, 'I am certain that my observations and conclusions regarding the source of the Sutlej will elicit interest among those who are fascinated by the evolving nature of our planet.' Amis smiled indulgently, and disappeared.

Yatris go to pilgrimages to fulfill spiritual needs and religious yearnings, to undertake rituals, to satisfy cravings for celestial communion. Some go to atone for sins, fulfill promises to pious parents, some to save their souls from damnation. Yet others would travel the much-trodden path to pilgrimage centres to imbibe history, art and culture. Once, a woman at a luncheon party commented facetiously, 'Some people would undertake these alternative holidays for the pleasure of recounting in drawing rooms.' This opinion perplexed me somewhat, for it was a great deal of rigour and danger to undertake for this puerile pleasure. But this remark did set my mind wondering as to what made us go to Tibet once again.

Prior to this journey, I had not met two members of our team, Rock and Mandy. Rock arrived from London, where he had lived for the past three decades working as an IT professional. Apparently, he had lived a life of excess and now felt the need for some restraint. He revealed, 'I am looking for spiritual upliftment . . . No, not revelations.' He expected, after reading Robert Thurman's book, *Circling the Sacred Mountain*, that travelling in this ancient land of practising Buddhism could prove to be the salve that his soul was seeking. He had spent six years in a seminary, but was now a self-confessed atheist. He was very well versed in the theories of religion. Rock and Medha often discussed the significance of rituals, shamanism and religious practices. I listened intently, impressed by their prodigious knowledge. In his preoccupation with spiritualism and photography, Rock had completely overlooked preparations for the rough physical aspect of the journey.

Medha was a maverick, very unconventional and a bit individualistic. She swore that she was going to Tibet again because she was spiritually drawn to Mount Kailash. She was a *tantric* Buddhist and a Shaivite Hindu. I did not question too much of what she said, primarily because I am apprehensive of all psychoanalysts. It surprised me that someone with a rational mind, with years of analytical training and experience, could so firmly believe that Shiva's abode was Kailash and she must physically reach it. She was a very imaginative person and a good conversationalist. She had a captive audience in me, listening to her postulating on the creation of the earth and universe, from the perspective of different religions.

One day, Medha admitted to me over the phone, 'You see, I must make this journey again, even though I was badly affected by HAS last time. It is important for my soul to go to Kailash. I have decided that other things are less important.'

'What happens to your soul when you are not at Kailash?' I asked innocently.

Medha thought for a while, then I heard her chuckle and laugh aloud.

We unequivocally accepted Ray as the commander of the fleet. He was well qualified for the position, and he took over this responsibility with unquestionable seriousness. He liked describing our journeys to Tibet thus, 'This is an external and internal journey, seeking physically the abode of Shiva and realising one's inner strength'. I sought clarification.

'The reason for the pilgrimage to Kailash being so perilous has perhaps something to do with testing one's own commitment and determination in completing it.' I listened and pondered over what he said.

'I am not convinced that commitment and determination can guarantee one's ability to complete this pilgrimage,' I commented. Unintended, it turned out to be a prophetic statement.

Anita was a senior executive in an enormous corporation. Her responsibilities of work and family were as enormous. So it was always uncertain till the end if she would accompany us on what she called her second Tibetan holiday. Although we were aware of Anita's special mission of a very profound nature on Kailash, we respected her desire not to discuss the matter. She planned to place some of her late husband Vir's personal belongings at Shivathsal, on the Kailash *kora*. This was where one symbolically ended one life and entered another. She did not aim to seek freedom from this life, but decided to perform the sacred act to free her mind from the 'human bondage' of the past. All who have known tragic separation from a partner early in life, know how tentative are the first steps in the life of a lone person. Anita was learning about this new life.

Anita and I had shared some interesting moments in Tibet earlier. Landforms interested us equally. We once saw a torrential muddy river flow into a hollow and disappear for miles before it reappeared in the lowest part of the basin. This meant nothing to the others. We were enthralled.

Once she said to me, 'I have dreamed of a white horse, a mountain and a large lake.'

Feigning serious mental exercise, I interpreted her dream. 'Now let me see. The mountain was Everest, the lake was the Dead Sea and the horse was the *Pankhi Raj Ghora*,' referring to the mythical King of the Flying Horses.

But Anita was unimpressed and dead serious.

'Is that the reason for going to Mount Kailash and Lake Manasarovar?'

She thought for a moment and said, 'Partly. The lake was beautiful and serene, but the mountain was frightening.'

'And the white horse? A horse or a unicorn?' I was sceptical.

Anita answered hesitatingly, 'I don't know. I have had these dreams for twenty years now.'

'Do you think you dream of them because you would like to go there?'

Anita was firm in her reply. 'You know that Kailash and Manasarovar must call before you can reach there.'

'Perhaps the white horse would carry you there,' I commented flippantly.

Another friend of many years, Lola, was also on a holiday to the Tibetan plateau. She too was a business executive, and additionally, a successful publisher of a journal on international issues. She was travelling away from her very protective family, leaving behind a great deal of worry and concern for her safety. She said to me, 'I am now convinced that the time is right for me to join you all on this trip. I am letting things flow as they are and I would let myself be carried by events as they happen.' Uncharacteristically, Lola had exercised hard to prepare for this journey. She was extensively travelled and her international network extended to influential people, who were happy to help her while on the trip. Why was Lola going on this mission to Shiva's abode in the face of strong opposition from her family? That was the enigma, which was never resolved, and she did not offer an explanation.

From the other end of the globe had come Mandy, a practising lawyer, and Lola's friend. She had visited India earlier but I had not met her before. At the request of some in the group, Mandy had arrived in Delhi armed with melatonin and sun block cream from New York. She was pleasant and easy to befriend. But I was quite unaware of her reason for travelling to Tibet. Like Rock, she too was meeting most of us for the first time at Lola's house, where there was a 'bon voyage puja' for all of us, before we departed in search of ourselves.

In a way this *puja*, which has been translated by some as 'prayer-worship', was the event that set my mind to focus on the nature of the trip to follow. We were going for what ostensibly was a pilgrimage, and that too, a very arduous and fairly perilous one. I felt somewhat ashamed that I had reached late and noted the serious intent with which the *puja* was conducted. The *pujari* tied red thread on our wrists, as is the custom at prayers. He was enjoying the attention being lavished on him by this multilingual, multicultural group of worshippers.

With great flamboyance the *pujari* told Mandy that this would be a very auspicious journey for her as her name began with the same letter as the lake Manasarovar. I was a wee bit miffed that he did not seem to notice that my name *was* the same as that of the lake. But knowing that all well-wishers present were praying for our successful venture and safe return, I left with a feeling of all-encompassing purity of thought. And fairly convinced that although the reason for my travel was not religious, it was blessed.

I admit to a most terrible failing of nature . . . the need to be pioneering. I am also unashamedly in love with this utterly romantic idea of exploration and travel to remote corners of the planet. And when there was not much worthwhile left to explore and pioneer, except perhaps in the complex domains of nanotechnology, astrophysics and biotechnology, I chose to solve the mystery of the alternate sources of the Sutlej.

I was returning to Tibet to search for the true source of the Satadru — the ancient name of the Sutlej mentioned in the *Rig Veda*, meaning hundreds of streams. In the penumbra of mystery associated with life-giving rivers, mysticism attributed to stones, lakes and mountains, inaccuracies arise from different interpretations of the same facts. Somewhere between all this lies the truth. And it was my endeavour to discover the truth about the source of the river Sutlej.

I was certain that this journey would unfold a wonderful world that I had so far only imagined. I hoped that it would enrich my travel experience like no other earlier journey had in the past. I was impatient to reach the Sutlej and hoped to return home in control of my mind and life. Somewhere deep inside me, I told myself that if I could complete the *koras*, then I would be able to circumvent the problems and stumbling blocks of life. It is true that the rational mind does not see a link between the two, but at that time, this was my intrinsic belief.

Many pilgrims travel long distances and undertake hardships to reach sacred places. So, it was not at all surprising that Anita, Medha, Ray and Lola, who genuinely believed that Kailash was the abode of Shiva and had faith in His powers, were making this pilgrimage. Except for Lola, the others were going to Kailash for a second time. It was the ultimate act of devotion for them. But I had no such deep faith or overt religious feeling, though I was touched deeply by the devotion I saw among others.

I was committed to writing a book on our travels, for I planned to share with others the rigour and the excitement of our travels. I knew many who envied our luck to be able to travel to so many different places in the world. Several religious Hindus and non-Hindus had told me how they would have liked to have been a part of a pilgrimage to Kailash and Manasarovar, but had neither the energy, nor the circumstances to undertake a long journey.

As I got acquainted with the civilizational facets of this remote part of the world, I found that learning new terms was fairly challenging. I learnt that *la* was a mountain pass, *tso* a lake, *lungba* a valley and *chu* a small stream. Slowly, the list began to grow. At the end of this book, there's a glossary of non-English words that I have used.

Western Tibet, in this account, broadly comprises the Ngari province. This is the high plateau extending from Lhatse in the east to the Indian Ladakh border in the west. The southern limit is the Himalayan range and the northern, the Chang Tung plateau. In this vast region, Far West Tibet comprises the area west of the watershed between the Tsangpo and Sutlej, marked by the ridge astride which is the Mayum La Pass. Besides its topographic identity, Far West Tibet is also significantly different from eastern Ngari in that it is more forbidding and sparsely populated, a stony and isolated high-altitude desert.

There is no dearth of books and travelogues on Tibet, but most of these focus on eastern and central Tibet. These regions of the country are far more accessible now than before and packaged tours to these destinations are well publicised. The *National Geographic* conducts high-profile photographic treks to Lhasa, Shigatse and Gyantse from Bangkok that are very popular among a certain section of tourists. My personal interest was in Far West Tibet and the focus of my writing was to document these details for the future travellers to this remote area. I was certain that one day I would share these incredible experiences with others, just as many explorers of the past had left behind records for us to delve into and paved the way for adventurous trekkers to follow.

In early times, when there were vast expanses left unexplored, cartographers marked uncharted lands and seas with the words, *Here Be Dragons*. It was a warning to travellers of the potential of dangers in these places. This evocative phrase played on my mind while reading accounts of travels, watching films on *Discovery* and walking on lonely paths in faraway lands. Through my years of growing up with paper maps and later working on digital maps, I occasionally thought about its significance as a cartographic symbol. In consequence, when it came to choosing a name for this book, it occurred to me that nothing could be more natural than to borrow from this phrase and transpose it to the land of the yaks, where it could appropriately be applied even today.

What follows is an account of our second visit to Tibet, culled from the jottings made in my journal during the expedition.

The journey began, as all journeys must. In undertaking any long journey, our elders have advised us to remember our objectives, reflect, plan for the worst and hope for the best. These sagacious words of our elders were ignored. In the tradition of people who have mundane busy lives and suddenly find freedom from deadlines and meetings, the couple of days in Kathmandu, on the way to Lhasa, were spent being carefree tourists. Our passports were being inspected by the Chinese embassy and the Group Visa for travelling to Tibet was being arranged in Kathmandu. This left us with some time to shop at Thamel and meet acquaintances.

A poster of Mount Kailash, represented in a three-dimensional photograph taken by one Kami Tshering Sherpa, completely mesmerised me. We spent many minutes in animated discussion, trying to guess from which angle the photograph had been shot. Of the four of us, who had been to Kailash earlier, there was absolutely no unanimity on the position from where the Sherpa could have taken the photograph. We were also undecided if it was an orthophoto [a photographic map] or generated on the computer.

The Shangrila Hotel had charmingly left a copy of *Lost Horizon* in the room in place of the expected *Holy Bible* or *Bhagavad Gita*. James Hilton's imaginative book was set in a secluded mountain valley and an isolated monastery on its slopes. Life in the valley of the Blue Moon was idyllic and the lamas in the Shangri-La Monastery had learnt the secret of extending their youth and their lifespan. Hilton kept the mystery alive by never really positioning the valley and Shangri-La in space on a map, although it was referenced in time.

In its heyday, the book was more than popular, and in 1937, was made into a successful film by Frank Capra. In his book, *The Search for Shangri-La*, Charles Allen dipped into history to identify the source of the myth that could have been the inspiration for Hilton's book. He professed the germ of the idea was taken from Shang Shung, the Tibetan Bon Civilization that predated the widely recognised historical civilization that evolved in the Yarlung Valley. Scholars believe that Shang Shung was probably located in the upper Sutlej Valley.

It was almost preordained that I read the book till late into the night and thoroughly enjoyed the food at the Kilroy's eatery by day. We had involved discussions on the book during meals. There were pointless guesses as to where the idyllic valley of the Blue Moon and the Shangri-La Monastery could possibly have been located.

'I believe *Lost Horizon* was filmed twice,' said Ray.

'Have you seen the film?' asked another.

'Why yes, I saw the Frank Capra version. Weren't Chang and Ronald Coleman truly impressive?' I asked no one in particular. 'Tibet was vaguely mentioned in the film, but not any known place in the country,' I remembered.

'It could be Tsaparang,' said Anita.

'Or perhaps near Kyunglung, just below the Tirthapuri gorge, as Allen seems to suggest', said Medha, referring to his book, *The Search for Shangri-La*.

'That's his view after investigating Shang Shung, but Hilton talks of the Tien Shan mountains . . . ' was my information from the book under discussion.

'True, but the Chinese are promoting a place in the east as Shangri-La,' informed Ray.

'Rubbish. It's all propaganda,' Anita had the last word. Anita's family were host to the Dalai Lama and his followers in Shimla in 1959, as they fled the invasion of the People's Liberation Army (PLA) in Tibet. She had heard of terrible stories of persecution and had memories of atrocities on the Tibetans.

Just as other trekkers and mountaineers visiting Kathmandu, we too wrote our names on foot-shaped plaques at the trendy restaurant, Rum Doodle. This restaurant was, of course, named after the 40,000-foot-high peak in Bill Bowman's farcical tale of blundering mountaineers. In preparation for the ascent to 12,000 feet, from the Valley of Kathmandu to Lhasa, we began the 'Diamox' routine one day before we flew up to the plateau. We knew that this medicine would help us to adjust to the elevation with the least discomfort. On our last evening in Kathmandu, we enjoyed high decibel music till the early hours and boarded the flight to Lhasa the following morning.

The flight was exhilarating. It was a clear sky and we saw enormous alluvial fans gushing out of the Himalayan range and high peaks beyond. Quite suddenly, snowcapped and grand, appeared the Everest. And you knew instantly, and certainly, why it should still be called *Sagarmata* — Mother of the Sea (of snow), as the Nepalis had called it for centuries. While saluting George Everest for being the fine surveyor that he was, Britain could have refrained from rechristening the highest point on earth. The Tibetans, of course, still call it *Chomolangma*, Mother of the Universe.

We moved from a landscape of stupendous heights and depths to the Roof of the World, the high plateau where the ranges looked diminutive and the valleys shallow. For a few fleeting moments, we glimpsed Yamdrak Tso (Scorpion Lake), spreading its brilliant azure tentacles into brown stony land. Unknown to the unsuspecting Tibetans, the scholar-surveyor-spy Sarat Chandra Das had surveyed this lake in 1881. In a few minutes, the airplane made a very rapid descent to Gongkar Airport, entrepot to Lhasa. The airport was daintily fitted into a flat space between two spurs of the Himalayas, jutting into the Tsangpo. I regretted spurning my elders' advice while I threw up in the sickness bag, but immediately felt better. I wondered, was this an omen for the expedition?

The most unlikely group of trekkers had reached Tibet once again. Now here we were, a motley assembly of seven people from different avenues of life, undertaking a journey seeking answers to unspoken questions embedded deep in our minds. Some were on holiday, others were exploring the sacred spaces and yet others were saving their souls. Each had a different mission, but our paths on this journey naturally converged, planned along the same route, leading to the faraway hidden world of Far West Tibet. Would we end the journey together without mishap? Could we find self-fulfillment along the way? Would I find the true source of the Sutlej? Only time would tell.

Manosi Lahiri

The stark north face of Mount Kailash, or Kang Rinpoche,
holy to Buddhists, Hindus, Jains, and Bons.

FIRST CHALLENGE

Any and every place in the world has a past. This is even truer of Tibet than most other places. However much one would like to live in the present, the background of the past appears repeatedly against the events of the present. The kings, lamas, *bodhisattvas*, deities and sentient beings of the many kingdoms that have flourished in the land, engulf a tourist to Tibet. So, as one moves from one place to another, local lores abound about beings, sometimes mythical, sometimes historical, and these stories are narrated with predictable regularity. And all these legends are treated like firm truths that exist along with the physical reality of the contemporary state of occupation. The overriding clash of civilizations that visitors to the country notice is that of overpowering Chinese presence and subdued Tibetan Buddhism.

The story of modern historical Tibet began with King Songtsen Gampo in the first half of the 7th century. The king occupied and united many factional small provinces into a unified Tibet. He was a great statesman and politician, for he realised the importance of living at peace with his powerful neighbours. He married a Chinese princess from the north and a Nepali princess from the south, both Buddhist women. It is thus possible that the state supported Buddhism during Songtsen Gampo's reign, though the influence of the religion waxed and waned over the years in response to the level of royal patronage. At different times, learned Buddhist teachers were invited from India and many monasteries were built. Over time, Tibet became a theocratic state and several different sects appeared. Powerful institutions of the Panchen and Dalai Lamas were established and the Dalai Lama evolved into the highest religious and political sovereign.

The recent history of Tibet is replete with stories of the strain between the Panchen Lamas of Tsang province in the north and the Dalai Lamas of U province in the south. The First Dalai Lama was a disciple of the great scholar Tsongkhapa. The institution of the Panchen Lama in its present form has existed since 1642, when the Fifth Dalai Lama honoured his spiritual master, the then Panchen Lama, by conferring on him the name and the Tashilunhpo Monastery. The word Panchen originates from the Sanskrit *pandita* (scholar) and Tibetan *chenpo* (the great), together making Panchen. In the monograph, *The Lives of the Panchen Lamas*, an interesting point is made on the relationship between the two institutions:

'Each lama in their lifetime is not only involved in the search for the other's reincarnation; but also assumes the role, firstly as the disciple, and later in life as the master, of the other . . . A relationship between an all-powerful sovereign and a subject of near equal eminence would always be a difficult one, especially when the subject is considered by many to be spiritually superior to the other.'

What a fascinating connection, and so easily exploited by other nations over the centuries!

By the 19th century, when the British and Russians were inching towards the frontiers of Tibet, the country responded by closing its borders to Westerners. Except for the Chinese, Lhasa became the Forbidden City of the world. Tibet's xenophobia under the Lamas in the last couple of centuries was no less impressive than during the Cultural Revolution under the Chinese. For years, even when explorers were able to cross the forbidding high passes across the snow barriers of the Himalayas, or cut across the deserts from the north and then enter Tibet, they seldom reached Lhasa. If they did succeed in befuddling the border guards, they were intercepted by district officials and sent back forthwith. Some returned disappointed and others perished on the way.

As early as 1627, two Jesuit missionaries, Father Estaevao Cacella and João Cabral, reached Shigatse, passing through Bhutan. Shigatse was then the capital of Utsang (Central Tibet). Their intent was to establish a Christian mission and preach the gospel in Tibet. Here, 'the Great Lama, with the King's approval, issued a proclamation permitting them to preach religion without let or hindrance.' But, the difficulty of communicating with their mission at Hugli was great and the lamas spread the word that the missionaries 'had only come to pull down their pagodas and destroy their religion.' So the Jesuit fathers concluded that 'the risks were too great, the promise of success too uncertain.' By 1635, the mission was relinquished.

Although the early Christian missionaries' efforts in Tibet had come to naught in Shigatse, and further west at Tsaparang about the same time, they were not forgotten. On September 24, 1714, Father Emanuel Freyre, who had lived in India for twenty years, and Father Ippolito Desideri, a young student who had recently arrived from Rome, set off from Delhi to re-establish these missions. They approached Tibet from the west through Srinagar and Leh. Inconceivable as it seems today, they knew about Little Thibet or First Tibet (Baltistan) and Great Thibet or Second Tibet (Ladakh), but not the greatest of them all, Principal Thibet or Third Tibet that constituted the Plateau of Tibet.

The priests crossed the entire length of Far West Tibet, following the valleys of the Indus and Sutlej in sections, and completely missed Tsaparang. They then travelled through western Tibet along the Tsangpo Valley and on March 18, 1716, reached Lhasa. Freyre, who was worn out and unaccustomed to the intense cold, shortly left for India through Nepal a month later. Desideri, who was enchanted by the land of the Dalai Lama, stayed on for another five years. He learnt to read and write Tibetan, and wrote four volumes on his experience in the country, which unfortunately remained unpublished for many years after he returned to Italy.

The information of Desideri's experiences in Tibet had reached a few in the Society of Jesus through his letters. His manuscripts were found in 1875 and published, in Italian, only in 1904. Desideri's great contribution lay in documenting all aspects of Tibetan religion, customs and 'lamaism' at a time when there was little knowledge of the country in the west. It is history's great irony that even when it was all documented and available, it did not reach readers till many decades later. And so the mystery of the land and its people were well preserved for a while longer.

In 1774, George Bogle and Dr. Alexander Hamilton arrived in Tashilunhpo via Bhutan on behalf of British India, to explore the possibilities of trade. They lived for several months in Tibet and befriended the Third Panchen Lama's family. An influential trader, Purangir Gosain, whose name appears in several expeditions to Tibet, was proficient in Persian and Tibetan, and thus was the interpreter and writer with the team. Bogle spoke in Hindustani to the Lama's mother, who was from Kashmir. However, the British were not given permission by the Dalai Lama's office to go to Lhasa.

In the 19th and early 20th century, the race to reach Lhasa first was largely among the Western explorers, for it was widely known by 1885 that Sarat Chandra Das had already reached Lhasa twice at the invitation of the Panchen Lama. He later published *Journey to Lhasa and Central Tibet*, a most interesting account of life in Tibet and its capital city. The official who had helped him on his two clandestine visits, without knowing that the British employed him, was punished with death by the authorities when this became known. Haree Chunder Mookerjee in Rudyard Kipling's *Kim* is said to be modelled on Sarat Chandra. Other Indian secret agents, the *'pandit'* Nain Singh and Kishen Singh had surreptitiously reached Lhasa even earlier, in 1866 and 1880 respectively, but this was not then known to the world outside the Great Trigonometrical Survey of India (the scientific survey and mapping of the Indian subcontinent undertaken by the British colonisers for several decades in the nineteenth century).

The military expedition to Tibet headed by Francis Younghusband came in 1903. When they finally reached Lhasa, after the infamous attack on Gyantse Fort (remembered now by a tableaux in the fort on the hill depicting ruthless British forces torturing peaceful Tibetans), they found the Dalai Lama had fled to China. The British returned after signing a treaty and extracting trade rights from the Regent.

The quest for Lhasa continued. A few adventurers from the West did reach the Forbidden City and these were men of grit, usually disguised, so as not to be recognised as intruders. Peter Hopkirk narrates a gripping account of these inveterate travellers in his book, *Trespassers on the Roof of the World*. All his characters spent months on the road to Lhasa. In appreciably less time, we reached Lhasa in a Chinese airplane in about forty-five minutes from Kathmandu, flying over the Himalayas. Still, there was a sense of excitement to be able to reach the famous capital of a vast nation.

We stepped out of the airplane and alighted onto the flat sunny tarmac of Gongkar Airport. Unsmiling uniformed PLA personnel guarded the airport. Low, barren mountains marked the horizon. Besides being the entry point by air to the Roof of the World, Lhasa itself is a remarkable tourist destination. It provides a number of distractions by way of temples, monasteries and markets while one spends a few days acclimatising to 12,000 feet above sea level. German and Swiss travel agencies regularly bring groups to visit Lhasa, Gyantse and Shigatse.

At Immigration, we stood in the same order as we were listed in the 'Group Visa' document. Our passports were handed over in the same order. But since the Tourist Agency's list was in a different order, the officials had to infer which body went with which name, by checking the passports again. This ritual over, the visitors moved to collect their baggage. As on our previous visit, this time too, the passport officer did not stamp our passports. There is no mark on my passport to indicate that I have been to Tibet in the year 2,000.

A familiar face peeped through the small crowd in the lounge waiting to meet the passengers. Pema, the Tibetan guide who had travelled with us for over two thousand and five hundred kilometres across the plateau earlier, had come to meet us. She welcomed us near the baggage carousel, garlanding each of us ceremoniously with a *khatak*, the gauze-like white silk scarf. Following international (read capitalistic) practice, we were now charged Yuan 2 for a trolley. The Diamox tablets had worked well and none of us were subject to any respiratory problems. Pema took great pains to emphasise the importance of being discreet in word and deed when dealing with 'Authority.' She forbade us to mention the word DL or carry His pictures.

We set off to Lhasa in two Land Cruisers. Crossing the Tsangpo, the road hugged the banks of its tributary, the Kyi *chu* (Lhasa river). 'Why this fuss about the Dalai Lama's picture?' Pema was asked once we were settled in our seats.

'The police is very angry with Dalai Lama picture,' she warned. 'You no give to Tibet peoples.' We swore that we would obey her instructions and do no such thing.

The air outside felt dry and the girdle of mountains around were stark in the bright sunshine. There is a very special quality about the air on the high plateau of Tibet that no tourist can overlook. The sky was the clearest, deepest blue. On that day, there was not so much as a whiff of cirrus cloud. The earth and sky together reflected white light and showered powerful ultraviolet rays all around. We drove for about an hour and a half, with a short stop en route. And from then on we dispensed with the constraining four walls of a toilet and quickly got used to running behind boulders.

As we drove to Lhasa over gently rolling plains, one could almost forget that we had reached the highest plateau on earth. Even the Himalayas looked dwarfed, their relief unimpressive from there. I reminded myself that we were more than two miles above sea level. A short walk was enough to make me feel dizzy and pant for breath. I slowed down immediately.

On the way to the city, enormous figures of Sakyamuni Buddha, the great 11th century Buddhist teacher Atisha, and the protector of Tibetans, Tara, are painted on a rock cliff on the side of the road. In spite of the realities of its recent political past, it is clear that Buddhism is all-pervasive in the lives of the people of the country. Symbols are seen by way of painted images on hillsides, *chortens* (stupas), cairns and prayer flags along paths and roads. Also, people go about their daily business while repeating their prayers soundlessly and working diligently on their prayer beads. We stopped at the painted frescoes to take a look at the vibrant colours and serene faces. A few kilometres away was Netang, where Atisha had preached, meditated and died.

'Wasn't Atisha from India?' someone asked.

Sakyamuni Buddha painted on a rock — on the way from Gongkar airport to Lhasa.

Pema vehemently objected, 'No, no. He Bengali.'

'Which means he was Indian,' I explained.

But Pema would have none of that. She insisted, 'He from Bengal.' This innocuous exchange amused me considerably, since Atisha was from today's Bangladesh.

'He was born Prince Chandragarbha, later named Deepankar Srigyana, by his guru, meaning, Light of Knowledge. But Atisha was the more popular Tibetan name, meaning conqueror — conqueror of early Bon influences on Buddhism,' I pedantically informed the others, having recently read about it.

Atisha is perhaps among the few men in history who have been revered for a millennium by the people of their adopted country. Like Sakyamuni Buddha, he too was born a prince. That was in the year 980 A.D. at Bikrampur, in the Kingdom of Gaur (Bengal). He was the second son of the famous King Kalyanshri and Queen Prabhavati. While still young, he was trained in the sciences, philosophy and religion and became an accomplished hunter. Later he studied under several gurus and discoursed in metaphysics at Nalanda, then a famous university. His own fame as a *pandit*, a scholar, spread far and wide. At that time, a great guru was the abbot at the monastery in Indonesia. Atisha spent twelve years studying under him, before returning to India to the monastery of Vikramshila on the river Ganga.

Atisha had passed his prime when he ventured forth to the Land of Snow. In the year 1042 A.D., at the invitation of the King of Guge in Far West Tibet, Atisha went there to revitalise Buddhism. The then King of Guge, Lha Lama Yeshe-O, had sent thirteen monks to India to study Sanskrit to enable them to translate the scriptures into Tibetan and report on the status of Buddhism in the country. The Indians who went to Tibet were interested in trade, and many, while there, passed themselves off as teachers.

As an ordained Buddhist monk, Yeshe-O was deeply concerned with the degeneration of Buddhism in Tibet and differences surfacing between the many sects. Of the thirteen he sent to India, only two survived the rigours of the journey. They returned with the news of flourishing Indian Buddhism, the active universities and the wisdom of the great teacher Atisha. But when the King sent gold and a promise of fame for a teaching position at the monastery in Toling, Atisha refused on the grounds that he wanted neither gold nor fame. It was only later, when the dying wishes of King Yeshe in his enemy's prison dungeon were reported to Atisha, that he relented and left for Tibet.

A detailed account of Atisha's life, travels and achievements in Tibet appears in Sarat Chandra Das's *Indian Pandits in the Land of Snow*. Many pandits who went from India to translate scriptures and establish the Indian form of Buddhism are mentioned by name. Atisha travelled across Tibet from the west to the east, teaching and reviving Buddhism in a land where it had lost its purity from the time it had been introduced by the early disciples of the Buddha and later masters like Guru Rinpoche in the 7th century. Among his famous disciples was Rinchen Zhangpo, the abbot of Toling Monastery. Another was Dromtonpa, who established a monastery at Netang, near Lhasa, which remains in superlative condition till today. It was there that the famous debate between Chinese and Indian forms of Buddhist practice was conducted, where the proponents of the latter won. Atisha died in 1054, at Netang, at the ripe old age of seventy-three. Today, this remains one of the most well-preserved monasteries, as a result of the Bangladesh government's active negotiations with the Chinese to ensure its protection during the Chinese Revolution.

Back in Lhasa, I was astonished to see the change. There were many more shops, buses and lights in the city now. Tall buildings blocked a clear view of the Potala Palace, traditionally the palace of the Dalai Lama. This was regrettable because the site for Potala was chosen by Songtsen Gampo, the great ruler of unified Tibet in 637 A.D., on a hill in the middle of the wide Kyi *chu* river basin, so that it could be seen from afar.

We chose to stay at the Shang Bala, a hotel in the Tibetan quarter of Lhasa. It is a reflection of the times that the Tibetan capital today is so predominantly Chinese, that only this historic corner of town is referred to as the Tibetan quarter — an irony that does not escape the visitor to the city. There is a faraway ring to the name Shang Bala, a perfect place in the mind that you would never see on earth. It is the unearthly Paradise that you reach through Enlightenment after limitless series of life, death and rebirth. But there was nothing remarkably Tibetan about the Shang Bala Hotel, decorated by hanging Chinese lanterns and managed by the Chinese staff. It was a comfortable stay and now they also offered a Western breakfast.

Pema offered us some liquid, a Tibetan medicine that looked like water stained in blood, to counter HAS. She spoke earnestly, 'It very good. I breathe nicely,' she said, thumping her chest. I declined her offer, but the others regularly gulped down mouthfuls of the foul-tasting and evil-looking medicine packaged in glass ampoules that reminded me of chicken extract dispensed from pharmacies in Delhi. It is ever popular among local people who travel to higher altitudes.

Lola keenly swallowed the medicine and I recall her saying, 'I'm really looking forward to reaching Manasarovar and Kailash.'

'Well, that's at least another week. Three days of acclimatisation here in Lhasa and another four days on the road. Then, heaven.'

It was a hot day and Tibetan buildings do not have fans. I kept the windows in my room wide open. Large buzzing flies inspected the interior and flew out. As I leaned out of my window, I could see the Potala Palace, partially marred by a monstrous new construction. Several traditional two-storeyed houses, built around cobbled courtyards, had simple heating devices installed on their roofs. These were made of curved metal sheets that functioned as reflectors. The sun's rays reflected from the sheet and focused onto the kettle hanging above. This method of tapping renewable solar energy using simple technology has much to commend it for countries with cloudless sunny skies.

We exchanged notes at lunchtime. Ray said, 'I have a slight headache,' and several others were breathing deliberately. Medha complained, 'My chest feels tight.' An elaborate many-course meal was laid out. The Chinese restaurant manager was very efficient and pleasant. She also spoke a smattering of English, as she informed us, 'I take order for dinner.'

I sorely missed my compatriot Sarat Chandra Das's *Tibetan-English*

Dictionary. Truth be told, I have never consulted it but read references to it. But clearly, it was the need of the hour. At every meal, we placed orders for dishes that inevitably produced surprises. Lola asked, 'Do you have chillies? I like hot food.' Someone else wanted, 'veggies only.' Yet another said, 'I'll eat fish but not chicken.' And, horror of horrors, there were those who could not eat with chopsticks. We were served Chinese tea and food. Tibetan fare was not on offer.

The cobbled road was lined with stalls selling kitchen utensils, luggage, clothes, umbrellas and fruit. There were several Internet cafés, advantageously located within a stone's throw of the hotel. This made our connection to the outside world affordable, but we found access was very slow.

Little boys in monks' habits sat on the sidewalk along the pavement and recited scriptures in one voice while passersby dropped coins into their mugs. They did not look particularly reverent but did reveal great proficiency in memorising their scriptures well. Although the Chinese discourage begging, it is not considered demeaning here and collecting alms by reciting prayers is quite acceptable. In fact, it is an act of faith that adds merit to one's life. There is merit too for the one who gives alms. The accumulated merit enables one to move towards a release from the cycle of rebirths. Earlier, this practice was greatly frowned upon by the occupying government, but it has now relaxed a little after widespread criticism from within and outside the country.

Next morning, at breakfast, we met a team of Americans who had arrived the previous evening. One of them asked us, 'Where are you headed?'

'Kailash and further west till we reach Tsaparang, and then through Chung Tung eastwards and down to Kathmandu.'

'Isn't that the mountain that we saw towering on our left?' the woman in the American group asked one of her companions.

Dismissively, he replied, 'Yeah. We drove past it.'

'Did you circle Kailash?' we enquired enthusiastically.

'No. We're not Buddhists,' he answered.

'And why are you here?'

'We're geologists. We flew in to Kashgarh and drove through to Ali. We've come by the Southern Route. We've been driving for days in the dust.' He gave the impression of being someone who was bored by what was all in a day's work.

The Jokhang Temple, a stone's throw from the Shang Bala, is arguably the most revered of all temples in Tibet. It is the oldest Buddhist temple and said to have been built by Princess Bhrikuti, the Nepali wife of King Songtsen Gampo, in the middle of a lake. Although temple craftsmen from Nepal built it in the mid-7th century, the famous Buddhist teacher Tsongkhapa extended it in the early 15th century. The image of the Buddha instituted by the Princess is still worshipped today.

After the systematic desecration of the temple and defacing of images in the 1950s, through the '60s and '70s, it has been renovated in the last two decades. Visitors like us could hardly notice the ravages of the past, so well has the interior of the temple been rebuilt over the original built by Nepali craftsmen. The face of the Buddha in the many different manifestations appeared shadowy in the glow of the lamps. Everything was enveloped in the distinctive smell of yak butter and *vanaspati* used to light lamps. The air within the temple carried the weight of the fumes and the vibrations from the sounds of chanting. A special prayer, sponsored by a rich merchant, was being conducted in the central hall of the temple. Rows of monks, sitting cross-legged on the floor, were swaying forward and backward as they recited scriptures. There were huge bowls of offerings and incense being burnt on the altar. Everyone entered the temple wearing thick-soled shoes.

We walked along the *barkhor*, the circular path around the temple. Trinkets made of imitation mountain corals and artificial turquoise were displayed on carts. 'Buy old and cheap,' pestered stall keepers, aggressively hawking their wares.

The mean trick then was to demand, 'Give me new and cheap.' This was usually enough to dissuade persistent sellers of junk. But one shrewd salesman was not deterred. He showed me an identical piece, 'New and cheap.'

I know when I am outsmarted, so I conceded, 'Okay. Give me old and cheap.'

'Take. Very pretty,' he said, and transaction completed, we moved on.

I doubt that the bazaar atmosphere of the circular cobbled path of the *barkhor* around the temple has changed appreciably over the centuries. However, the courtyard at the Jokhang Temple complex had been paved and was much cleaner than before. The stalls along the *barkhor* exhibited a shade of regimentation in that all had similar red, white and green pleated fringes on their awnings. They were loaded with inexpensive Chinese goods for the common man. Stalls were heaped with clothes, bags, belts, shoes, enamel plates and bowls, and more. I bought a delicately woven broad-brimmed, foldable hat to protect my head from the sun.

The temple courtyard was enormous. People bought juniper incense sticks and burned them there, outside the temple. This was the same temple courtyard where many Tibetan monks and worshippers had been killed in the turbulent 1990s. People still recalled the brutal force with which unarmed persons were attacked by the PLA. But Tibetans have long known what it is to be humiliated for being just themselves, for that seems to be the lot of occupied people everywhere. But on that day, the Jokhang was bustling with people and there was no obvious sign of disruption in their way of life.

A little boy came up and spoke to me in English. He asked, 'Can I come to meet you in the hotel?' I was impressed by his fluency, but unnerved by his attitude.

I asked, 'How old are you?'

'I am six years old. I go to school next year,' he said. Something was amiss. Six-year-olds do not ask unknown foreigners to visit them in hotels.

The strong scent of juniper incense wafted through the air and filled every nook and corner of the temple complex. Many pilgrims gathered in front of the main entrance of the Jokhang Temple, prostrating and praying. They used narrow foam mattresses and practical padding for their thighs and knees to protect themselves from scraping while prostrating on the ground. Many of the worshippers looked impoverished. We circled the two enormous brass prayer wheels at the entrance of the temple.

A Chinese-American boy sat among a group of young monks and held their interest in whatever discourse he was holding. He spoke to us in English, 'I am ashamed to admit that I cannot speak Tibetan well, but that is so.'

'Where are you from?' we asked.

'I'm Chinese. I go to college in America. Have you been here before? This is my first visit to Tibet. What an incredible place,' said the boy.

'Yes, some of us have been here before. We're back because Tibet just fascinates us. Its past and present are equally captivating. . . '

'I may want to return to Lhasa next summer to spend a semester here.'

We wandered around to see the other parts of town. We explored the modern streets lined with new department stores and offices. The stores were impressive but empty. The Chinese men and women wore Western clothes. The Tibetans, especially women, wore the *chhuba*. The older women still wore their striped aprons and heavy jewellery made of silver and stone.

We were interested in visiting a nightclub, specifically the one tastelessly constructed in front of the Potala Palace. We invited the guide to join us, but she declined the invitation, saying, 'Only Chinese peoples goes to disco. Tibet peoples goes to teahouse,' referring to the many tea parlours along the streets. Tibetans drink many small cups of salt butter tea in a day.

Next day, on the way back to the hotel, a small girl dressed in a pink pinafore came up to us at the Jokhang Square. She too spoke to us in fluent English.

The girl said, 'I am seven years old and will go to school next year.' We noticed how precocious she was.

'Your English is excellent. Where did you learn to speak it?'

'My grandfather has taught me to speak English. I know that you are staying at the Shang Bala. Can I come over in the evening to meet you in the hotel?'

We side-stepped her offer of inviting herself over, saying, 'We're busy this evening.'

'I would have liked to bring my grandfather and speak with you in English,' the girl said. She was not certain about my origins, but asked Mandy, who is tall and white, 'Are you from America?'

Mandy answered, 'Yes, from New York.'

The little girl was truly impressed and exclaimed, 'Oh wow!' in a pronounced American accent. To this day, I can remember the wonder in the eyes of the little girl. She had made personal contact with someone from the land of the free and prosperous. Mandy was quite startled.

Much later, we learned that police have used children as conduits to keep an eye on foreigners and get information of subversive activities that tourists may be attempting, in collusion with local people. But there is an interesting phenomenon on in the cities of eastern and central Tibet today. Missionaries come as English teachers and actively evangelise, usually without much restraint from the government. But the net result is that quite a few people now speak in English, though conversions are few and mostly limited to the Chinese immigrants.

The Jokhang Temple was as magnetic as it has always been. The charm and attraction of Jokhang lay in its incomparable atmosphere made up of the central ancient living temple, the profoundly religious pilgrims and the noisy activity of trade in the surrounding bazaar. The courtyards hummed with the droning of the monks reciting prayers. Lines of people walked along the *nangkor*, the inner circular path within the temple, touching the one hundred and eight brass prayer wheels. Many sat on the stones in the courtyard and near the doorways, moving fingers over

Prayer service inside the Jokhang Temple draws many worshippers.

Roof of the ancient Jokhang Temple.

the prayer beads on the rosary, while their lips repeated prayers.

In the sanctum sanctorum, the lamps burned continually, while the faithful poured yak butter and *vanaspati* to keep the flames burning. Buddhas and *bodhisattvas* sat unperturbed in the midst of the bustle. An old couple sat in the doorway to a bolted and chained door, chatting away while the dogs played by their feet. Sheep were tied by the covered well. The temple was teeming with people cutting queues and hurrying along to see their deities before the temple doors closed for the day.

The bell at the Jokhang, mentioned in David MacDonald's *Twenty Years in Tibet*, was nowhere to be seen. I asked a monk, 'Is there an old bell?' He claimed confidently, pointing to a door, 'It is enclosed in wooden panels in that chapel. But the chapel is now locked and closed for the day.' It is said that there once was a Jesuit Cathedral here that was burnt down in a fire. But my belief is that it was probably a Capuchin church, since the latter had representation in Lhasa. Ippolito Desideri represented the Jesuits in Lhasa and had lived in the city for five years from 1716. But he was required to return to Goa, while the Capuchins were entrusted by Rome to take Christianity forward in Tibet. Apparently, the markings on the bell were in Latin.

We put our ears to the rock that was said to rise from the lake on which the Jokhang Temple was built. 'You hear water?' asked Pema. I shook my head doubtfully. We were told that we would hear the ripples below — but there was so much ambient noise that if the sound of ripples was conducted through the rock, it was lost in the babble of tongues and the shuffle of feet. I could not hear the water although I was intrigued by the possibility.

In the Jokhang courtyard, we saw a broken tree trunk of great antiquity, enclosed within stone walls. 'Why would anyone want to make a monument of an old tree trunk? No one seems to pray to it.'

'It's not the tree but the stone tablet that is being protected.'

'What's so important about the stone tablet?'

'It records a historical treaty between the Chinese and Tibetans. The inscription on the tablet states that each country would respect the other's sovereignty and that the sphere of influence of each would be only within its own territory.'

'It's flabbergasting! It does not make any sense that it should be protected, in view of the present circumstances.'

'Well, it is. Only for historical interest.'

The guide had no interest in the tablet and was not aware of the inscriptions on it. At the Tibetan Museum in McLeodgunj [near Dharamsala, India] is a memorial to those who have died as a result of the Chinese occupation. There is a stone monolith with a small brass plaque inscribed with the text of this treaty.

The Ganden Monastery, important to the Yellow Sect, was about an hour's drive out of Lhasa. We decided to go to Ganden. The scholar Tsongkhapa founded it in the late 14th century. He was also the first abbot of the monastery. Ray was suffering from a headache and remained in the hotel, hoping a brief respite would help quicken his adjustment to altitude.

All along the road to Ganden, we saw crops growing in the valley floors along the Lhasa river, but little cultivation elsewhere. Massive shelling during the Cultural Revolution had destroyed this monastery and even today the scars remain. However, most of the chapels and the Hall of Audience have been rebuilt and a small seminary exists. We were able to see a lesson in scriptures in progress. But the portly teacher neither scared the demons in hell or heaven with his weak clapping and gentle foot-tapping.

On our previous trip to Lhasa, we had been to the Sera Monastery, where we heard from a distance the pupil monks practice debating in the garden. They clapped and stamped so hard that we could hear them from outside the monastery. The difference in the attitude of the students in these two monasteries was quite striking. While the worldly wise Sera monks were clearly used to attention and seized of the moment to be photographed, the Ganden monks appeared bashful of admiring visitors.

Mandy and I walked along a *kora* around the hillock on which the monastery was built. The others explored the chapels and courtyards. The *kora*, or circumambulating of a temple, hill, lake or *stupa*, is universal in Tibet. Ganden is about 1,000 feet above the road from Lhasa. The Ganden *kora* began at a small opening in the hills on which the monastery is situated. As we stepped across this tiny pass, we were unexpectedly rewarded with a grand view of the valleys and Lhasa river embracing the hill. While walking, we made small talk along the way, as if this would distract us from the discomfort of the trek.

'I'm sure the monastery's location was selected for strategic reasons.'

'It must at one time have depended heavily on the produce of the villages in the valley along the river.'

It was clear that Tibetan farmers used every bit of cultivable land to grow crops. Each little spur that jutted into the river and had soil on it was covered with luxuriant green fields of crops, usually barley and mustard.

'I'm sure the lamas exploited the farmers, forced them to join their armies and feed the monks.'

'Naturally. Isn't that how it always is? But they must have taken care of their souls in return.'

Both of us were somewhat out of breath in sections of the walk, but I thought that on the whole, we had conducted the *kora* with ease. As later events showed, I had underestimated the impact of the stress of walking the *kora*.

We returned to the hotel and were faced with a serious problem. Ray was definitely not well and worse than yesterday. Immediately on our arrival, he said, 'I have a severe headache. The intensity of pain seems only to increase, irrespective of medication.'

'What do you want to do?'

'I must return to lower altitude soon. I have called the travel agent to split the Group Visa.' While this was the only option available to Ray, I was a little shocked at the unexpected turn of events. The travel agent arrived and informed us that splitting visas was a cumbersome process.

We wanted to know how long it would take.

'It can take two days, but sometimes it takes longer,' she said.

'Two days or longer!' we were dismayed.

She added reassuringly, 'The Group Visa goes to four agencies, but yours may be processed quickly because it is a medical case.' And because, I believed, the agent was proficient in terms of her networking. Notwithstanding the official process that the papers would need to go through, she promised to do her best and get the visa split quickly.

'It goes to the Tibet Public Security Bureau, the Tibet Foreign Affairs Bureau, Tibet Tourism Bureau and the Border Army. The last normally takes one day to clear papers,' she said.

'So when could Ray plan to fly back?'

'There are only two flights a week to Kathmandu and the next one is tomorrow morning.'

'So he should be on tomorrow morning's flight to Kathmandu.'

'I will try. He must leave at 4.30 in the morning and pick up the ticket at the airport.'

After a brief but thorough checkup in the hospital, the doctor recommended that Ray go back to lower altitude immediately. His blood oxygen was low and there were signs of oedema in the brain. He was asked to breathe in oxygen for an hour before returning to the hotel. Sitting by his bedside, I heard him talk of his now unachievable desire to recite prayers for world peace at Drolma La on the Kailash *kora*, in the manner of Lama Govinda and Thurman.

Ray was wistful. He said, 'I also planned to say prayers for my father at Gauri Kund.'

On our previous visit too Ray had suffered from HAS. He was disoriented and lightheaded at 15,000 feet, but did manage to acclimatise later. But on this occasion, he had a severe headache at 12,000 feet. The others were informed from the hospital that the doctor had confirmed our worst fears. On being asked if I would like to continue the journey,

I reiterated without hesitation, 'Of course, I will.'

An enormous paved square has for many years now replaced the meadows in front of the ramparts of the Potala Palace. The palace is a riot of colours: ochre, white and deep red, perched atop a hillock in the midst of the flat Kyi *chu* Valley. Tourist buses and vans were parked in the square under a sky overcast with a flurry of cotton wool. The steps leading up to the fortress-palace were lined with stalls selling *tankhas*, books, metalware and T-shirts. Rock bought a couple of beautiful paintings of Green and White Tara, the two protector deities of Tibetans, born of the tears of the compassionate Buddha. Salesmen enticed us with singing bowls made of five metals that reverberated with a low droning sound well after being struck with a wooden stick.

As always, the Potala, with its thousand rooms in thirteen storeys, was brimming with tourists from distant lands. Its ornate paintings, scrolls of scriptures, dazzling golden *chorten* intricately embossed with jewels, *tankhas*, and multiple images of the Buddha and *bodhisattvas* were impressive beyond measure.

Many Tibetans lit lamps and incense sticks in front of the enormous gold tomb *chorten* of the Fifth Dalai Lama, who was the founder of the theocracy that lasted in Tibet till the Chinese occupied the country in 1951. The institution of the God-King was attributed to him and he was the one who made extensive additions and extensions to the Potala Palace in the mid-17th century.

Rooms with high ceilings and yawning dark corridors stored ancient scriptures. As Tibetan monks have been literate for centuries and knew the art of paper manufacturing and block printing for long, their religious texts were recorded in scrolls of paper and strips of wood. Many of the religious texts have survived as a result of the practice of sending copies to various monasteries across the country. This was not the case of the medicinal texts, which were stored in the Tibet Medicine School that was razed to the ground during a frenzy of destruction sweeping the country during the Cultural Revolution. At the time of our visit, there were twelve worshipping monks who lived in the Potala, but we also saw many Tibetan and Chinese uniformed men from the security forces.

The 1,000-foot-high Potala Palace, seen from the forecourt.

The monks in the chapels were cordial, but did not enquire from Indians about the Fourteenth Dalai Lama, who has taken refuge in India since 1959. We saw his bedroom and chapel, neatly preserved for posterity.

Martin Scorsese's film *Kundan,* based on the life of the Fourteenth Dalai Lama, does not do justice to the grandeur of the Potala Palace. But then it is true that the film was perforce filmed elsewhere. While it brings to the world the practice by which a Dalai Lama is chosen, trained and instituted as King and Reincarnate Buddha, the images of the palace are less than enhancing.

Today, only a few temples are still used for worship. Here visitors light lamps, leave behind donations and carry back offerings of blest barley and white scarves. Every so often you see Western tourists suffering while climbing up the 1,000 feet to the roof of Potala before being fully acclimatised. The Potala Palace is now a World Heritage site. Some of us purchased an attractively illustrated and beautifully produced book on the Potala from the gift shop in the palace.

Potala roof.

Tibet is no longer a country ruled by religious leaders. Today's instruments of government are anything but theocratic. Notices from the offices of the Beijing government now replace the edicts from the offices of the Grand Lamas. The Potala Palace is now more of a rich museum of Tibet's glorious past than the splendid monastery of the Head of State.

Though the monasteries that were earlier the centres of power and influenced all aspects of the lives of the local inhabitants still remain intact, they are subject to Chinese propaganda and widely known to have been infiltrated by the political cadre. Besides, new nonreligious institutions have come into being. The most telling sign of control and fear among the lay Tibetans was their reluctance to talk about the sanctions that have been imposed on their traditional way of life or discuss the ever-increasing Chinese immigration to the Tibet Autonomous Region. It is not easy to engage Tibetans in conversation about the Chinese occupation. They are always afraid of being overheard or reported.

Ray was deeply disappointed. He had read extensively on Tibet and planned meticulously for this trip, taken every initiative to interact with the travel agent and included all my special requirements to survey the upper Sutlej Valley in the itinerary. Ray's imminent departure caused much distress, and some chaos, among the group. Lola and Mandy also decided to discontinue the journey. Though somewhat surprised at their prevarication and decision to depart, I tried to assess the situation dispassionately and conceded there was merit in their decision. At the cost of sounding unduly dramatic, I must still record that a pall of gloom descended on the entire group and for some hours even the very possibility of continuing the expedition was in question.

Mandy reasoned, 'Group dynamics may come under stress in the absence of the leader.' Lola did not offer a reason for her decision, but was firmly of the view that she could not continue in Ray's absence. Perhaps they were insecure in the knowledge that even minimal medical service would not be available for most of the journey. Early next morning, long before the sun appeared on the eastern sky, all three had departed.

These events left Anita distraught. She admitted, 'I'm not certain about the correctness of my decision to continue.'

'Come on, Anita. You've done this route earlier. And survived,' I tried to reassure her.

Anita was deeply hurt and felt abandoned by her friends. We talked for several hours into the night. She said in some distress, 'How can they leave me and go away so abruptly? We planned this holiday together.'

I tried to placate her. 'It's best they left Lhasa because they realised early that this was not a holiday they would enjoy, particularly when the going would later get truly rough.'

Anita did not appreciate my directness. She repeated, as though convincing herself. 'I must go to Kailash. I have come so far to go to Kailash, Manas and beyond.'

I reaffirmed and spelt out my resolve, 'I will remain a part of the expedition as far as I can. Be firm in your resolve to continue.'

After a while, Anita said, almost to herself, 'But should I? I prayed for Vir last time at Kailash and he was gone in less than a year.' Then, more coherently, she revealed her hopes for a catharsis on this journey to Kailash and Manasarovar, a desire to be happy and complete once more.

I commiserated and agreed philosophically, 'The truth is we must learn to accept that each of us has to be content alone. But naturally it is good to have the company of friends, particularly on a long, lonely journey such as this.' And all the while I thought, 'Perhaps I will wake up tomorrow morning and find that she too has decided to fly back to Kathmandu.' The truth was that beyond a point in this journey, there was no escape route.

As for me, I would miss Ray's companionship. He was one of our group to Manasarovar and Kailash in the year 2,000. Some years earlier we had also travelled in Xinjiang along with his wife to Heaven Lake, Turfan, Kara Khoja, Kashgarh and other remote places on the Silk Road. I have borrowed books on Tibet from him occasionally. Once I saw inscribed in his hand on the front page, 'Bought in New York, summer 1999, in anticipation of next year in Manasarovar. Will it happen?' Did he perhaps have a premonition about what lay ahead? But I could not fathom Mandy's and Lola's compulsions. And I was also astonished that I never suspected Lola's travel plans were dependent on Ray's and Mandy's on Lola's.

We were all fretful because we did not know how many days we would be required to wait in Lhasa before we received our modified travel papers. We were losing time and this would impact on our tight travel schedule.

The truck carrying provisions and the Nepali staff would be waiting for us at Lhatse at a prearranged time and place. As of now, there was no way to communicate with them, as they were already on the way from Kathmandu along the Friendship Highway.

I reminded myself that one of the purposes of this journey was to learn to function with control under difficult situations and keep calm under all circumstances. Our motto for the remaining days would be, 'Stay cool.'

While we waited in Lhasa, my search for the bell with the Latin inscription took me to Jokhang four times. 'A bell? No. No bell,' said an English-speaking monk on the last occasion. No one seemed to have seen or even heard about it, except for the monk mentioned earlier, who was now untraceable. I did not read of it in any guidebook either. But I believed that the bell-shaped stone within the temple was a possibility. However, it was plastered through the centre. So the mystery of the bell from the Cathedral persists until someone solves it.

On our last evening in Lhasa, we walked over to the post office from where we phoned our families and friends and informed them about our diminished group. Rock was in sandals, he tripped on a loose cobblestone and limped in pain. A group of girls watched and laughed aloud. During the same walk, he tripped twice more. Leaving the post office, we put him on a rickshaw and sent him off to the hotel.

We walked into enormous glitzy department stores filled with branded symbols of modernism. The younger folk were in pants and hats. PLA and military fatigues were the preferred style of the day. There were few people in the stores and fewer still buying anything. Anita got a big box of chewing gum for the road and I got myself a notebook with a pink plastic cover to write my journal.

Standing by the window in my room and looking out at the silhouette of Potala in the moonlight, I reviewed the situation dispassionately. We were a very diverse set of people and, right then, very far from both home and our destination. Even before we had begun our land journey, three members of our group of seven had already departed. Whichever way you looked at it, it was a grim situation. Anita clearly preferred to be with her friends Lola and Ray. She might yet return to Kathmandu from Lhasa.

Medha was emotionally independent and so determined to reach the abode of Shiva that she would probably continue, irrespective of physical discomfort. On our previous sojourn, Medha had suffered severely from HAS for the first few days in Lhasa. But this time she had followed the 'Diamox' prescription meticulously and was distinctly better. Rock could have wished to, but be unable to continue because much depended on how soon his ankle repaired. His foot was in a crepe bandage in the hope that it would heal in the next few days while we drove in the Land Cruisers over the Tibetan Plateau.

Many months later, over a relaxed convivial repast, Medha confided that on that momentous evening, she was as uncertain as I had been about what would unfold the next day. She was prepared to reach Kailash all alone, although she was hesitant to jeopardise her safety in the process. Earlier that evening I had been the first to commit myself to the planned trip, but she was not certain that I would honour my commitment the next morning. That night, my hope was that the *raison d'être* for us being in Tibet, the unstated quest for self-fulfillment, would be the fuel that would propel our journey forward. That would be until such time as we were assailed by HAS, or flash flood, landslide, accident, nervous breakdown or other unavoidable events that lay in the domain of the unforeseen and the unexpected, which form the deliciously unpredictable components of an expedition.

That night, after very many years, I prayed.

2

ON TASAM HIGHWAY

Our plan was to stay in Lhasa for three days. That would have been adequate time to acclimatise to the high altitude of 12,000 feet. After adapting to the elevation, sights, sounds and smells of Tibet, we planned to drive west to Lhatse via Shigatse. Here we would meet with the supplies truck, near the Lhatse petrol station.

We lost another day, waiting at Lhasa, completing the formalities relating to changes in travel plans. It was a tense and uncertain wait till the end. We were aware of the slow and discretionary nature of the bureaucratic processes and did not know how soon the paperwork would be completed.

'Do you think our travel papers will be ready by lunchtime?' we asked.

'No,' replied Pema emphatically.

'By afternoon?' we persisted.

'Don't know,' she answered without enthusiasm.

'Can we leave today?'

'If paper come by three,' was the terse reply.

'Have you spoken to the agent since morning?'

'Yes. I talk to travel agent.'

'What does she say?'

'Paper with Military Police,' informed Pema. 'Military Police' was her blanket term for all security departments under the Chinese.

The papers did not arrive by three in the afternoon. We reconciled ourselves to spending another night in Lhasa.

Next day, the journey continued. We were glad to pack our bags into two Land Cruisers and leave Lhasa behind on a hot, dry day. Very quickly we left the town behind, went past the rock painting of the Buddha and Atisha near Netang, and approached the long bridge over the Tsangpo that we had crossed earlier on the way from the airport. I looked in awe and wonder at this river that flows across southern Tibet. The river and its tributaries had long been an essential part of the fabric of Tibetan economic life.

So it was not surprising that Pema told us at this point, near Chushur, that the *bodhisattva* Thang Stong Rgyal Po had spent his life building chain iron bridges and ferries across rivers that were difficult to cross. That was in the 15th century. Later, I read in an unlikely source, an eru-dite discourse on *lhamo* by Tashi Tsering of Amney Machen Institute, Dharamsala, that the suspension bridges and ferries built by Thang Stong Rgyal Po and his disciples were an impressive 52 iron bridges, 60 wooden bridges, 118 wooden ferries. This was Tibetan Buddhism at work, where spiritualism and concern for mankind are intertwined inextricably. *Bodhisattvas* were real persons here: men and women in flesh and blood, who had reached enlightenment, but voluntarily delayed *nirvana* for the benefit of fellow beings.

A long 400-kilometre drive to Lhatse was ahead. This distance had to be completed on paved but reasonably bumpy mountainous roads in one day. We planned to bypass Shigatse, the seat of the Panchen Lamas, to make up for lost time. After all, our destination was Far West Tibet and we had had a very satisfying tour of the fabulous sprawling Tashilunhpo Monastery on our earlier visit to Tibet.

The supplies truck with the Nepali staff on board had been dispatched from Kathmandu via Zhangmou. Indiscriminately termed the supplies truck, we knew that this four-wheeler was more appropriately described as our lifeline. Ensconced in this truck were the Sherpa, who spoke our language and Tibetan, and also had enormous experience in high-altitude trekking and mountaineering. Our support system, consisting of these men, drums of petrol, sacks of food and bottles of water, were all packed into this vehicle.

A steep single lane road follows the Bhoti Kosi stream from the plains of Nepal, past Zhangmou and the squalid hill town of Nyalam. In Tibet, this stream is called Nyalam Tsangpo. At Zhangmou, the border town between the two countries, the Sherpas had transferred all supplies from the Nepali truck to the Dong Feng (East Wind in Chinese) truck. From here they would drive up the Friendship Highway to Lhatse via Nyalam and await our arrival from Lhasa in the Land Cruisers.

We were now on the historical Tasam Highway that broadly follows the wide east-west trough between the Tsangpo-Sutlej rivers in the south and the Nyenchen Tanglha-Gang Te Se (Kailash) ranges in the north. It is a loosely defined road connecting the westernmost corner of Tibet from Gartok to the capital, Lhasa. It is most unlikely that anyone would be able to point to you the Tasam Highway, because it is now referred to as the Southern Route that cuts across the Tibet Autonomous Region. This ancient thoroughfare of the Roof of the World was named after the *tasam* or stage posts, which it happened to connect. From the 35 stage posts along the highway, transport officials supplied fresh animals to government officials carrying mail. There is hardly any map today that would show you the positions of towns annotated as *tasam*, although this was the norm at one time.

This was the same road that had been used by many intrepid adventurers, traders and pilgrims over the centuries. The Italian priests, Ippolito Desideri and Emanuel Freyre, travelling from Leh to Lhasa, had followed this route with the same kind of care that the Tartar princess' entourage did in the freezing winter of 1715. The Bhotia *pandits* had worn Buddhist monks' habits and attached themselves to traders' caravans on the same road. In the event, many of them helped in filling the 'white patches' in atlases of Asia. None was more successful than the Swede Sven Hedin in achieving this, and no other explorer spent as much time on the Tibetan Plateau, crisscrossing it on horseback. Between 1906 and 1908, he travelled from Leh as far as Shigatse along the Tasam Highway and mapped a great deal of central and Far West Tibet, although several details recorded by him proved imaginary when we explored the same areas later. Irrespective of these minor aberrations, Hedin's contribution to the knowledge of Tibet in that era was incomparable.

Among the Orientals, besides the Chinese, Mongols and Central Asians, it was the people of the Indian subcontinent who had a long and traditional association with the Tibetans. Pilgrims and traders had traditionally used the high passes of the Himalayas to approach the plateau from the south. For the last thousand years, there have been well-established routes along the entire mountain chain from Kashmir to Arunachal Pradesh. Pranavananda mentions fourteen popular mountain passes that were commonly used by pilgrims and traders.

Groups of people crossed the Himalayas from the south and usually joined the caravans that regularly followed the main highway of the plateau. Even when Tibet closed its borders to Westerners, Central Asian merchants still had access to Lhasa. So all through the last millennium, the east-west Tasam Highway had been in active use. It is for this reason that when India, as a British colony, was no longer welcome to send men to Tibet, the Survey of India sent the Indian *pandits* in disguise as Bhotia and Tibetan pilgrims. This made them unobtrusive.

The Japanese monk Ekai Kawaguchi had crossed into Tibet between the Dhauladhar and Annapurna peaks. Disguised as a Chinese priest, he often lived with migrating shepherds between 1900 and 1903, till he reached Lhasa in search of Buddhist texts. His highly readable book, *Three Years in Tibet,* records his experiences on this journey. It is peppered with occasions when he met brigands, his resistance to the charms of a gypsy maiden who fell in love with him and how he often lost his way in that enormous geographical space.

That was the era of some sensational writing about this faraway and unknown corner of the world. In 1897, the Englishman, Henry Savage Landor, along with his Indian servants, reached as far as Shigatse before he was captured, tortured and managed to flee back to Indian territory. His two-volume account of the journey, *In the Forbidden Land*, is a lively account of Tibetan punishment. Some would question his claims, but he has been honoured by having a hill station in India, Landor, near Dehradun in the Garhwal Himalayas named after him. G.E.O. Knight, who was the leader of the British expedition to Tibet in 1922-23, left from Darjeeling and reached Yatung, but was denied a visa to Lhasa.

Later, in 1930, Knight wrote in *Intimate Glimpses of Mysterious Tibet and Neighbouring Countries* that pillory was common in Tibet. He also recorded that he personally had a supernatural experience. He wrote about a vanishing yogi who walked up to a hilltop with them. 'We had heard of the many things *yogin* could do — would he float in the air and disappear from mortal vision for the benefit of the White Man? We were asked to watch for a moment or two. With a few peculiar movements of the body, the *yogin* disappeared in a very mysterious manner. We could not vouch for any feat in levitation, but he certainly did disappear on a piece of level ground with no obstacles within 50 feet of the observer. No trace of the *yogin* could be found. Then, suddenly, out of the ground as it were, he reappeared.'

On this expedition, Knight also met 'Madame Noel, a French Buddhist lady travelling in Tibet.' This was in all probability, Alexandra David-Neel, who reached Tibet from China in 1923, becoming the first Western woman to visit Lhasa.

Alexandra David-Neel is my idea of the most fearless and noble adventurer. Highly educated, she had learnt Sanskrit and Tibetan at the Sorbonne University and was a practising Buddhist. She spent fourteen years travelling in Asia. Her book, *My Journey to Lhasa*, published in English in 1927, created a sensation in the West, particularly in the U.S. And why would it not? She spoke of flying lamas and learning to raise her body temperature through yogic meditation. She once took recourse to using this knowledge when she dried a flintstone that had become wet, to set fire to some sticks in the snow. The French woman spoke Tibetan like a native. Dressed like a beggar with a revolver hidden in her *chhuba*, she had walked across Tibet with her adopted Tibetan son, and lived undetected in the Forbidden City for two months.

In *Magic and Mystery in Tibet*, Alexandra wrote, 'Tibetans do not believe in miracles, that is to say in supernatural happenings. They consider the

extraordinary facts, which astonish us, to be the work of natural energies, which come into action in exceptional circumstances. . .' There
are many in the West who would agree with her today. The grand old
lady of exploration died at the age of a hundred and one in France; her
ashes were immersed in the Ganga.

This is the 21st century and we were on the Tasam Highway. We were
travelling on four-wheel-drive Land Cruisers. It was comfortable travel
compared to walking, horseback, or travelling on the back of a yak. We
had taken care of our physical needs for the next several weeks and made
full use of modern portable amenities in as diverse fields as food, lights,
medicines, clothes, bedding and tents. To that extent, there really was
much less unpredictability and danger in our journey when compared
to those who had undertaken it a hundred years earlier.

However, once we got out of the Cruisers and began walking, which
would be for approximately two hundred kilometres, our experiences
would be close to that of our pilgrim fathers and transcontinental adventurers. We were aware of it and eagerly awaiting the day we would
begin trekking. But in the meantime, for me, watching the land pass by
my windows was no less engrossing. I observed and wrote my journal.
Sometimes, I even wrote how I felt. That was a bit demanding for me,
for I am shy of disclosing my emotions.

Out of Lhasa city, for the first hundred kilometres, we drove along the
valleys of the Kyi *chu* and Tsangpo. Rich farmlands cultivated with
crops were everywhere. The plots were small and hugged the flat slopes
along the river.

'Is this a desert? This place is so lush,' said Medha.

'How green are my valleys!'

'That's true about the valleys. But look beyond and see how arid the
slopes are.' A geographer always observes this striking juxtaposition.

'The Chinese have done a great job of planting trees.' There was much
evidence of forestation along the roads.

'And also of cutting them down. Look at those trucks carrying logs.'

Hamlet in a verdant river valley enclosed in barren mountains.

There were many Dong Feng trucks plying on the highways carrying supplies to the remotest parts of the plateau, at least to those connected to or near the highways.

'What's that?' I asked pointing to a large modern but unimpressive building.

'Chinese Military School.'

Several times, when I asked Pema, 'What does it say on that building?' or a similar question about a prominent structure, it elicited the same answer, 'Chinese Military School.'

The Chinese institutional buildings are larger than the Tibetan ones, the Chinese characters on the signposts more imposing than the ones written in Tibetan script. Significantly, the Tibetan language still holds monopoly on the objects, where the mantra, *Om mani padme hum*, is written. This is the most mysterious and yet ubiquitous mantra of Tibet, repeated universally, hundreds and thousands of times a day, even today. Uncannily similar to the Pali script, it is carved or painted on boulders, rocks, stone slabs, doors, walls and even hill slopes and mountain passes.

Swami Pranavananda wrote, 'Tibetans assign certain colours to each letter of the mantra and they believe that the utterances of this six-syllable formula extinguishes rebirth in the six worlds of gods, men, titans, animals, hells and infernal hells, and secures Nirvana. The colours of the letters are white, blue, yellow, green, red, and black respectively.' We saw stones painted and embossed with this mantra, meaning simply, 'Hail, Jewel in the Lotus,' all along the way.

Long hours of travel within the confines of the Cruiser were anticipated, and yet, on the first day I was restless. The inaction was debilitating. We listened to music in the background, while Dorji, our driver, and Pema chatted incessantly, raising their voices over that of the engine. Dorji drove with seemingly supreme concentration, while she simultaneously spoke, prayed and worked feverishly on her rosary.

Every so often I scanned a map and tried to read the names of places that we crossed. This was easier said than done. There are silent letters in the Tibetan alphabet that are written but not spoken. So it was quite normal to find Horey spelt 'Hor Que' and 'Zada' written as Tsamda. I am not certain why the silent letters were written in English spellings. It added to a great deal of confusion. You were further confounded when you did not guess that Zarang and Tsaparang were the same place. Now the confusion has further been aggravated by the fact that the newer American maps had only the Chinese equivalent, but no mention of the Tibetan names. But on reaching a hamlet, we usually found that the local people only knew the Tibetan name.

After a few hours of travel, Pema declared, 'I listen *Gabi Gushi Gabi Gam.*' Her desire was to listen to the music from the Hindi film, *Kabhi Khushi Kabhi Gam.* 'My girlfriend and I see film in Lhasa,' she said with a smile.

'In the cinema?' I asked. It was a stupid question.

'No, no. On VCD. I know song,' Pema giggled with pleasure. She hummed, and sang aloud, 'O my Sona.'

Back home, my daughter Radha too enjoyed the same 'You Are My Sonia' song and dance sequence. The film was vibrant, full of fabulous looking young things and high energy, a family drama that must appeal to Asians. We were all aware of the popularity of Hindi films in these parts.

While Pema spoke of the many musicals she had recently enjoyed, my mind was scouring the landscape that I associated with the upper catchment of the Sutlej. I was eagerly waiting to reach Far West Tibet and planning out a strategy to pick up the greatest amount of evidence in the least amount of time to be able to understand the changing nature of the land in the Manasarovar-Rakas Tal area. Suddenly, the ride seemed unbearably long.

The supplies truck and the Nepali staff were waiting at Lhatse. Several large drums and the truck's tank had been filled with fuel from the petrol station located there. Much recent development and complete Sinofication had taken place in the town in the last few years. Buildings on the main road looked spanking new. Rows of shops lined the street, their walls covered in ceramic tiles in white and blue, as is popular in

The ubiquitous Mani mantra, painted on a wayside boulder.

the new sections of towns in China. This was the town to restock food and water for those aiming west.

At Lhatse, we bought hundreds of litres of mineral water bottled from springs in faraway China. From carts parked along the roadside we bought among the best temperate fruit that I have seen anywhere in the world. Full of flavour, large and juicy peaches, pears and cherries were placed in neat rows in cardboard boxes transported from long distances away. Beijing was five thousand kilometres from a point near here, a milestone declared.

A flourishing whorehouse operated from the stone hut opposite the petrol station across the road. The Madame was middle-aged with thin black-pencilled eyebrows and clearly successful in running business in the world's oldest profession. Her staff was made of young Chinese girls from the faraway poor districts. The pretty young 'knitting ladies' were knitting away sitting on low stools outside their business premises, patiently waiting for customers from among the truck drivers visiting the petrol station.

The parlour was decorated with plastic flowers and the walls pasted with posters of nubile young men and women in pre-coital embrace. The men were all Chinese and the women were Caucasoid with blonde hair. Discreet lace curtains enclosed tiny cubicles along the far wall. This is the image of a standard whorehouse almost anywhere in the remote areas of western China and Tibet.

The Nepali team led by the *Sardar*, Pradip, had arrived in the supplies truck. Pradip was immensely resourceful with experience in trekking to great heights, including climbing on Everest. He spoke Tibetan fluently and was the unofficial dragoman on the trip. Pradip was a born organiser and as ingenious a Sherpa as one has ever known. It was his voice that awoke our consciousness of every new day.

Devi was the cook, unimaginative but completely reliable. His talent lay in being able to produce a hot meal under the most inhospitable conditions — rain, hail, blizzard, dust storm or gale force wind. Cooking food at high altitude takes some talent, for water boils at lower temperature than on the plains. His kitchen was well equipped with modern conveniences, like a pressure cooker, cooking gas cylinders and stoves. He could hardly be faulted for flavouring everything in garlic. After all, that was the chief ingredient to keep HAS and evil spirits at bay.

Ramis was strong as an ox and had the most beatific smile imaginable. He was an old hand at trekking at high altitude and in Tibet he was a joy to have around. Ramis helped Devi in the kitchen. The other two Nepalis, Kumar and Kuman, were sturdy, young and new to Tibet. Kuman was an active member of a music group with ambitions of becoming a pop star. Both hoped to work for an American mountaineering and trekking club some day. They also aspired to climb the Everest and speak English, in that order.

On the first evening, we camped near Lhatse on a small grassy patch near a fresh water stream. Shortly after the tents were pitched, young Kuman appeared and stood at attention. He had been working hard to spruce up his communication skills in English. With utmost concentration he uttered these words, 'Do you like to have tea?'

'Thank you Kuman. Indian tea for me, Tibetan for the others,' I answered in fun.

Kuman disappeared into the kitchen tent and reappeared shortly. Once more he stood to attention and spoke with a great sense of purpose. 'Do you like to have Nepali *chia*?' Before I could answer, and confuse him further, Medha took charge and said, 'Yes Kuman. We do like to have Nepali *chia*.'

By dinnertime, it was clear the stomach bug Rock had picked up in Kathmandu was far more virulent than he had imagined. We insisted that he eat bland food and get on a course of antibiotics. He submitted willingly. His introduction to Tibet had not been fortuitous, but he was not complaining.

The sky was clear and the magic of the boundless, intense black of the night touched me. The Great Bear appeared just above our camp. High on the Roof of the World, it seemed all you had to do was reach out, and you could almost touch a star. We saw several shooting stars streak across the sky and I would not put it beyond each of my companions

Beginning of the desert near Lhatse: sand blown on a hill slope along the Tsangpo River.

to have wished upon them! The sparklers, shooting through blackness, dazzled our eyes. I quickly shut my eyes when a flash of moving light went across the sky and wished for a safe journey and fruitful end to my personal mission to find the true source of the Sutlej. After which I felt happy, ridiculous and childish!

Morning broke, crisp and clear. Tiny yellow flowers formed a carpet all around. Accompanied by the clatter of aluminum mugs from outside the tent, Pradip shouted his wake-up call, "Good Morning, tea is ready.'

It was Kumar who spoke next, "Vasing vater,' referring to the hot 'washing water' that was served in aluminum basins for morning ablutions.

I could hear Medha call out, "Pradip, Pradip.'

There was no answer.

Medha called again, her voice more insistent than before, "Pradip, where is my coffee?'

The question was met by silence from Pradip but it was Kuman who answered. "Do you like to have *chia* now? Coffee in breakfast?'

"No. I want coffee now. I brought my packet of coffee especially from New York. I explained to Pradip how to make it.'

There was much loud conversation in the kitchen tent. Then Pradip appeared with an aluminum mug and stopped outside Medha's tent. "Good morning, Mada madam; coffee is ready.'

After a quick breakfast, we packed into the Cruisers once more, ready to move on. Suddenly Tsering, the driver, switched off his Cruiser and stepped out. Without a word, he took a spade from the rear and dug a small hole. He picked up the few bits of paper and kitchen refuse that were lying around and buried them into the hole. This became a routine and I marvelled at the ecologist in him, with a natural desire to protect the pristine environment.

From Lhatse we began our journey once more, heading west, broadly following the Tsangpo Valley upriver. Everywhere, the valley had signs of human settlement marked by people, small hamlets, roads, cultivation and small orchards. Beyond the valley, as far as our eyes went, there were barren rocks. Soon, the golden yellow mustard fields in the valleys were replaced with barley. Trees lining the roads were fewer, with less foliage, and the groves were smaller. Freshly painted two-storeyed houses gave way to single-storeyed huts with dirty and peeling paint on their walls.

The road surfaces along the Southern Route are often in poor condition. In the rainy season, when rivers are in spate, many valleys are inundated and navigating through the quagmire can be a nightmare. It is often associated with helping other drivers whose truck tyres may have lodged deep in mud or rocky craters, deceptively covered with water. Roads along the banks of the rapidly flowing and swollen rivers wash away for many miles at a stretch. Ferries are suspended. But this was summer and the landscape was transformed. The enormous bodies of fast flowing water were now mere trickles. The roads had been repaired, waiting to be washed away by the next lot of flash floods.

These were the early days of our excursion. I heard the names Rock Sir, Nida (Anita) and Mada (Medha) repeated often. Manosi was conspicuously absent among the names that were easily rolling out from Tibetan and Nepali tongues. On questioning, I was told that my name was difficult to remember. So I set about giving them all a one-minute lesson on pronouncing my name.

'What is the sacred lake called?' I asked.

'Manas-sarovar.'

'What does that mean?' I enquired, not really expecting a correct answer.

'*Manas* is mind and *Sarovar* is lake. A lake that is born in the mind,' said Pradip knowledgeably.

'My name is Manas-i,' I told them.

'Manas-i?'

'Manas-i, she who is born in the mind, someone the mind imagines.'

But Ramis was not convinced. 'You said you are Manosi.'

'That's true,' I agreed. 'As a Bengali, I call myself Manosi, which is also the way we pronounce it.'

Fairly soon, as we travelled, we got to know our companions reasonably well. Once on the way, it took no time observing, learning and getting acquainted with each other's idiosyncrasies. Soon enough, I could tell who believed which shot was imperative to photograph. We tried to instill a new sense of responsibility for the success of the expedition and look out for each other. Many hours at a time were simply spent sitting in the Cruisers and occasional 'pee stops' and 'tea stops' were reserved for stretching legs.

'There's not a tree in sight.' Rock was somehow surprised by this.

'We've seen the last tree for many weeks now. The next tree we probably see would be on the day we leave the plateau behind!'

We were now above the tree line and life here revolved around this fact of nature. Firewood is in extremely short supply in Western Tibet. Food is not cooked as in other places. The staple is *sampa*, which is simply roasted and powdered barley. All one does to prepare a meal is to mix the sampa with water or yak butter tea. Fire for brewing tea is from dried shrubs.

Every so often we espied a group of Tibetan travellers by the roadside collecting dry thorny shrubs to light a fire to brew tea. In the cold, no fuel is wasted in heating water to bathe. Winter heating is provided by burning dried yak dung. When we drove through small dusty hamlets, we saw yak dung was stored in mounds as high as a tall man.

At one stop, a father and his two lovely daughters walked up the steep slope with effortless ease and approached us. They were shepherds and lived in the village nearby. The girls were in ethnic, traditional clothes, probably in their teens, blooming with health and life. He wanted us to take pictures of his daughters and also a photograph of himself between his daughters. We obliged him happily, but the complicated part was to explain that it would be weeks before he would receive the pictures. He knew about instamatic Polaroid cameras, so it was hard for him to

Young girls in traditional costume.

appreciate the need for us to return home, process the films and then send him the prints.

While my friends explained all this to the father, I silently watched the girls. Every movement and manner of expression reminded me of my girls, Pia and Radha. And my heart cried. Beyond any logic, my heart cried, this could be Pia, Radha and Joy. But now he would never be in a photograph with them. There could never be a Joy insisting, 'I want a picture with the girls by my side,' like this father in the middle of a desert plateau. I stood silently and smiled at the girls.

My friends often thought that I was uncommunicative and distant. I could not explain to them the whirlpool of emotions raging within me. How easily they could be triggered to unleash uncontrolled havoc in my heart. I had not yet come to terms with the ultimate loss: death. I could not speak because tears trickled down my eyes to my throat. My throat muscles hurt, because I did not cry visibly and permit others to share my grief. When the shepherd and his daughters walked away, we moved on in the opposite direction.

For a while, we traversed enormous circular basins, with lakes at their lowest points and girdled with mountains. These lakes were usually very scenic but the waters were brackish. Yaks and sheep are the only ones that drink this water. Tibetans prefer the meat of animals fed on brackish water, holding the belief that such meat tastes better. People living in the villages around the lakes, on higher ground, drink water from mountain springs. Further west, the water in these lakes completely disappears and is sometimes replaced by sparkling white sheets of salt.

One lake basin is linked to another through connecting cols. These cols are marked with numerous cairns built by passing pilgrims, who have also tied colourful flags to send prayers to heaven, to ensure a safe journey. We crossed these passes and shouted '*Lhaghya Lo*' (Victory to the gods) and the drivers vociferously echoed '*Soh, so, so, so*'. Sometimes we stopped on the higher passes to build cairns in deference to custom and the unknown. This was a gesture to beg protection from deities and ensure evil was kept at bay. Sometimes the drivers took smoking stops, when they huddled together, sitting on their haunches and talking loudly. In the process, the Cruisers and the supplies truck missed each other, though we had instructed all three drivers that we would move in tandem.

After waiting for a while for the truck, Pema stated, 'Truck meet teahouse, Shi Ga Tse Ta Menu.' This implied that we would have to wait for the truck at the teahouse at the Sang Sang crossroads. The teahouse was tiny, dark and cool, and clearly the local centre for exchanging gossip. The shop stocked salted butter tea in tall flasks, canned fruit drinks, *chhang* and salted meat. After a wait of a couple of hours, there was still no sign of our supplies truck.

Inside the shop, a few men dropped by to chat and drink tea. Tibetans drink Chinese brick tea, which they brew before adding salt and yak butter and then churn it with a bit of soda. When the men had emptied their cups and left, a couple of passing Cruisers stopped outside. The two men driving the Cruisers entered and ordered *thukpa* for lunch. This is perhaps the second most popular dish besides *sampa* in Tibet. It is a soup made of bits of meat and *sampa* boiled together. The men also ordered *chhang*, a light beer made from barley.

I asked the teashop owner if she had *momos*. But she shook her head to imply that she did not serve any. Instead, she pointed to an array of meats lying uncovered on her counter, some fresh, others dried, boiled or salted. In the meantime, Tsering bought a large dried leg of yak from the teashop. He threw it into the back of the Cruiser. Anita, a recent convert to vegetarianism, was much agitated by this action! My earnest explanation of the food chain and energy cycles in nature did nothing to impress her. She gave me the piteous 'You insensitive, stupid person' look and imperiously turned her face away.

Our supplies truck showed no sign of appearing even well after the prearranged meeting time. This was a testing time for our patience under the fierce and brilliant sunlight, with not a tree in sight for shade. It came to me with force that this was a desert, a world without trees and grass. Accusations, unveiled, were made on the exact instructions given to the driver of the truck.

Pema insisted, 'Driver stop teahouse.'

'Did you ask him to stop at the teahouse?' we asked.

'Driver stop,' she affirmed.

Out of sheer anxiety, someone asked, 'Could he have gone ahead?'

'No. He stop teahouse,' Pema repeated.

While we waited, children with layers of dust and mucus in their nostrils peeped into the Cruisers with open curiosity. Tibetan children are very friendly and ask for nothing except pens. That would probably be their most prized gift from a visitor.

The Cruisers were parked along a little brook next to a culvert and we gave ourselves up to waiting for the truck. A couple of feet above the surface of a little pool of water below the culvert, a white and grey pied kingfisher hovered, almost motionless for minutes, waiting to plunge, dive and catch an unsuspecting fish. And suddenly it flew away, mission not accomplished.

A walk along the brook's banks was amply rewarded by the sight of beautiful ducks of a rich orange-brown colour, with white heads and black tails. They appeared to live in families of an adult couple and a few ducklings.

'These are the Brahminy ducks.'

'Brahminy?'

'Brahminy ducks are unusual in that the couples remain lifelong mates. Faithful till death do them part.'

'It is said that when one of the pair dies, the other pines and dies too.'

Brahminy ducks (Ruddy shell duck or Ruddy shell drake) are the commonest waterfowl of southern Tibet. They are about half a metre in length. The adults moved in pairs, making loud trumpeting sounds. Later, we saw many families of Brahminy ducks, swimming in the ponds and loudly talking to each other. They were quite unafraid of people and did not fly away when we approached them. It was early summer and the chicks were old enough to swim with their parents. Sometimes, the chicks would float on water and the ducks waddle along on their webbed feet along the water's edge, honking loudly.

The stationary Cruiser now had Rock sitting, with his ankle still wrapped in a crepe bandage, and about ten shepherds, big and small, surrounding him. The driver, Dorji, had taken the keys away. Rock was helpless and angry at being left immobile among a group of very smelly and dirty peasants. He had been the cynosure of many rustic eyes, who had spent about half an hour peering at him and demanding things.

Pema and the two drivers, Tsering and Dorji, had driven off to investigate a possibility that other drivers would bring word from our truck driver, using the informal but effective Highways Driver Network. This organically developed system works by word of mouth. Facts are picked up from drivers on the highway and messages are left at nodal points, like teahouses, where truck drivers stop regularly. Expectedly, the team returned shortly from Shi Ga Tse Ta Menu.

Pema's information was, 'Truck problems.'

Pradip confirmed that the truck indeed had problems negotiating heights and steep slopes.

'What is the problem?'

'Bad Lhatse petrol,' insinuating that the problem arose from spurious and adulterated petrol from the Lhatse filling station, since the mechanics of the truck were in perfect order.

We waited. A herdsman appeared, riding a contraption powered by a noisy motor. He had a cart on wheels attached to his motorbike. On it was a gnarled, dry tree trunk. I could not imagine how far he had travelled to collect it. I had not seen one tree as far as my eyes scoured the landscape. The attention of several children was now diverted from Rock to the cart. With mucous running over their lips, they leaped whooping into the cart. Then they were driven away, with many spluttering starts and stops of the motor.

We waited some more. I commented casually, 'We're tired having waited just a few hours.'

'It's not exactly a pleasant wait,' Anita pointed out.

'Can you imagine what it was like for Montgomerie's men?' queried Medha.

'Montgomerie's men?'

'Captain Montgomerie of the Survey of India.'

'What of him and his men?'

'He was a British Intelligence Officer and was credited with the idea of sending Indian surveyors in disguise to Tibet in the 19th century, when Europeans were debarred from entering the country.'

'Oh, you mean the *pandits*?'

'Sure. They walked on this very route for months, and some for even years, before returning home.'

'There's a riveting section on the *pandits* in Hopkirk's book.'

'He's written so sympathetically about Nain Singh, Kishen Singh, Kinthup . . .'

'But there were many other unknown *pandits* who never returned home.'

'After a great deal of searching, I got a copy of *Indian Pandits in the Land of Snow*. Only to be informed that it is an account of Teachers of Religion and not those who were sent by the British in disguise to be passed off as *pandits*.'

When Tibet closed its borders to Westerners in the 18th century, the British sent Indian spy-surveyors in the employ of the Great Trigonometrical Survey of India to chart the country. The Indian surveyors, called *pandits*, literally walked along this road for months, counting their steps, to measure distances between places. These missions were surreptitiously undertaken to gather information about Tibet.

Many a *pandit* had stealthily moved on these roads. Disguised as Buddhist pilgrims, they scrawled notes on lengths of rolled paper, hidden away in the prayer wheel. While we use thermometers, they carried mercury in conch shells to record temperature. They hid miniaturised instruments, fabricated in the Survey Office at Dehradun, within false compartments in their trunks. They recorded the boiling point of water to infer elevation. We, of course, made use of Rock's GPS receiver, received as an 'Off to Tibet' present from friends, for a similar purpose. And clearly, we covered many more miles with ease in the Land Cruisers than the *pandits* could ever have imagined.

'Did you know that they doggedly measured the plateau by walking a measured two-step pace of 33 inches? And kept tally of 100 paces by dropping a bead on a 100-bead rosary.'

'Oh!' an exclamation of appreciation came from Rock.

'Were these scientific surveys?'

'Not in the context of current fixation with accurate measurement and standardised instruments.'

'But certainly best under the circumstances.'

Our lifeline, the supplies truck, valiantly driven by little Jaunty in the Red Cap, finally arrived with support staff, tents and food five hours later, coughing and wheezing. The driver was a thin, small quiet man, who we felt was the product of malnutrition. He never stopped amazing us by his ability to effortlessly manoeuvre the truck through hairpin bends on the mountains. The Toyota Land Cruiser drivers, Tsering and Dorji, on the other hand, were well built, jovial men radiating good health.

Our convoy drove a little further on and we chose a very pretty spot to camp for the night. From here we caught a glimpse of the snowcapped peaks of the Himalayas. Rock's GPS instrument showed it was 15,800 feet. We debated on the wisdom of an overnight halt at such a great height within days of reaching Tibet. But as the sun went below the horizon at 9 p.m., we set up camp there, for it was too late to drive to a lower camping site. It was cold and we wore layers of clothes, caps, boots, gloves and mufflers to cover all parts of our bodies; but the wind attacked the only bit that was unprotected, our faces. All night, the tents flapped and the water in the stream, not five feet away from my head, gurgled noisily.

Morning broke warm and sunny. I looked out of my tent. On a tarpaulin sheet, spread out on the ground, was just about every part of the truck's engine that could be dismantled. Little Jaunty in the Red Cap was quietly busy, reassembling the innards of the truck. After the previous day's experience, he wanted to ensure that the truck would be able to face the rigours of the next few weeks.

Pema took her job as a guide seriously and suddenly said, 'Gang Te Se,' pointing to the range of mountains, the eastern extension of Sven Hedin's Trans-Himalayas. Away to the north, snowcapped and picture perfect, it lay parallel to the Himalayas in the south. We were almost there. Another day or two and we would be in Far West Tibet.

3

LONG ROAD WEST

It was the summer solstice, June 21, the longest day of the year. We planned to make the most of the extended daylight hours to compensate for lost time. We had now left Central Tibet behind and entered the eastern section of Western Tibet, straddled along the Yarlung area of the plateau. The pre-Buddhist Bon civilization was believed to have originated and existed here for many centuries before Buddhism overtook it. This was the historical seat of the early Tibetan kingdom and first dynasty from about the 2nd or 3rd century B.C., long before Lhasa became the seat of the nation.

Buddhism is believed to have arrived in Tibet with Kashmiri and other Indian *pandits* (teachers of the laws of religion) about 400 A.D. Bon and Buddhism were practised simultaneously and both influenced each other, till King Songtsen Gampo united Tibet in the first half of the 7th century. Both his Chinese and Nepali wives were Buddhists and used royal patronage to promote Buddhism and extend its influence. Later, in the 8th century, King Trisong Deutsen emphatically supported Buddhism. This caused great anger amongst the Bon practitioners, especially because a religion from a foreign land was replacing the indigenous religion of Tibet.

About the year 900 A.D., the royal prince Langdarma, a Bon, began persecuting the Buddhists, and withdrawing the tenure to the monasteries. This led to many Indian *pandits* leaving the monasteries. In 1907, A.H. Francke wrote about Langdarma in *A History of Western Tibet*, 'He was not without humour in his anger. Half of the many Buddhist monks had to become butchers, and the other half hunters. Whoever did not show a liking for his new profession was decapitated. But when Langdarma thought that he had succeeded in annihilating Buddhism, the snake, which he thought he had crushed, bit him. A Buddhist hermit put on a robe, black on the outside and white inside, because only black clothing, (the colour of the Bon *chos*), was allowed to be worn in those days. But underneath his coat, he kept a bow and arrow in readiness. He approached the King, as if he were a supplicant, and threw himself down on the floor. When Langdarma walked up to him, he suddenly rose and shot the King through his heart. Then, in order not to be recognised by those who had seen him enter in black, he put on his dress with the white outside and escaped.'

The Buddhist descendants of Langdarma fled west and established the western Tibetan kingdoms, including Ladakh and Guge. But more of that later.

It was another day of long hours of travel through enormous mountain basins under a remorseless sun. There are no large towns or trading centres today in western Tibet. All the towns that we crossed were no more than a cluster of huts, mainly in the valley of the Yarlung Tsangpo or its tributaries. Many of these had their origin in the *tasams* of yore and even today sported simple guesthouses for the tired traveller seeking a place to rest for the night, just as the messengers of yesteryears had rested at the *tasams*.

Those special messengers carried letters, edicts and visas between Lhasa and the county offices. The mail was tied to their bodies and the belt around the inner jacket sealed under the *chhuba*. Only designated officials at the destination could break these seals. The messengers were excellent horsemen and rode for miles every day. At the *tasams*, they exchanged their tired horses for fresh ones and rested for a few hours. Quite often, they were robbed and murdered on the way. The entire official machinery was dependent on them to carry orders, visas and other documents to the officials in remote places. These men performed the same function as the runners of India, who carried messages across the mountains, plains and forests before the network of roads and railways were established.

There were also the wealthy merchants, royalty and high officials who travelled in large groups with the protection of armed guards. Desideri wrote of the Tartar princess's caravan that he had joined. 'At the head of our caravan rode a number of the Princess's servants and some squadrons of Tartar cavalry, followed by the Princess and her Tartar ladies, all on horseback, her ministers and the officers of her army; then came more Tartar cavalry with whom we generally rode; the rear guard was composed of cavalry, partly Tartar, partly Thibetan, the baggage train, provisions, and a crowd of men on foot and led horses.'

Tibet is a land of vast spaces and great distances and Tibetans are a nation of long distance walkers. You see nomads with all their possessions stacked on yaks, walking in the middle of nowhere. You see groups of pilgrims and lonely travellers walking apparently from nowhere to anywhere. Travelling westward, we saw more shepherds, nomads, sheep and yak. The 'Chinese Military Schools' were fewer and the populace looked decidedly poorer than those in Lhasa. Many more of the houses were of the traditional kind, made of sunbaked mud bricks and in various stages of disrepair. The more prosperous houses were whitewashed and had wooden designs painted on their doorframes. Prayer flags on the roofs, suspended on flimsy flagstaff, were universal.

Nomad family on the move.

Anita was playing some haunting music.

'What are you listening to?'

'Shiva and *Gita shlokas*.' The primeval music appeared to blend with the ancient mountains around.

'All the old, eastern religious music sounds similar. Zoroastrian and Buddhist prayers also sound like *Gita shlokas*.'

'A friend once told me that verses from the Vedic era were based on a series of three or four notes, unlike contemporary music that is based on an octave. That is why they sound similar.' Trivia often provided much-needed relief in breaking monotony.

The sensitive words and lyrical poems of Rabindranath Tagore that I played for a while were terribly stilted on the Tibetan highland. They sounded out of place in these raw, primitive, and elemental surroundings.

The Cruiser bumped along, and I sat musing on the nature of religious persecution. Today it seemed as fierce in its intense condemnation of what it would not tolerate as it did many years earlier. About a millennium after Langdarma, the PLA were equally effective in persecuting the Tibetan Buddhists and vicious in their attack on the monasteries.

Just as the *pandits* had then returned to India, in 1959, the Fourteenth Dalai Lama and other monks turned to India. Earlier, the Thirteenth Dalai Lama had also sought refuge in India for three years. I am told there is no such thing as historical inevitability, but history does seem to repeat itself.

On the long road, polite conversation was made, often veering on the prosaic. Anything to relieve the tedium of sitting in the Cruisers for several hours at a time.

'Did you sleep well?'

'Oh God, no! Didn't sleep a wink all night.'

'Did you have difficulty breathing?'

'Terrible. Used the can a few times,' was the answer, referring to the oxygen can. 'My finger tips are tingling.'

Anita said, 'You should drink more water to stop that.'

Medha called attention to herself. 'See how my face, hands and feet are swollen? It's water retention.'

'Don't stop taking the "Diamox". And keep drinking loads of water.'

'It was so cold last night. I used a liner inside my sleeping bag,' I said.

Anita added laconically, 'My sleeping bag is made for the Arctic. I perspired till I shed some clothes.'

In some ways Anita and I were alike. Just as I did not like talking about Joy, she too did not like discussing Vir. I think our reticence to discuss our recent losses was the result of our upbringing. We went to similar schools — convents run by European missionaries who taught us to be strong, upright, dutiful and unemotional, at least publicly. So we both were now responsible professional women, who diligently bore our familial and social responsibilities and seldom shared our personal sorrows with our friends and family. And in some complex way, while we empathised with each other, we never spoke about the vacuum left in our lives.

But I for one knew how she felt, for I was certain that she had known unconditional love and now cherished her fond memories. But we did not share these intimacies with each other. The nearest we had come to it was when she had felt that her anchors for the journey had abruptly been withdrawn.

Medha was a free soul. There was no place for hypocrisy in her life and she lived life by her own rules. She was my opposite, completely confident, uninhibited and with very clear views on most matters. A psychoanalyst by profession, she was perceptive and never succumbed to the weakness of letting someone else decide for her, nor would she take on others' burdens. While she was forever willing to listen to others speak, she was never judgmental. Strangely though, on our earlier visit to Tibet, Ayone showed inexplicable antagonism towards her manner and was often abrasive, though she ignored this. Medha has been a 'whacky' friend of Soma and Ray's for years, and they were responsible for connecting all those with the common thread of interest in Tibet.

Each of us had many years of life and varied experiences behind us. If we were able to spend six weeks this time in close proximity cordially, in spite of our divergence and some differences at times, I would put it to our desire to conduct the pilgrimage graciously, without precipitating any untoward situation. I knew it was quite possible that I would have minor disagreements and tiffs with Anita and Medha, but they would not be too serious to be a threat to the trip.

Rock was the unknown factor for me. An epitome of politeness and understatement so far, I had met him briefly at Lola's in Delhi, but now had got to know him better. He was easy to converse with and spoke affectionately about his children. I got the impression that like the rest of us, he too was making adjustments to changes in his life. He mentioned a broken marriage, children growing up and leaving home and his recent retirement from active work. All in all, this was a momentous period in his life. With so much happening to him just before he left for Kailash, it was no wonder that he was quite unprepared for the journey. He too was bashful about discussing his personal life. He had given up Christianity earlier, at least the ritualistic part of it, and for some time now found the simplicity of Buddhism attractive. It was clear from his general statements that he believed a pilgrimage to the land of practising Buddhism would bring peace and order to his life and awaken a new enthusiasm for the future.

Near Zhangboa, where the Himalayas are very close to the highway, we stopped and took pictures. But, of course, the range was probably more than a hundred kilometres away. Distances are deceptive in this clear air. A few months earlier, the Karmapa Lama, along with some trusted followers, had fled Tibet through the Himalayan passes near here into Mustang in Nepal. This led to intensely negative publicity for the Chinese government in the world press and upset Beijing a great deal. The snowcapped ridges here were now much higher than the rolling hills we had passed through the previous day.

'Look, sand dunes.' West of Zhangboa, we saw a Saharan landscape of fresh ripples on sheet sand and shifting dunes. The older sand, covered by short grass in places, was nature's way of stabilising their movement. My personal favourite was the family of *barchan*. These crescent-shaped dunes imperceptibly move forward along their concave curve.

'Looks like a graphic artist is slowly elongating the two tails of the crescent. Can you hear the hiss?' I heard the silence broken by the hiss of fine sand moving in the air. It was like the faintest hiss that can be heard when dousing a fire with water. But it was continuous and disturbingly soft, the kind you need to strain your ears to hear. 'You're imagining the sound,' I was told.

I had read about and seen pictures of these *barchans* many times and was bent on photographing them. But Rock, a keen photographer, informed me, 'Your point-and-shoot camera cannot handle this bright light.'

I could not understand why. I had especially brought this camera for this trip. And I would certainly like to photograph this surreal landscape that was more like a Salvador Dali painting than anything else I could describe it as. Every barchan seemed to be alive, whispering and moving imperceptibly forward.

Rock instructed, 'Take off your Polaroid glasses and see what it actually looks like.'

I did and I understood. It was difficult photographing anything during the day; the sunlight was so bright. Here, it was more so, because the white sand scattered all the incoming light rays right back into the atmosphere. In the event, my little point-and-shoot camera did a competent job of recording the splendid naturescapes. Notwithstanding the glare and my shaking hands, the little gadget produced some excellent pictures. Expectedly, the better ones were all the handiwork of my companions.

While bumping along in the Cruiser, I read the *Lonely Planet* guide to Tibet. The guide labels Tibet a 'harsh and uncompromising landscape best described as a high-altitude desert'. It was a completely accurate description, and yet the country was much more of an inviting destination than what that statement would imply.

Crescent-shaped barchan dunes, west of Zhangboa.

Even if you were to forget Lake Manasarovar and Mount Kailash, which are invested with centuries of mystic aura, Central and Western Tibet are the most perfect experiential laboratory for the lover of landforms and landscapes. The novice explorer or professional geographer, environmentalist or geologist, would all find much more than they had bargained for. For me, the added bonus was the emptiness and anonymity that are an intrinsic part of being in Tibet. Those who live in densely populated lands and value solitude would certainly understand what I mean to convey.

'Why do people live here?' wondered Rock.

'They know no other world. These people have always lived here.'

'Life must be hard.'

'Surely. Survival is fraught with risks.'

'Isn't that true for all isolated communities?'

'True. And as elsewhere, here too the breakdown of the traditional systems would be the cause of worry for the future.'

'Did you know that thousands of shepherds and animals died in the years when the Communists tried to convert the nomads into sedentary farmers by settling them on farms?' someone asked after reading from the guidebook. That would have interfered with the nomadic economy based on feeding a few animals on extensive pastures, moving from valleys to higher hill slopes in summer.

'Recently, we heard of plans to build an airport at Ali,' said Anita.

'And whispers of a plan to pave the *kora* route of Kailash,' added Medha.

'Wonder if we have seen the last of the pristine *parikrama*. Anyway, who are we to question the wisdom of bringing modern transportation and communication to people who have long been denied the fruits of development?' I asked.

At one 'cigarette stop', Tsering and Dorji gave us a theatrical performance of Tibetan tap dance, very similar to that we had seen at the gardens of Nobrulingka, the Dalai Lama's Summer Palace on the outskirts of

Lhasa. Dorji, the more unlikely of the two to be the artiste, rolled his eyes expressively and flung his legs about with gusto. The dance had such remarkable similarity to the Scottish Highland Fling that I would not be surprised if it were the only remnant of the Western culture introduced to Lhasa in the aftermath of the British invasion of 1903. A treaty between the British and Tibetans followed this invasion. There had been some years of modernisation and military training of the Tibetan armed forces, which were only partly fruitful. But training of the army band in Western military music was part of the process. That, too, would explain the tap dancers of Nobrulingka dressed in their kilt and bagpipe ensemble.

Back in the Cruiser, sometimes I would fall asleep, only to wake up when we went through a rough patch. I dreamt of my childhood, travelling in the train with my brother, sister and parents. When I awoke with a jolt, I realised it had been many years since I had dreamt about my childhood. Something surely was happening to me. I was able to relax and delve deep into my life; reminiscing happy, carefree days of long, long ago.

I was transported faraway to a seashore at the other end of the world, to another era, where I had stood holding my father's hand. That had also been a long land journey, on a train that was dragged along by a puffing steam engine. A train that made a different sound when it chugged over a bridge on a river. A train that took us to new lands and long seashores. I stood by the water and felt the swaying motion of the waves and rising tide.

That was also when I saw the first seashells, the strange hard, beautiful shapes that were thrown up by the sea. I was sure my father would hold me if the waves were to rise above my ankles, or if a shark came to claim me. With that reassuring feeling of certitude, I awoke once more to a sea of sand. I wondered absentmindedly if Pema or Dorji could imagine the salt in the damp air, pounding waves and an unending sea of water rising and falling, all day and all night.

Medha enjoyed listening to some techno-chanting, which I was unfamiliar with. The music sounded very modern and metallic, with repetitions of the same strain for long stretches of time. 'It's very popular in the West, you know?' she explained to the uninitiated. 'It is similar to religious chanting and is recorded by a practising European Buddhist.' I was unable to appreciate the acoustics and opted to sit in the other Cruiser. Besides, Medha often wanted to invite the 'environment inside', by lowering the windows. The environment did not respect my need for clean air and brought in sand through the open windows, making my eyes sting and water. In my childhood, when on a train, we normally travelled with the windows open, for there were no air-conditioned compartments. But over the years, my eyes seemed to have become sensitive to dusty air.

At night, we camped on a large hump on a sandy plain adjacent to the town of Paryang. The sun set at 9:25 p.m., five minutes after we reached the spot. The actual time for sunset was about two and a half hours earlier by local time at that longitude, but all of China, including the Tibet Autonomous Region, is on Beijing time. In another fifteen minutes it was dark. And then the infamous barking dogs of Paryang arrived on cue. Packs of healthy stray dogs slinked around the periphery of the camp quietly and sat upright like motionless sphinx through the night.

Next morning, they were still patiently waiting for us to pack up and leave, so that they could monopolise the leftovers from the kitchen. I got out of my tent and found one wagging its bushy tail. 'Hello dog! I am not certain how you acquired your unfair bad reputation for howling through the night. You deserve the leftovers,' I conversed with the canine and instantly it let out a blood-curdling protracted howl!

Beyond Paryang, there were no roads. The red double lines marked on the maps only indicated that you could drive through the area. The lines were not positioned correctly. You could not really use them as absolute indicators of position or distances. My training in cartography and association with surveyors had conditioned me to respect map scale and conventional symbols. I quickly unlearnt the importance of meticulousness and happily referred to the maps in hand only to interpret approximately where we might be. I smiled as I recalled heated arguments at seminars on 'precision' and 'accuracy' relating to position of map features.

Passing through an undulating country, I observed gently sloping and rounded mountains. 'Just look at those mountains. They look like sleeping dinosaurs.'

'Earlier you said that they looked like elephant's legs arranged in rows!'

'And so they were. Their form changes because of the minerals the underlying rocks are composed of.' But we were tiring of seeing mountain after mountain and were hoping that the one mountain that we had travelled so far to circle would soon emerge out of the Gang Te Se range.

Rock was interested in plants, but those were in short supply. So when some brilliant flowers lit up short stretches along the way, he would rouse himself energetically and hobble across to photograph them. 'Look here,' he pointed out once, 'some of these flowers appear to be erupting straight from the soil.' But for almost all the days from then on, the only vegetation we saw were thorny shrubs in every direction. These thorny shrubs grew on coarse sandy patches on gravel, like a sea of upturned dark green shallow bowls.

The supplies truck was waiting behind another truck that was immobilised by a stream overflowing with brown muddy waters. We took a tea break in a Khamp trader's well-appointed tent. It was a spacious shop that doubled up as home for his family. There was absolutely no sign of any other habitation for miles around this tent. The white tent was embroidered with the flowing continuous lines of the 'Knot of Eternity' in royal blue.

The tent had an oven in the centre and all walls, floor and beds were covered with rugs. There were stacks of cigarettes, canned drinks, kettles, bottled water, bottles of *chhang*, pots and pans for sale. Unlike our drivers, who were dressed in trousers and shirts, the trader was dressed in a *chhuba*, like the shepherds we saw on the way. He had the air of one who knew he was prosperous and his gold teeth sparkled as he spoke. He pointed to the old woman with a toothless grin and shining eyes lined by deep crow's feet.

'She has a daughter in the next town,' the trader informed us.

The woman said, 'I want a ride in your truck.'

'Okay,' she understood the English word. 'Come along.'

'I'll go to the next town.' She noisily bade farewell, '*Tashi dalek, tashi dalek*', to everyone in the small crowd that had collected around the truck stuck deep in mud. Then the Nepali boys hauled her up in our truck and carried her off to her destination, a few miles ahead.

For the scientist, the Tibetan plateau must be among the best preserved places to study natural physical processes. There is widespread evidence of past glacial activity. And yet there are no glaciers here today. The interesting thing about geological history, unlike human history, is that it leaves behind evidences for eternity. It is not dependent on human memory, interpretation and writing.

In Tibet, much written text has been destroyed deliberately in the latter half of the last century. The present political cadre has also foisted significant social change on the populace. Most Tibetans would not mention exploitation or oppression. They just would not speak about the Chinese presence for fear of being inappropriate, particularly if there is anyone within hearing range. As such, one might say that tomorrow's historian would have very sketchy evidence to interpret contemporary Tibetan life. This is not so with the land. It always leaves behind evidence of changing climate and landscape that can be interpreted eons later. And often their impact is far more palpable today than human history of a few millennia earlier.

A young Chinese boy in an army uniform manned a long bridge. On exiting the bridge, we entered a muddy patch. A truck, full of Tibetan pilgrims, their animals and kitchen, blocked the approach to the bridge. The truck had painted on it a swastika, a conch shell, a bow, and a quiver of arrows, a lotus and other symbols of religion. Several kettles hung from the rear top frame of the truck.

There seemed no urgency at all in making an effort on either side to make way. People got off their vehicles and there was affable exchange of news. Some pilgrims sat by the road and lit up a fire, fanning the flames with bellows. A kettle was removed from the truck and tea was made. A tall, good-looking man in long boots, broad-brimmed hat and plaits, the stuff of outdoor action heroes of films, was clearly in charge. He said, 'We are from Ali in Far West Tibet.'

Our drivers asked, 'Where are you now coming from?'

The outdoor action hero answered, 'We are on a pilgrimage. We have just completed the *kora* of Kailash.'

'And where are you going now?'

'We are travelling further east.' With a twinkle in his eyes, he invited me to leave my friends and join his retinue. The women sitting at the back of the truck laughed and talked loudly. Then they all waved goodbye and the truck moved on.

River crossings on the Southern Route are always involved and complicated. In places where there are no bridges, fording rivers without mishap is a craft honed over years of experience. Drivers get out and check the many wheel marks that lead to the river. The crossings are treacherous and often even experienced drivers end up selecting the incorrect set of wheel marks.

Numerous prayer flags and cairns made by travellers mark the Mayum La Pass (16,958 feet), the well-marked watershed between the catchments of the Tsangpo that flows east and the Sutlej that flows west. From the pass, we had a 360-degree uninterrupted panoramic view of the mountains and as we crossed it, we looked into the expanse that was Far West Tibet.

Looking westward, I could hardly contain my excitement, for finally we had reached the secluded Tibet of my dreams. And right then facing west, as I looked to my right, I was certain that I saw Amney Machen gallop in from the north on a handsome steed. There he was in his flowing dress and felt hat, charging across the nomad lands and sending off clouds of dust. He pounded across the high plains and then disappeared into the mountains in the west, waving his *khatak* as he went. And I knew that this was an invitation to share in the magic and mystery of his lands.

This was Far West Tibet, far from the tourist trails of the east I often had read about recently. This was the land of the pilgrim, who was attracted to it by a force stronger than could be explained away as a religious need. This was a far cry from the conducted tours of the fabulous Potala in Lhasa, the Kumbum in Gyantse and the Tashilunhpo in Shigatse. For in Far West Tibet, pilgrims went not to visit beautiful temples of gods and monasteries for men of religion, but to be in communion with nature; to contemplate and walk around a lake and a mountain.

As we swerved downhill from the pass at Mayum La, the mountains gave way to sandy plains. The tracks were not bumpy anymore. They were jumpy. We found our way following earlier wheel marks, avoided broken culverts, forded streams and finally and definitely reached our destination, Far West Tibet. We had left behind the east-flowing Tsangpo and its many powerful tributaries. We were now in the land of the west-flowing Lanchen Khambab or Sutlej. The very awareness of this fact made me observe everything around me with a keenness that was altogether new. In some ways, it was a reawakening to a younger self, left many years behind; a self which found pleasure in discovering little things and happiness in watching the world around.

For about fifteen kilometres along the driving track was the long and narrow Gunggyo Tso lake. This lake was known to connect to Lake Manasarovar by the Samu *chu* stream, even as late as the 19th century. Sven Hedin said that according to Chinese lama-topographers, the Gunglung glacier fed the lake through subterranean channels. The Chinese emperor Kang Hi had this area surveyed between 1711 and 1717. I walked over to see it from the top of a high sand dune. Many birds and animals wandered on the banks of this lake. The old outflow channel was now choked with sand and there was salt encrustation around the lake. It is possible that during the rains, there may have been some water in this channel for a short distance, but it would not connect to Lake Manasarovar today.

When I returned from my inspection of the outflow channel of the lake, Rock was listening to Shubha Mudgal's songs on the Cruiser's music system. This was an aberration, for he was committed to his Walkman. But shortly, Tsering changed to Tibetan opera, whose words he knew by heart. Sometimes, he was so moved by the music that he would sing along aloud. The music sounded like it was strongly influenced by Western opera. His other favourite was music from the Hindi films *Lagaan* and *Hum Kisi Se Kam Nahin*.

Although Tibetan folk opera (*lhamo*) has a 500-year-old history, it is seldom seen in its pristine Tibetan form now. It was discouraged by the Chinese officials as traditional in Tibet along with *gifu* in China during the Cultural Revolution. Later, in the 1980s, when it was tolerated under Deng Xiaoping's liberalisation policies, the Chinese officials edited and altered the scripts to suit Occupation sensibilities.

Jamyang Norbu, renowned for his detective fiction, *The Mandala of Sherlock Holmes*, writes that the modern *lhamo* has been influenced by Chinese opera, which has itself been much impacted by classical Russian opera. No wonder I thought Tsering's opera music was Western in form! The gifted and versatile iron bridge and ferry builder, Thang Stong Rgyal Po, was also a great patron of *lhamo* and is credited with raising money for his construction work for society through opera. Apparently, women were the first to take part in these musical performances.

Rock asked, 'How much longer?' His patience was wearing thin.

'A couple of hours more before we see the lakes, if I recall correctly.'

'I need to stretch my legs,' he said. Rock had not been able to walk much because of his hurt foot.

'How does your foot feel?' I asked solicitously.

'Better. I'm bearing up all right,' he smiled. Which was impressive euphemism from someone who had a sprained foot, a stomach bug and was suffering from the dry heat and rarefied atmosphere.

The Gurla Mandhata mountain of the Himalayan range appeared suddenly on our left, towering over the earth. On that day, the peak looked magnificent with huge sweeping slopes glittering with clean white ice and snow. In a very short while, we got a splendid view of the turquoise waters of the Mapam Tso (Lake Manasarovar). The Cruiser circled the flagpole attached to prayer flags that had been left by pilgrims on the way to Mount Kailash and Lake Manasarovar. Painted across the sky was a brilliant spectrum around the sun, an aureole of such intense hue that it could be captured on camera.

Pema suddenly stopped talking to Dorji and said, 'There. Kailash.'

'Yes, we know that's Kailash range. We've been driving along it for two days,' said Rock, exasperated.

'No. Mount Kailash. Kang Rinpoche.'

'Where?'

'There,' Pema pointed in the direction of the peak.

'Oh, it looks tiny from here. Is it really over 22,000 feet?' asked Rock.

'Let's get nearer and then you'll see it in all its glory,' we assured him.

We then caught the first complete view of the pyramidal peak of Mount Kailash, majestically dominating the lesser eminences of the Kailash range. The Himalayas have many pilgrimage destinations, and Hindus consider Mount Kailash the ultimate pilgrimage among these. However, the Gang Te Se (Kailash range) is topographically not of the Himalayan family and the Kailash peak is not in the Himalayan mountains. The thirty-kilometre wide Barkha plain separate the two ranges.

By now, we had covered more than a thousand kilometres of bad roads in the last four days and had hardly seen more than four or five Land Cruisers a day. We had reached the very flat Barkha plain at 15,000 feet, strewn with coarse gravel and sand. There were no fixed river channels here and it was a nightmare to cross during the rains. But on that day in the *Ta-lo* of 2002, we had an army truck to follow, besides some well-entrenched wheel marks.

At Barkha, papers were checked and 'chopped' (stamped). The old *tasam* town of Barkha was clearly doing brisk business during the special Year of the Horse. Many little shops, teahouses, guesthouses and hotels catered to the local pilgrims. This little settlement, no more than a handful of huts and tents, had for centuries served the needs of pilgrims from India and Tibet going to Kailash. In the past, it was also an important *tasam*. From here we could see Mount Kailash clearly defined against a blue sky.

'How like the pictures in the coffee-table books,' commented Rock.

I agreed wholeheartedly.

'That shape. Sven Hedin described it well when he called it a tetrahedron.'

Even from this distance, we clearly saw the horizontal striations and the vertical cleft along the southern face of the peak.

'It's these horizontal lines cut by the deep vertical cleft that prompted the early Bons to call it the Swastika Mountain,' remarked Anita.

Suddenly, everyone was silent as we drove by the mountain. In our minds, the unspoken question was, 'Will all of us be able to circle the Swastika Mountain? Will any one of us have to return disappointed?'

But none of us voiced these concerns aloud, for the very mention of any apprehension would be enough to set in motion a series of negative thoughts and vibrations!

'Thank God,' I said, 'we are finally in the catchment of the Sutlej. Now to look for its true source and banish all suggestions of alternate Lanchen Khambabs.'

4

SHORES OF MANASAROVAR

About four centuries ago, Ippolito Desideri had written a short description on his journey from Leh to Lhasa. On reaching the Barkha plain, he wrote, 'We came to a plain called Retoa, where there is a lake (Manasarovar) so large that it takes people several days to walk round. It is believed to be the source of the Ganges. But from my own observation and from what I heard from various people, who knew this country and the whole of Mogol, it seemed that the above mentioned mountain Ngnari Giongar (Kailash) must be regarded as the fountainhead not only of the river Ganges, but also of the Indus. Mount Ngnari Giongar being the highest point of this region, the water drains off on two sides. To the west, it flows through Second Thibet to Lesser Thibet until it reaches the Mountains of Kascimir, and finally, near Lesser Guzarat, forms the wide, navigable river Indus.'

He then continued to describe the second river. 'On the eastern side, another large body of water flows into Lake Retoa and eventually forms the river Ganges. This agrees with the detailed accounts in old writers about the gold sand found in the Ganges. They must have lied if the source of the great river is elsewhere, for it is only on the banks and in the sand of Lake Retoa that any large quantity of gold is collected, being washed down from the Mountain Ngnari Giongar by heavy rains and melting snow. If it is admitted that the fountainhead of the river Ganges is on this mountain, then the old writers speak the truth, and my observations confirm their words. Thibettans and merchants come there from time to time to search for and collect the gold sand, to their great profit; and as I have already said, this superstitious people make pilgrimages to the lake, devoutly walk round it and think thereby to gain great indulgences.'

When I read this, I was amazed at Desideri's interpretation of three different geographical enigmas of the time. He correctly stated that the Kailash Mountain was among the highest places in that part of Tibet, long before Sven Hedin had informed the world about the Trans-Himalayas, his name for the Kailash range. Desideri then proceeded to document the existence of gold in the region, near Lake Manasarovar. The mines still exist today on the isthmus between Manasarovar and Rakas Tal. It was the myth about the source of the Ganges that stumped him. For that was a puzzle which was solved almost two-and-a-half centuries later.

Off the northwestern shore of Lake Manasarovar is a little *gompa* (monastery) on a rocky crag. This is Chiu *gompa*. In Tibetan, *chiu* means sparrow or a little bird. No other name could be more appropriate for this monastery perched on the rocky outcrop about three-quarters of a kilometre from the lakefront. When you stand on the terrace of the *gompa* and look east, you get a bird's-eye view of the wind-swept undulating hills around the deep blue waters of Manasarovar. You can scan the flat Barkha plain and the Gang Te Se range in the north, and the Gurla Mandhata peak in the far south. Because the air is so clear, the mountains appear deceptively near. When you walk down the narrow steep stairs, you spy mounds of dry roots of scrub, dry yak dung and beer bottles stacked on the open terrace, in preparation for a long and severe winter ahead.

Inside the *gompa* are dark eerie recesses with idols of Urgyen or Padmasambhava (Guru Rinpoche).

'Urgyen meditated in this *gompa* on his way to Mount Kailash,' said the monk who lived at Chiu.

'Just look at those eyes. How enormous they are!'

'That's because he was Indian. Padmasambhava came from Udiyana, now in Pakistan.' Padmasambhava is depicted in paintings and idols with large, bulging eyes and a curled moustache to distinguish him from the Tibetans.

The monk continued with pride, 'The master came to Tibet in the 7th century at the invitation of King Triesten Detsen. He spent a great deal of time in this *gompa* on his travels through the country spreading the word of the Buddha.'

It is believed that the birth of Padmasambhava was miraculous. He was found as a fully formed child of eight, in an enormous lotus in a lake in Udiyana, in present-day Swat in Pakistan. His name means 'born of a lotus'. He is said to have appeared with a *vajra* (thunderbolt, to banish evil) in one hand and a lotus in another.

As with other historical characters relating to Tibetan Buddhism, even today the line between fact and fiction is not clearly marked. But from our conversations with the local people, we realised that the imaginary attributes of historical persons were given much credence. No wonder the Chinese occupation found the Tibetan penchant for continued acceptance of traditional and irrational beliefs frustrating, so completely in contradiction to the thoughts they espouse.

Nearby were *chorten* (stupas, shrines) and walled enclosures for sheep. Several shepherds lived there and would come down to meet tourists who camped nearby. Once, a strange young shepherd, uncharacteristically wearing brown goggles, followed us about. Tibetan faces are wrinkled early because of the strong ultraviolet rays and no one wears dark glasses to protect their eyes, although many wear hats. So the shepherd's idiosyncrasy made him quite noticeable. He was a vagabond and loafed around the camp. One day he appeared on a bicycle, a very unusual mode of transport in this part of the world. He smiled lecherously and made lewd suggestive gestures. Before we could react to his indecent proposal, he rode off at great speed. We next saw the man a few days later, right on top of Drolma La at 18,600 feet!

We were not able to camp at our planned site because we could no longer dig into the Ganga *chu* channel and get fresh water. Earlier, the seepage from the lake fed a few shallow pools of water at the mouth of the stream. Now the *chu* only carried some mineral water from the hot water springs at the village. So we moved further south along the shore of the lake and camped past the new government guesthouse, between the shore and the raised pebble beach. The years-old *chorten* at the confluence of the Ganga *chu* and Manasarovar stands mute witness to the erratic changes in the flow of water from the lake into it.

I loved visiting Lake Manasarovar. For long, I had known that one day I would reach this mountain lake. It was my destiny since my parents had christened me perfectly. My mind had imagined a placid, watery blue sheet, but not this brilliant paradise. It was the largest sheet of water that temperamentally changed colour in a matter of minutes, reflecting the hues of the sky and tracking the warm and cold currents within it. All the blues and greens of the spectrum that one could imagine streaked it. And because it was so enormous, you could walk along its shores for miles without encountering anyone.

The truth is that few pilgrims, other than the Tibetans, actually circumambulate around this lake. Many more do the *kora* of Kailash. Indian pilgrims usually stop by the lakeside on the way to Darchen, or on the way back home after the Kailash *kora*. The chief reason for this is that it takes much longer than the outer *kora* of Kailash. But recently, the practice for the Indian government groups, arriving from Purang, has been to divide into two groups. While one undertakes the *kora* of Manasarovar, the other circumambulates around Kailash.

The lake had lost a little of its serenity and the beauty that comes from remoteness. Inaccessibility and difficulty in reaching this height had made it one of the most desirable pilgrimages both for the religious and the seeker of peace. Man's unquenchable thirst and quest for new knowledge seems to have conspired against Manasarovar's pre-eminent place in mind share. From the generally acknowledged highest freshwater lake, it has now been superseded in that position by Nam Tso, also in Tibet. At present, the lakeside near Chiu *gompa* is dotted with tents and houses, including the new guesthouse. When we visited, tissue paper, chocolate and biscuit wrappers, plastic containers or broken bits of Lhasa Beer bottles were littered around.

And so many people must also leave behind their footprints and wheel marks, which have destroyed sections of the raised beaches. A newspaper article once reminded us, 'When Sir Edmund Hillary and Tenzing Norgay climbed Mount Everest in 1953, the peak was breathtaking in its virginal beauty. Today, if Everest takes one's breath away, it is because of the magnitude of garbage and litter left behind by tourists. Everest is known as the world's highest junkyard.' This succinctly encapsulated my feeling about Manasarovar at Chiu that day. Unfortunately, the article further reminded us, it so happened that budget destinations were always the first to suffer environmental degradation. So it was with this area, for it was the most popular with budget overseas pilgrims and tourists, who normally did not walk around the lake. Fortunately, they had not yet intruded into the marmots' underground world, from where the creatures inquisitively peeped out of their burrows.

'What's that rodent? Looks like a rat,' came from uneducated me.

'It's a marmot,' said Anita.

'Are those marmots' holes? There are so many along the lakefront here!'

'My. Aren't they terribly energetic and healthy-looking,' commented Medha.

'I cannot imagine how they survive in the winter when their burrows must be frozen.'

'And no vegetation left on the land either.'

'They probably fatten in summer and hibernate underground in winter.'

There were waterfowl as well. So far, I had not seen swans, but many other graceful ducks, geese and birds.

We had prepared to walk around the lake as far as possible and had planned to spend at least a couple of nights camping at Trugho, at the foot of the Gurla Mandhata. That was, of course, incumbent on being able to transport the tents there, provided the supplies truck could reach the proposed campsite. The success of the *kora* was also largely dependent on the condition of the various channels and the delta formed at the confluence of the streams flowing into the lake. Sometimes, they are impossible to cross along the lakeshore and one must follow the streams up, and then follow their course down again, before continuing the *kora*. But we were now into high summer and expected to walk around the lake along its smallest circumference.

The *kora* of Manasarovar was one of the most important items on our agenda. Each of us had spent hours reading personal accounts of the circumambulation of the lake. We had planned it for months. We mentioned it so often in our conversation that no longer did we refer to circumambulation as *parikrama*, in the Hindu way, but *kora*, in the Buddhist manner. That seemed like an abbreviation, which it was not.

We had a fair idea as to where we would camp and how many days it would take us to make a complete circle of approximately seventy-five kilometres in summer. The *kora* of the lake is much larger in the rainy season because of the flooding at the mouth of the streams that flow into it. Needless to say, from the word start, we realised that our information base was incomplete. The *Lonely Planet* guide is undoubtedly the best source of data for those planning on undertaking this *kora*. It is a 'must read' to avoid debacles such as often occur. But unquestionably, the best factual account of the *kora* and the lake is found in a book now out of print and seldom found, even in old bookstores. This is *Kailas-Manasarovar* by Swami Pranavananda.

By far, the most interesting account of the Manasarovar and its shores is by the Swami. He is, perhaps, among the last great explorers of the area from India, or elsewhere. His account has details that could only be given by one who knew the land, its flora, fauna, language and people, intimately. He had surveyed this area with the scientific inquisitiveness that characterised just a handful of explorers. He exploded the myth of the 'Blue Lotus' and swans that the imaginative poet Kalidasa wrote about and which generations of Hindus have imagined on the waters of the lake.

Interestingly, the Swami said that the best time to circumambulate the lake is winter when the water is frozen, and most Tibetans do their *kora* of Manas at that time. Perhaps it is for this reason that we saw so few Tibetan pilgrims in the height of summer. I find Pranavananda's description of the frozen lake most intriguing, especially his mention of the subterranean hot springs leading to temporary melting pools of water and crevices on the ice sheet. His recording of the fact that sputum from the lips formed icicles before reaching the ground on a December morning is quite believable! He mentioned eight monasteries along the shores of Manas, but we saw no more than five *gompa* and the *chorten* at Chirkeep.

We began walking from Chiu *gompa*. I had a vague sort of awareness that I was doing something that a good Hindu is expected to do, certainly once in a lifetime. We had, of course, trekked a part of this first lap earlier — but this time I meant to complete the *parikrama*. As we walked away from the camp, I reminded myself that it was Full Moon, and surely that must be an auspicious day to begin so important a journey. While I tried to convince myself that there was no contradiction between the actions I was taking and the rationale of my mind, I crossed three women in salwar-kameez, who had already completed the Kailash *kora* and were on their way back home to India. They said, '*Om Namoh Shivaiah*.' Somewhat startled by this overtly religious salutation, after a moment's hesitation, I replied self-consciously, '*Om Namoh Shivaiah*.' Walking along the marshy shoreline of Manasarovar, I noticed that the raised pebble beach was very well formed at this point.

For several years now, an agreement between the governments of India and China has made it possible for Hindu pilgrims from India to visit Manasarovar and Kailash in small groups. The present group of twenty-seven had walked up over the Lipu Lekh Pass in Uttaranchal in India and into Tibet near Purang. All these pilgrims had undertaken this hard journey, walking and on horseback for twenty-one days, because of their fervent religious belief. Kailash is Lord Shiva's abode and a pilgrimage to this mountain is a means of purging oneself of sins committed in this lifetime. A dip in the waters of Manasarovar is similarly ordained to help you move towards a release from the chain of birth, life, death and rebirth.

I asked myself, why was I there? I did not have a satisfactory or convincing answer. I was certain I was not there to just walk around a lake and a mountain. I knew that each of us was seeking something beyond a *kora*. I was just not very sure what that 'something' was for me. I told myself I was there because I was among the blessed few who had reached this sacred place. The truth was that I was making a quick escape from routine, and had a well-planned series of activities for solving a mystery. While I walked along the lakeshore, I formulated a rough workplan and absentmindedly watched an Indian woman in a magenta *sari* and *choli*, changing after a dip in the lake. She asked me, 'Where are you from?'

When an Indian asks this question, the answer is, 'For all practical purposes, Delhi, although I am Bengali.' When a foreigner asks the same question, the answer is, 'I am Indian.'

The woman volunteered, 'I come from Aurangabad.'

'Are you with the government group?' I asked.

She answered, 'Yes. I am with the Indian group. We are returning now.'

'How do you feel after the Kailash *parikrama*?'

'Very good indeed! It's special. You'll know when you get there.'

On the raised beach, on the left bank of the Ganga *chu*, an interesting ceremony was underway. A lama from an eastern monastery was conducting a prayer and burning incense on a pyre. Devotees had collected around him as he waved scarves and scattered handfuls of barley into the air and prayed to the elements. Some of his followers covered the pyre with damask and beautifully embroidered cloth. They were worshipping along with him.

There is something wonderfully unfettered about a *kora*. I experienced the most powerful liberating sensation on the first day of the *kora*. I had not yet fallen into the rhythm of breathing, walking and soliloquies. Thinking and talking to oneself seemed to be the most pleasurable and natural thing to do on long treks. You could happily transport your mind to the remotest corner of the world, the farthest from where you were, and yet observe yourself plod on from a distance. While on a *kora*, it was easiest to take yourself out of your body and become a lama, an artist, an astronomer, an ascetic or a *yatri*. You did not need to carry in your mind a scheduler or calendar. Your *kora* was over when you reached the end, which was the starting point. It was not a race; you did it at your own pace.

The trek from Chiu *gompa* to Seralung was long and difficult. The first few kilometres from Chiu to Langbona are along the foot of a line of cliffs. On the trekking maps, it is indicated as a continuous smooth line. It is, in fact, made up of several rocky headlands and tiny coves. The beaches along the coves are sandy. Walking is slow and although a stick is not essential, it is useful to steady oneself. A few twists of the ankle are quite likely in this section of the trek.

Shortly we came across blocks of slate with carvings of *Om mani padme hum* on them. From here we moved on to the point marked 'Chirkeep' on the map and identified on the ground by prayer flags and a *chorten*. This is one of the most remarkable and universal features of Tibet. There are important Buddhist landmarks known to all pilgrims, but you do not see people there. The lake was rich with waterfowl. The cliff face provided numerous natural hollows for birds to make homes in. Tibetan twite, finch and Tibetan lark were seen in large numbers. They were all fawn and grey-brown in colour and easily lost sight of on the rocks. You noticed them only when they flew out of their nests forming a perfect V in the sky. We spied several dark reddish-brown crag martins sheltering in the clefts in the rocks along the cliffs.

Rock and I sat on the boulders while the birds flew in complete abandon over the lake. For about an hour we watched a command performance of twenty-one Brahminy ducks.

All I could say in wonder was, 'See how the birds glide over the water.'

Watching the ducks skim over the surface of the lake in some ways had the same wondrously soothing effect on one's nerves as watching fish glide in an aquarium at home. They had the grace of ballet dancers and a perfection that was divine.

'Notice how they call out to their partners?'

These were noisy ducks, trumpeting and honking as they swam. They appeared to be reasonably quiet in flight though.

'Yes, indeed. They're protective of their young ones. They're quacking to reassure their chicks. Always have an eye on them.' Perhaps they informed the other birds of their right to their territory at the same time!

'I have seen these Brahminy ducks swimming in lakes earlier. I think there are many more in brackish water.'

I watched the birds with a sense of time moving in reverse. I was a child once more and I could see my mother's tin sewing box, with birds painted on it. As a child I had watched my mother take needles, buttons and thread out of this one-time candy box. She had embroidered these same ducks along the hem of my white organdy dress. Around the orange-brown ducks were embroidered green reeds.

'See how they skim over the surface of the water for such long distances. Aren't they a study in perfect aerodynamics?' exclaimed Rock, fascinated.

We walked by some caves along the lakeshore, and Rock said, 'I'm sure in earlier times, hermits lived in these caves. They must have stayed here to meditate without interruption.'

Several large hollows bore testimony to the old practice of barring a hermit into a small cave and building a brick wall across the opening, thus preventing him from ever setting foot outside again. I have read in David MacDonald's *Twenty Years in Tibet* that some of them walked out after a year or two to return to normal life, but most of them were quite disoriented by then, having lost touch with time and people.

'I believe some hermits stayed in the caves meditating till they died.'

'I'm sure these caves are used by shepherds now. There's a strong smell.' There was a feral smell within many caves.

'Can you imagine the hermits living in these caves, with blackness all around and the continuous sound of the lapping waves in their ears? I would easily have become deranged in days.'

'I say, what a powerful form of self-denial, to have a 'residence' at the most desirable site facing the Manasarovar vista, and never to see it!'

While I walked ahead, Anita and Medha took a devotional bath in the chilly waters of the lake. This action was born of a profound belief that all sins of a lifetime are erased after a symbolic washing away. Bathing in the Manasarovar is truly a feat in self-mortification: the ground is slippery, the waters freezing and the winds gusty. I found it too daunting. So I now have a new respect for my companions who undertook this act of faith. Rock, like me, did not feel the need to dip into the lake. Still, just to remain on the right side of Hindu ritual, I symbolically sprinkled a few drops of the holy water on my head!

Rock and I chatted amiably, waiting for Anita and Medha to join us. We hardly knew one another and used the opportunity to ask about our children, work and motivation for undertaking the journey. We found ourselves discussing life after death and belief in rebirth.

He asked me, 'Do you truly believe so?'

'I find it a very useful philosophy in deterring sinful activities and positively encouraging one to undertake good actions. After all, there must be some way to explain why good does not necessarily beget good in this life.'

'That's the problem. There does not seem to be a causal relationship.'

'Then again, how could one bring up children without giving them the satisfaction of seeing good results some time. It makes sense that the rewards of good actions could be savoured in the next birth if you missed them in the present one.'

After some thought, I continued, 'I believe the principle of rebirth can be a potent motivating factor in life to consider actions before precipitating them.'

Rock nodded. He understood my logic.

Then I asked him, 'Do you believe in miracles?'

He was quiet for a few moments and said after a while, 'If you are a Christian, at some level you must believe in miracles. But I am not one anymore.' And there our conversation ended, with both of us understanding each other.

Beyond here, up to Langbona Monastery, the path was a little more difficult but the litter was much less. There were fewer crushed cans marked 'Dispose of properly — please do not litter'. It was summer now and the sandy slopes were covered with aromatic scrub and thorny shrubs.

'This heady scent must have wafted into the noses of the hermits, meditating in the caves,' said Rock.

'And tickled their olfactory senses. I wonder if it distracted them?' I asked aloud to no one in particular.

We spent some time collecting specimens of aromatic plants.

I crushed the little fleshy leaves in the palm of my hands and the heady aroma had a strangely disturbing impact on me. I was reminded of an elderly aunt who lay on a bed, suffering from a severe headache. I had rubbed balm on her forehead as she slowly sank into slumber. That day, so many years ago, my hands had smelt the same as the aroma that wafted through the air along the lakeshore.

'Hey, doesn't this smell of the ever-popular Tiger Balm?' That was the omnipresent medicinal ointment used to cure aches and pains in China and Southeast Asia. Rock took photographs of a boulder face with black, rust, orange and green lichen. While he concentrated on the lichen, a couple of spotted doves walked about on the ground near his feet.

Langbona is clearly marked by a *chorten* that dominates the scenery. We had been on the road for seven hours already. We stopped for a snack. The guidebooks estimated seven hours from Chiu to Seralung. City born and bred, we were certain that it would take us another seven hours to reach Seralung. We had acclimatised well to the rarefied air and were not breathless while walking.

'It's marshy from here to Seralung and must be avoided, according to the guidebook,' said Rock, consulting the book. 'We have already walked about fifteen kilometres. Should we walk to Seralung, we would have to walk around the marshes and Sham Tso Lake for another fifteen kilometres.'

'That's the route taken by Buddhist pilgrims. See, Tibetans are walking around the Sham Tso,' said Pradip. We could see three maroon ants on the horizon. Tibetan pilgrims. No Yindus or Firinghees.

At this point, the European group we had met the previous day caught up with us. We exchanged notes. They were having a hard time extracting guidance from their guide, but cheerfully listed a litany of disasters that had befallen them.

'Our Land Cruisers are never to be found in the predetermined locations.'

'The positions marked on maps cannot be identified on the ground.'

'The guide has not been on this trek earlier.'

'Sand has piled up on the only tracks known to our driver.'

From experience we knew these were not matters to be addressed as problems, but inevitable. The Europeans moved on, looking for their Land Cruiser. Ours had now appeared with food and water at the appointed place. The sandwiches, made of dry crumbly bread, were the last of the loaves brought from Kathmandu by the kitchen staff. The fruit was dehydrated. But all this we ate with relish. Then we piled in and travelled at least another thirty kilometres, passing through Hor Que before we reached camp.

Medha continued walking, supporting herself with Leki sticks. For company she had one guide, one *Sardar*, one helper, one driver and one Land Cruiser. We pleaded and reasoned with her to discontinue her further walking venture for the day, but she was insistent, determined to continue on foot to the camp.

Camp was on a wide plain facing west, at the mouth of the now dry

Full moon reflected on Lake Manasarovar, seen from Seralung.

Sanu *chu*, five kilometres from Seralung *gompa*. This is an ideal site and the lake here has the expanse of a seafront. The land is low and rolling. Behind our camp was a pebbly ridge, probably marking the edge of the lake in earlier times. Behind this ridge was a large camp of a hundred and thirty Indians. The Shrestha Company managed this group, as it held packaged tours, with fixed itinerary, catering to middle-class Hindus.

Our guide, Pema, informed us that the Shrestha Company was from Nepal.

'Do you know them?'

'Shrestha Company guide Mr. Poddar my friend. Very nice man.'

'Perhaps he knows the truck route to Trugho *gompa*.'

'He know. He say truck have problem. Bad road.'

There is loose sand around Manasarovar, deep enough for tyres to sink.

'So how does our supplies truck reach Trugho?'

'Truck no go,' said Pema, with finality.

Mr. Poddar had solved several problems Indians face in undertaking this pilgrimage. He had cut down the time for the pilgrimage to eighteen days. This exhilarating drive up over 15,000 feet from Kathmandu to the Lalung La Pass, when undertaken in two days, is dangerous for people from the plains. Occasionally, the result has been fatal.

Mr. Poddar conducts the Manasarovar *parikrama* quickly in Land Cruisers. The only walks involved are from the campsite to the lake to take a holy dip. Shrestha also provides changing facilities on the beach for the modest *yatri*. As the Land Cruisers drive up from Kathmandu to Lhatse, people get the opportunity to acclimatise to the elevation by spending time at Zhangmou and Nyalam. The Shrestha Company offers a reasonably comfortable pilgrimage on a difficult route. It is affordable too. But I do not know how they manage emergencies, like illness and splitting of visas. Perhaps, they handle them from the local administration centre, Darchen, when necessary.

We heard voices and accents that we were familiar with: compatriots from South India and Mumbai. 'Our camp should be nearer the waterfront.'

'We're almost a kilometre away from the lake.'

'Still, it's lovely here. Like Marina,' said yet another voice in another accent.

A stark naked Firinghee completed his skinny dip at 15,000 feet, covered up quickly to avoid hypothermia and ran to his tent.

Rock, Anita and I sat by the lakefront and watched the dragons spit fire into the sky as the sun dipped behind hills, and the water in the lake reflected the yellow and orange of the sky. Then it became dark and we could hear the lapping waves till the full round moon rose over the lake and shone like polished silver. Rock, who is a very spiritual person, spoke of his attraction to the simplicity of Buddhism. He had been interested in Buddhism for a long time, having rejected the faith of his birth, Christianity, decades ago. He had rejected the institutionalised version of Christianity, not the basic precepts of the faith. So for him, the attraction was to see for himself some of the most sacred places of Buddhism outside of India. To a lesser extent, he was also interested in Hinduism's reverence for Kailash. Then there was the simple attraction of going to one of the most remote and starkly beautiful places on earth.

Anita once more told us that she had seen dreams of a large lake, a mountain and a white horse for twenty years. This time I did not laugh. I was certain that in her recurring dreams, the lake was Manasarovar and the mountain was Kailash. She was drawn to this beautiful lake that is in the heart of the sacred spaces for Bons, Jains, Hindus and Buddhists. And the white horse? Could it be a metaphor: the windhorse on the Tibetan flags that carry messages to heaven? The windhorse that carries the symbols of Buddhism on its back?

Medha was not back yet. There was concern for her group as it would not be possible for them to walk through the marshes in the semi-darkness of the moonlit night. Tsering drove off in search of the other Land Cruiser being driven by Dorji. We sat outside on the lakefront, drinking bowls of hot wonton soup. The shore was wide and the wind had rustled up large waves. The lake was shimmering in the moonshine. You could easily make believe that you were camping by the sea. With no sign of Medha and her walking companions, we retired to our respective tents long before they arrived in the Cruisers, exhausted and irritable.

Next morning we began walking early, with a plan to meet at Seralung *gompa*. The guidebook said it was half an hour away, but I knew for sure that it must be at least one-and-a-half hours walk away. It was not very hot yet, so we were happy walking along the shore. It was not easy. At that point, the shore was widely strewn by coarse deep sand and one section had large, irregularly shaped quartz boulders. Families of duck and geese abound and nest in these marshes. Many sat prettily on islands of floating weed.

We approached Seralung *gompa*, identified by the prayer flags and *chorten*. It was atop a sand dune. We saw a horse tied on the slope of the sand dune. Anita and I immediately decided to ride up to Trugho. Seralung is a charming monastery, with a small shop outside, selling cold drinks, cigarettes, water and small knickknacks.

It was the only time I saw someone fishing in the lake with a net. The fisherman stood in the shallow knee-deep water wearing long boots. He spread his net and waited. A little later, he gathered his net, slung it over his shoulder and walked into the *gompa*. The fisherman turned out to be the administrator of the *gompa*. The PLA had emptied this *gompa* of all its images, treasures and scriptures and dumped them into the lake. The story goes that later, when the PLA became less destructive, the Tibetans retrieved some of the artifacts from the lake and renovated the *gompa*.

Rock took a measurement on his Garmin GPS. Chiu was exactly twenty-two kilometres from Seralung *gompa*, as the crow flies. The European group had also reached it. The lamps were lit and there was a glow inside. The guardian deity had some link to my personal preferred deity, the Goddess of Wisdom, Saraswati. This made me happy, because I knew one prayer to Saraswati, which I was taught as a child. As I got on my knees to invoke this prayer, 'Jayo, Jayo Devi. . .' ('Hail, hail Goddess. . .'),

Pema informed me that a horse would be available. Saraswati, who clearly could read my mind, had already answered my prayer!

I came out and started negotiating. The owner of the horse spoke and Pradip interpreted. 'He can give two horses and one horseman for one day for Yuan 300.'

We said, 'Too much. Yuan 200 should be adequate.'

The owner consulted with the horseman.

'*Nando*,' said the horseman. We got the gist of his cryptic comment.

'Anyway, we want to reach Trugho, even if it takes more than a day.'

Nobody appeared to have any accurate information on how long it would take to reach Trugho on horseback.

'Okay, take us to Trugho and we will give Yuan 300,' we suggested to the horseman.

'I will ask the owner,' was the noncommittal reply.

We struck a deal at Yuan 300. This, we felt, was a better way to define the scope of work, because neither the guide nor any of us had an idea as to how long it would take to reach Trugho. They agreed that four of us would take turns riding because there were only two horses.

Rock thought this was all a big joke. The first horse arrived. It happened to be the chestnut we had seen tied on the slope when approaching the *gompa*. His back was covered with attractive carpets and he was decorated with beads and trinkets.

'Where is the other horse?' I asked.

'It come,' answered Pema.

And so it did in a while. It emerged from behind some sand dunes. At first, we saw an indistinct nucleus within a swirl of blowing sand. And then, as it approached us, the opaque centre of the sandswirl transformed to a horse. Was this an apparition? Was it an optical illusion? Was I too dreaming like Anita? A small white horse with flowing mane, not more than a metre high — a '*tattoo*' — came trotting past the dunes and halted at the *gompa*.

A white horse to bear Anita to Trugho. I suggested that Anita should get on the white horse. After all, she was the one to have dreamt about the white horse circling the lake, with a mountain in the background, for two decades now. But it was not to be. The horseman indicated that she must ride the bigger horse and I the smaller one. And then we set off. My white *tattoo* had a hard, small saddle, somewhat uncomfortable, but we were happy to begin riding along the southern shore of Manasarovar.

The white horse was immediately thirsty and wandered off for a drink. He was not interested in walking fast. Tufts of green grass, which they nibbled at hungrily, easily beckoned both animals. They completely ignored commands from their inexperienced riders. The horseman tied up the reins of both quadrupeds over their respective necks and dragged them along.

On the left were huge longitudinal dunes and on the right, swamps. The insects, which were found all along the lake's marshes, looked something between a fly and a large mosquito. They were also strangely territorial and attacked like a blizzard when you approached their area, but they did not follow, nor did they bite. The chestnut was particularly disturbed by the insects and rubbed his face several times on my legs.

The marshes gave way to sand banks along the shore. In the shallow lagoons were nesting birds. The sun got hotter all along and riding became less fun. The sand and the strong light were taking a toll on my eyes and I was riding with them closed for a few minutes at a time. The horseman too rested for a few minutes. He joined a couple of nomads brewing tea in a primitive kettle on brush fire by the lakefront. When teatime was over, the nomads bundled the kettle and cups in a cloth pack, swung it over the shoulder and began walking again. Anita took photographs of the horseman, nomads, horses and us, all quaking under the remorseless sun in the background of hazy sand dunes and the steaming lake.

Riding on land radiating heat and the sun's benevolent rays enveloping all that the eyes rested on, an oft-repeated theme in Anita's conversation was the comfort to be associated with her next hedonistic holiday. 'It's definitely going to be a spa. A health spa with the best food, massages, swimming . . .' Approaching the wooden bridge over the shiny sliver of the Tag Tsangpo stream, Anita moved onto the white horse, and Rock mounted the chestnut. But both dismounted at the lower reaches of the Tag Tsangpo, as Tibetan horses are very frightened of seeing water flow below a bridge and are known to panic and drop their riders on such occasions. This was a thought lodged in my mind after reading Sven Hedin's account of crossing a river in the western part of Tibet. The animal had fallen off the bridge in panic, but had swum to safety, fighting the strong and chilly currents of the river.

'The Gunglung glacier is quite close here, according to the map.'

'How near?'

'About ten kilometres away.'

'But there is only a trickle of water from the glacier in this stream.'

'There are springs a few kilometres up the Tag Tsangpo. Hedin and Pranavananda mentioned them.'

'Should we attempt investigating?'

'There's no controversy about the Tag Tsangpo bringing the meltwaters of the Gunglung glacier to Manas. So there's no excitement in investigating it.'

'But how long will it take to reach the springs?'

'At least three hours of walking and about an hour on the horses.'

'We'll never make it to Trugho before midnight then.'

In the midst of all this conversation and confusion, someone dropped a pair of sunglasses. After retracing a few steps to search for it, we reconciled to its loss forever in the sands of Manasarovar. Rock and Anita rode on the horses along the shore towards Trugho *gompa*, our next campsite. Medha and Pradip were many, many steps behind. I took a longer but quicker route, circling the lake from beyond the sand dunes, and reached Trugho well before the others.

5

AT THE FOOT OF GURLA

Trugho is the largest amongst the Manasarovar monasteries, against the backdrop of the gigantic Gurla Mandhata mountain, the easterly extension of the Ladakh range. The peak is said to have derived its name from Mandhata, a king in ancient times who prayed to the gods and undertook penance from the shores of Manasarovar. Traditionally, the approach to the lake over this range from the south has been across the Gurla Pass. At the time of our visit, the Tru Gho Monastery Democratic Management Committee ran Trugho *gompa*.

As I walked into the *gompa*, the monk said, 'One person, Yuan 10.'

I obliquely suggested that I did not plan to enter. 'I should like to pay entrance fee when I return with my friends.'

He repeated, 'One person, Yuan 10.'

I said, 'I am only looking for the shop to buy a drink.'

Gesticulating, the monk shut the door in my face. Not finding the shop and with no one around to direct me, I looked around for a while and then wandered off to the camp.

There are many mystical stories linked to Manasarovar. But the most enjoyable fable has remarkable parallels to a popular parable, The Emperor's New Clothes, which separates the pure-hearted from the rest. It is believed a holy tree grows in the centre of the lake. The story goes that the Fifth Panchen Lama once came to Lake Manasarovar for a pilgrimage. He stayed at Trugho *gompa* and on one occasion threw a

Gurla Mandhata, with majestic sweeping slopes, south of Lake Manasarovar.

khatak onto the holy tree. All the impure people around saw the *khatak* hanging in air over the water, because they could not see the tree. Only the pious few saw the *khatak* hanging from the branches of the holy tree rising from the waters of the lake. Needless to say, I saw no tree, either in the lake or on its shores.

There is another interesting myth about serpents that live in the lake along with their serpent-king, Naag. They are protected by seven rows of trees around Manasarovar and survive on the fruit of the enormous tree that grows in its centre. The fruit not eaten by the serpents fall into the lake, turn to gold and sink to the bottom of the lake. A marvellous yarn of trees and serpents in an area where there are none! It has been repeated for generations and one almost begins to believe that it may have been once so. Both Indians and Tibetans believe in the tree that grows in the middle of the lake.

The camp was next to the *gompa* by the lake. I took off my boots and drank some cold water, and surrendered myself to the serenity of the place. The campsite was on a glacial plain at the southern shore of Manasarovar, at the foot of the Gurla Mandhata range. As the clouds blew away, the snow on the highest peak shone in the sun. Presently, three men in Army uniform came from the direction of the *gompa* to check out the camp. One of the Army men was carrying a gun. He briefly looked into my tent but said nothing and all of them moved on.

Anita and Rock arrived shortly and a little while later Medha approached on the white horse. The hero of the day was the *Sardar*, Pradip, who was accompanying Medha, on the chestnut. He galloped at full force and had an enthusiastic audience cheering and approving of his performance. It was the same animal that had earlier refused to acknowledge Anita's and Rock's coaxing with the heels.

The horseman happily collected his money. He had walked for twenty-seven kilometres and stopped only twice: once to drink tea with some nomads and another time when we took a break. He gestured that he would eat and then ride back to Seralung straightaway. As for us, we exchanged notes on various degrees of discomfort in different parts of the anatomy as a result of the ride.

Some time later the same evening, the three Army men along with another man in mufti approached the camp from the direction of Gurla Mandhata. The civilian waved out to me, and I waved back. A few minutes later, all four were at our camp. Two of them were carrying AK-47 rifles. The one in mufti was fairly fluent in English.

'Hello. How are you?' asked the one in mufti.

'Very well, thank you. How are you?' I responded.

'Okay. Are you Yindu?'

'Yes. Join us for tea?' I asked the visitors, and they accepted our invitation.

'We are from the Chinese Frontier Army.'

'What is out there?' I asked, pointing to the narrow valley they had emerged from.

'A checkpoint along the border. We are posted at the checkpoint.' This was in the narrow valley, south of Trugho, on the border between Nepal and Tibet.

'You speak English very well,' I commented.

'Thanks. Learnt it at university.'

'Are you in the Army?'

'Yes, I am a soldier,' he answered. He was probably also an officer. His body language was disciplined. The others were deferential towards him.

After inquiring about us, the officer said, 'I have been at the checkpoint only ten days. Life in Tibet, especially here, is hard and lonely.' It's the same story in all the far-flung Autonomous Regions of China. The Chinese who go to settle or work there rarely realise before reaching them how hard life is and how strongly the local people resent their presence. With increased Chinese migration to Western Tibet, there are little clusters of exclusively Chinese houses, shops and offices that form the 'towns' along the main travel routes, while the nomadic Tibetans

Frontier Army men demonstrate the use of an AK-47 rifle to author over tea.

wander about with their animals across the vast plateau.

'Where is your home?'

'Near Xian, in a crowded area.' After a pause, he asked, 'Have you lived in the U.S.?'

'Not I, although I have visited the country several times. She lived there for many years,' I said, pointing to Medha.

'My brother is keen to go to U.S. Tell me about U.S.' After some discussion on life in the U.S. and opportunities it provides, Medha slipped away to wash herself in the tent especially equipped with a hand shower attached to a drum of water.

After a while, the officer said, 'I myself prefer to work in China. But not in Tibet.'

While I sat chatting with the men, I was given an inspection of the gun and for good measure was told that one of the Army men was a Tibetan. He could not speak Chinese and was being given lessons in the language.

Tea and biscuits were served. The Chinese gunman inspected his cup sceptically and closely. He finally asked, 'Have you mixed coffee with the tea?' It was only then that we realised the opaque Nepali *chia* served was quite novel and unacceptable to him. He was raised on Chinese tea.

Rock and Anita approached from the *gompa* side. They had gone there an hour ago. On their arrival I asked, 'Let's take a photograph with our guests.'

'But that would not be possible with the uniformed men, but possible with me,' said the officer in mufti.

So Rock took a few pictures. The officer wrote an email address on a scrap of paper and said, 'I am expecting to go home to China shortly and will see the photograph then. But in the meantime, leave might get cancelled if border tensions with Nepal escalate.'

I thought he referred to Maoist insurgency in Nepal. But he was actually referring to the tension between the two countries as a result of the young Karmapa Lama having escaped from Tibet across the border to Nepal, near Mustang, a few months earlier.

The Army men invited us to visit them at the checkpoint. We regretfully declined. Would we have the temerity to flout the Chinese rules? Our permission to travel included Trugho, but not the checkpoint. Besides, the guide was very particular that we should not wander away in that direction.

As if waiting for a cue, the officer asked, 'What is she like?'

'She's all right. Knows her way around.'

'I think I probably have seen her somewhere earlier, perhaps at Darchen during *Saga Dawa* a few weeks earlier.' *Saga Dawa* is the annual festival to celebrate the day of Enlightenment of the Buddha, during the full moon in the month of May.

It was not possible to forget Pema easily — she was a lively young woman, who spoke English and by Tibetan standards dressed immodestly. Her preferred dress on this trip had been hip-hugging tiger-stripe pants and a red sleeveless shirt on hot days. On cooler days, she half-covered her head and face in a black tasselled scarf, which gave her a very exotic Arabian look. She had many admirers and was now married to Tenzing, a temperamental guide educated in India, who also doubled up as cook for foreign adventure tourists.

'You know, you can practice speaking in English at the neighbouring camp. All the tourists there speak English.'

'Okay. That's a good suggestion. We like it.' The guests left after a brief goodbye and a reminder to send the scanned photographs by email.

It was a warm night, though windy. The Nepalis and Tibetans were happy, singing and laughing late into the night. I lay in my sleeping bag and thought of the day's events, but mostly of my children. All this effort spent to be far from home, but when sleep evaded, the first thoughts were of home. Strange are the ways of the heart and mind!

I planned to speak to the children from Darchen on the way to Tarpoche to begin the Kailash *kora*. At about 3:30 in the morning, there was a rumble from the ground, followed by a tremor for a few seconds. I jolted into wakefulness. The sound of the earth was like a prolonged growl from the core. From the floor of the tent, I experienced the earthquake nearer the ground than I had ever done before. A few seconds later, there was another rumble from below, followed by further tremors of lower intensity. The sky was covered with clouds, and the low full moon was hidden behind it. Yet the snow on Kailash was shining bright.

It was the 'Do As You Please' rest day. We planned to wake up late, relax, wash up and clamber over a few hill slopes. Medha had decided to walk along the lake on that day and rest the next. I was awake and lying in my sleeping bag. I had unzipped the front flaps of the tent and could see sunshine outside, though the sky was partly clouded. Beyond Trugho *gompa* was the blue lake and on the side, domes of sand dunes.

I could hear Medha speaking to the Nepali boys. 'How are you all feeling? Everyone okay? I want you to pack my breakfast. Two slices of bread with peanut butter, omelette and honey and some fruit. My bag is going to be heavy because I am carrying my woollens. The sky is clouded, so it may rain. I do not want to catch a chill. I'll walk as far as I can and the Cruiser should meet me after seven. You can give me packed lunch. I want to walk as much [as I can] to have my legs in good shape for Kailash. . .'

Medha was now ready to leave for the day and giving instructions, 'Pradip and one more person can accompany me because this would be a hard walk. Pradip, you can carry my bag and some water. And when I am gone clean my tent. And you can wash these. . .'

Medha left for the walk with the *Sardar*. It was a relaxed day for the rest of us. Breakfast was at a leisurely pace in the open. It rained a few fine drops. Later, Anita decided to go for a walk along the shore. As she went, she said, 'I'll return by two o'clock for lunch.'

The Nepalis completed their work and housekeeping for the day and sat around playing cards. Bags, mattresses and various other articles of travel were spread out and aired around them.

I sat on my haunches on the ground and poured a few mugs of water on my head, washing my dusty matted hair. As the water dripped down my forehead, I thought of Atisha, many centuries earlier, standing on the shores of Manasarovar offering oblations to the gods standing in the lake. The story goes, 'from the centre of his head a stream of water issued forth and fell back on the water of the lake. A number of *preta* now in the spirit world drank it and obtained relief from their suffering.' The story would have preceded him as he approached Toling, to be greeted by the generals of the new King, nephew of Yeshe-O.

This is the place that I would always remember for being nearest to Celestial Communion. If there is anything like 'spiritual vibrations', then it possibly is in the quiet and peace of this immaculate earthly paradise. The illusion of timelessness was all-pervasive. Perhaps because there were no trees, roads, houses and people. Perhaps because there was complete absence of sound. There was just a colossus of a mountain on one side and the expanse of a turquoise blue sea on the other. And we were in between. It was a place to be absorbed slowly and not a transit point for rushing through. With every breath of the clean thin air I inhaled, I awoke to a sense of self-knowledge. Metaphysics is not my forte and I seldom ask, 'Who am I?' and 'What am I capable of?' Hesitatingly, here I approached the meaning of *being qua being*, my existence, my life and beyond.

Rock, who was sitting nearby, poring over *Circling the Sacred Mountain*, suddenly turned and asked: 'You believe in God?'

'Is an indirect answer permissible?'

'Go ahead.'

'I am willing to believe that there is a supreme power. But I do not understand how he operates, how he plans, rewards, punishes. He sets terribly difficult tests and waits for one to trip. For now, I want to forget about all that. I have left behind all that is chaotic, incomprehensible and doubtful on the plains, for the duration of this trip. All I can say is that there is much that is yet unexplained.'

As a child I was confused when the nuns in the convent earnestly explained that Jesus had died to save us all from our sins. I was never quite sure what sin was. But I rather liked going to the lovely chapel with tall columns, heavy wooden pews and stained-glass windows. While there, we, the nonbelievers, were given Moral Science lessons. The very first section in the little book began like this:

Q: Where is God?

A: God is everywhere.

And to think that I needed to travel so far away from my familiar world to be convinced of His omnipresence! As for sin, if one willfully committed it, then having a dip to wash it off was a remarkably easy way to salvation. Medha and Anita had already washed away all sins of this birth with a dip in the Lake on the first day of the *kora*. I was not sure if I should have done the same. I toyed with the idea of going in for a dip the next day.

'What does the *Mani Mantra* really mean?'

'*Om mani padme hum*? Better ask Medha or Anita when they return.'

'Do you think it's repeated by most as habit, without understanding the essence of it?'

'Possibly. But it's beautiful when translated to 'Hail Jewel in the Lotus'. Mysterious, isn't it?'

Anita did not arrive for lunch. I strolled along the lakefront and foothills. When I returned, I was vaguely aware that it was well past Anita's time to return.

I remembered saying a few days ago, 'I am not ready to die yet, I have too much unfinished work to do.'

And Anita said with determination, 'I am ready.'

It was now four o'clock. With an ominous feeling, I climbed the moraines behind the tents to survey the landscape. I saw a small speck on the shore to the left and the Europeans walking in a row along the lake on the right. They were walking towards their camp, set up close to ours. I walked further left and saw the speck take definite form as I moved closer. It materialised to Anita. She was flaying her hands, but I could not hear her. I got nearer and she shouted, 'I am stuck. I can't move.'

I encouraged her, 'Jump over the channel next to you.'

But she repeated, 'I can't. I'm stuck in quicksand.'

Did I hear quicksand? That called for some quick rescue effort.

I returned to camp, broke up a game of cards and sent the two Nepali boys, Kumar and Kuman, with walking sticks to help her out of the marshes. After informing Rock, I followed the rescue team.

Anita came back furious. She said in anger, 'I have been entrenched in sand for more than two hours and no one went searching for me.' She ignored me royally but told the cook, other helpers and Rock, 'You should have gone looking for me at two o'clock. I have been in quicksand, thigh deep. I saw a carcass.'

There was the carcass of a dead sheep near where she was immobilised. She was mortified she would end her life the same way. Rock and I felt guilty and irresponsible. We swore to look out for each other with more alacrity.

We had one more day to complete the Manasarovar *kora*. My mind was brooding on Mandy's warning about 'group dynamics'. It was beyond my comprehension as to why Anita could not see that I had found her. There was no way to appease her. Clearly, we were at fault for not looking out for her two hours earlier. Even so, I did arrange for help when I saw her stranded. Anita did not speak to me for the rest of the day. In silence, she expressed her displeasure.

I ignored Anita's behaviour. I was humming, 'Om...' but not the *mantra* on the stones and walls of Tibet. I relaxed and sang the Beatles anthem of the 1970s, thanking the Good Lord for saving us from HAS, earthquake, accident and the portents of 'group dynamics.'

> *'Om, Jai Guru Deva...*
> Nothing's gonna change my world,
> Nothing's gonna change my world,
> *Om, Jai, Guru Deva...*

Pools of sorrow, waves of joy,
Dah, dah, da-dah,
Passing through the Universe,
Om, Jai, Guru Deva . . .'

An hour before seven, I climbed into the Land Cruiser and drove west towards Gossul to meet Medha at the appointed hour. From here the road followed a nineteen-kilometre track beyond the sand dunes, which was several more than along the shore. Medha and I silently sat through an uneventful dark drive back.

At breakfast the next day, Rock announced that he was better. He was given boiled potatoes for breakfast, which he had with minimal fuss.

Medha said, 'My lips are swollen by UV action.'

Anita said, 'I think it is the result of frostbite.'

I said, 'I think Medha's lips are less swollen today than yesterday.'

Anita did not speak to me. When she was in her black moods, I often wondered who and what she was thinking of. There was always an explanation for aberrant behaviour: some undocumented manifestation of HAS.

There were dark clouds and rain on Gurla, but we were eating breakfast on a sunny plain in the open. We saw the first rainbow of the trip, a baffling extravagance of nature. High on Gurla Mandhata, a complete circle of VIBGYOR [violet, indigo, blue, green, yellow, orange, red] appeared in the sky.

Hindu scriptures say that a pilgrim must spend at least three nights in a place to earn blessings. Now I knew why. It takes at least that much time to imbibe the mystic spiritualism of a place. In plainspeak, it takes time to unwind, relax and enjoy the serenity and communicate with oneself, to truly appreciate solitude.

I was enjoying the solitude at the foot of Gurla like I had not enjoyed anything for a long time. I sat looking at the mountain and the sea. I did not think and I did not worry. Was my mind a vacuum? Very far from it. For my mind seemed to have unobtrusively begun delving into the mirages of the past and reviving long-forgotten memories.

The quality of the pale diffused light, so unlike what you normally see under the cloudless heavens of Tibet, reminded me of the afternoons spent in my grandparents' house during school holidays. The best part of the day was the afternoon, which I spent in a cool dark room with my old grand-aunt. I sat in her cane easy chair with a book on my lap, reading in the diffused light, which filtered into the room through the latticed window. I read simplified narratives about Brobdingnag and Kon Tiki with equal fervour and always imagined that some day soon I too would go on a faraway adventure. Had I ever imagined such a timeless world then?

From our camp at Trugho to Gossul was a difficult trek with swamps along the southern shore and large round pebbles on the west shore. White bushy-tailed hare ran between aromatic thorny scrub, which grew selectively on sandy round drumlins. Moving north, there was dramatic change in landscape. All along the shore were low scarps dotted with smooth round pebbles. Several *chorten* were stacked with skeletons and enormous curved horns of yak and sheep. These indicated the active practice of animal sacrifice.

These were Bon worshipping points. Here we came across the family of Tibetans who had met us earlier at the camp. We exchanged *tashi dalek* and they smiled and waved as they passed by. They were resting on the rocks with the two children and would complete the *kora* in the next few hours. Tibetans complete the *kora* of Manasarovar on foot in two days. It takes us four to five.

The ancient Gossul *gompa* sits on the most weird and wonderful cliff. The cliff is formed of round pebbles and the cementing material has been extensively blown away, leaving behind hollows and caves. In time, the *gompa* may collapse with the supporting ballast being eroded. There are two large caves below the *gompa*.

'How black the walls are. This is soot from smoke-fire.'

'The caves are probably home to nomads and shepherds.'

Bon worshipping site stacked with sacrificial remains on the shore of Manasarovar.

'It is said that Atisha stayed in one of these caves for a week in the early 11th century.'

'Well, it's possible. But you hear so much about Atisha and Milarepa wandering and living in caves in these parts that you don't really know how seriously to take these historical snippets as facts.'

'Quite. But it indicates that these caves have existed at least a thousand years now.'

Although there were marshes from Gossul to Chiu along the shore, they were easily negotiated. Birds and ducks nested here and many of them could be seen high up on the cliffs. Countless larks, Mongolian finches and Tibetan twite! Quite unexpectedly, a number of birds fluttered on the cliff face and flew out over my head and across the lake into the sky. Some pieces of loose grit fell and sand blew into the air.

I watched the straight wall from which the birds had flown out, noisily fluttering their wings. I remembered where I had heard the same panicky flutter of bird wings echo and knew the same feeling of being trapped in time. That was another time and another place. I was standing in the courtyard of the Agra Fort and the tourist guide was spinning the most romantic story of lovelorn princes and unattainable princesses, who sent notes to each other tied to the feet of carrier pigeons. Even as he spoke, a group of pigeons fluttered and flew past me. The walls of the fort were as bare, straight and steep as the walls of this cliff.

The cooing pigeons had suddenly fluttered their wings and flew past in disarray, to settle down on the floor of the courtyard. But the sound of their wings echoed in the enclosed space for several minutes after they had settled down. The whiteness of the heat was the same. And the birds rode the hot air currents with the same ease. Time stood still, but space had expanded. At Manasarovar, the birds sought the expanse of the lake and the sky.

Ducks sat on individual weed nests and floated in safety about ten metres from the shore, a safe distance from human and other predators. Grey-brown gadwalls, smaller than the Brahminy ducks that we had seen earlier, swam quietly in the water. Their low whistle broke the quietude at times. The water was clear and we saw shoals of fish swimming in the lake.

Tibetans normally do not go fishing, but the dead fish of Manasarovar are in high demand for divination and medicinal purposes. Pilgrims collect the fish that die from being battered by strong waves and float to the shores of the lake. Pema confidently informed us, 'Manas fish good for stomach pain.' How did she know? Why, everyone knew. This was faith, you did not question it. This was about faith healing. In the case of healing by faith, does it matter how much of the means has a scientific basis and how much is just the power of suggestion?

Climbing the raised pebbly beaches about six-feet-high, at the confluence of the Tsering Madan Valley and Manasarovar, we got an excellent view of the lake, Chiu, Kailash and Gurla. Here we met Maya, who was part of the European group. Our rather elaborate lunch was spread out and we talked about Dharamsala. Devi had churned out vegetables, momos, puris, green beans, a slice of yak cheese and boiled potatoes, the last keeping in mind Rock's needs. The Europeans had a shortwave radio and they listened to the BBC. We were content being cut off from civilization intermittently. Maya said that she had heard on the news that there had been locusts in Afghanistan and an earthquake in Iran.

Medha knew Maya's architect mother. 'It's such a small world,' they agreed. They were both psychoanalysts and in their conversation mentioned people they were both acquainted with.

Maya wanted to know, 'Why have you returned?'

Without any hesitation, Rock cynically stated his perception of the reason, 'Madness.'

Anita and I were silent, but Medha answered for us, 'It's compelling.'

Then I asked Maya, 'How did you entertain your Army guests?'

She was surprised by my query. 'How do you know of the visit?'

'We had also been visited.'

'The Army men are convinced that many foreign tourists are spies.'

'That's the problem with security forces. They distrust everyone equally.'

'There are probably some spies in the garb of tourists.'

'Very likely. But the Chinese in Tibet spy on the local population. They do not consider it spying, because they've occupied the country.'

The short interlude and rest over, we continued our trek. From here to Chiu was only about five kilometres along marshy ground edged by low cliffs and clouds of flying insects, who neither bit, stung nor hissed, only flew straight into your open mouth and nostrils. Tsering sensibly put a plastic paper over his hat and tied it around his throat. Normally this would choke and kill, but on this occasion it saved him from the ever-active bugs. Somewhere between there and Chiu was a small jetty. There was a motor placed on it and a water pipe led from the jetty into the cliff alongside.

'You see this pipeline? It carries pumped water from Manasarovar to the gold mines on the isthmus between this lake and Rakas Tal.'

'How do you know?'

'Well, you can infer. Although the pipeline is covered with earth and debris, it can be identified on a good satellite image. Now if I mention this, it may be wrongly construed that I am spying.'

The Tibetans refused to comment on the matter. 'Not good for Tibet Peoples,' was all they would say.

'Wonder what punishment would have been given by the *dzongpa* in the old days for disturbing the spirits of the lake?'

Stories of Tibetan punishment abound in literature because of their cruel and extreme nature. The *dzongpa* who could not stop the Englishman Mr. Drummond, Commissioner of Bareilly, from boating in the lake in the mid-19th century, paid with his life for his inability to stop him. Later, of course, both Hedin and Pranavananda sounded the lake for depth from their boats, but in the process incurred much displeasure among the local people.

The drivers whispered, 'Chinese peoples pump Mapam (Manasarovar) water for gold.'

And Pema added in a hushed voice, 'Tibet peoples not get Manas gold.'

'Why not? Especially if it's likely to be taken away by others.'

'Gold from special fruit tree. Only for Lake gods.'

'Bad luck for other peoples.'

That evening, we completed the Manas *kora*, walking and on horseback. Then we went off to the gushing springs at Chiu on the banks of the Ganga *chu*, to soak in the luxury of a natural jacuzzi of hot mineral water. But right then I was beginning to feel impatient. I needed to physically investigate and record observations of the Ganga *chu* while we were still at Mansarovar. After all, my survey of geological literature on this area of Tibet and study of satellite images had pointed to the little stream holding the key to the mystery of the alternate sources of the Sutlej.

Later, we collected water from Manasarovar for folks back home. We had brought strong PET plastic bottles from India to transport Mana-sarovar water, because the flimsy jerry cans from Drachen had a way of leaking in transit. Our families and friends sprinkled the holy water in their homes and on themselves, and blessed us many times over for carrying the water back for them.

In recognition of our completing the *parikrama* of Mansarovar, we were also treated with quiet respect by them. At such times, I often wondered if the feeling of achieving a milestone in life was justifiable, or was it a futile victory in one's ambition to seek freedom from oneself.

6

THE SUTLEJ CONUNDRUM

From the mountain ranges over the Mayum La Pass to the Ladakh range of the Himalayas in the west is the catchment of the river Sutlej and its many tributaries. The tributaries are truly very many, and the pilgrims who visited Kailash-Manasarovar in the days of yore knew that well. The river was then called Satadru, a combination of *sata,* meaning hundred, and *dru,* river.

In the 10th century, the descendents of the anti-Buddhist pro-Bon King Langdarma fled the Yarlung Kingdom and migrated to Western Tibet. Nyima Gon, a Buddhist descendant, was the first to found and consolidate a kingdom in Ngari *khorsum.* According to Tibetan texts of the time, he sent out surveyors to reconnoitre the provinces. This is what the surveyors had to report about Mangyul province, generally covering the Rakas Tal-Manasarovar area: 'The territory looks like a hollow land filled with lakes and surrounded by snow mountains. The people resemble frogs.'

This is a remarkably accurate description of the morphology of the area and of particular interest to my study. For, irrespective of what others have recorded in the past, even today it is just as described by Nyima Gon's men. The lakes occupy the lowest parts of the hollows. So, the rivers from the surrounding mountains flow into the lakes and not out of them. As regards the people looking like frogs, some things are best left unexplained.

From time immemorial Lanchen Khambab, the source of the Elephant river, or Sutlej, had been known to be near Dulchu *gompa*, northwest of Rakas Tal. But in the last two-and-a-half centuries, the 'scientific' view had veered around to Lanchen Khambab being at Gunglung glacier, southeast of Lake Manasarovar. The prevailing belief is that the Gunglung glacier source is the genetic source, that is, the river originates there. However, for religious purposes, the traditionally known source is the spring near Dulchu *gompa*.

What happened in between these two Lanchen Khambab, fifty kilometres apart? If the genetic source view were to be taken, then the following happened. The waters from the Gunglung glacier melted and were carried to Lake Manasarovar. Then the waters from the lake flowed through the Ganga *chu* to lake Rakas Tal. From a channel in the northwest of this second lake, waters of the Sutlej then flowed to Dulchu *gompa* and continued further west. But did that actually happen? Did water flow, even seasonally, through this entire link? Was there a case for alternate sources of this mighty river? That could be answered only after an investigation.

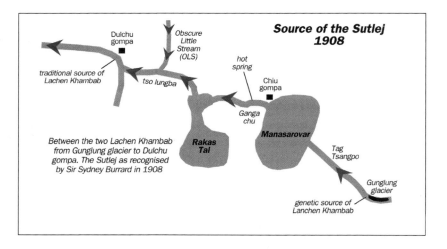

Legend has it that two golden fish lived in the freshwater lake of Manasarovar. One day, they quarrelled and one chased the other through the Ganga *chu* to the Rakas Tal, whose water was undrinkable. Once the fish entered Rakas Tal, the waters of the lake magically became fresh and drinkable. This is yet another interesting fable. It reaffirms the statement handed down in oral tradition regarding water flowing from Lake Manasarovar through the Ganga *chu* to Rakas Tal.

'That's a charming fable, except that . . .'

'There could be no gold fish . . .'

'. . . except that the tale deviates from one widely acknowledged fact. That no Tibetan would, even today, ever drink the water of Rakas Tal.'

'This doesn't make any sense.'

'What doesn't make any sense?'

'Why is this insignificant *chu* called by the name of the mighty Ganga?'

'Because, for the longest period in history, pilgrims thought it was the Ganga.'

'They believed that the Ganga's source was Manasarovar and this was the only visible outlet from the lake.'

'So, naturally, it was concluded that this was the Ganga.'

'It's hardly two hundred years since the myth's been exploded.'

'Thanks to the British surveyors.'

In the early 19th century, the British in India conducted several surveys in the Himalayas into the catchment of the two tributaries of the Ganga: Bhagirathi and Alakananda rivers. The surveyors moved up the Ganga from Haridwar and Rishikesh in the foothills, up the traditional pilgrim routes to survey the many tributaries of the river. It was conclusively proven that the Ganga did not originate in the lakes across the Himalayas in Tibet. No one seriously believes today that the Ganga is linked to Manasarovar or Rakas Tal, but the name given to the *chu* between the two water bodies remains.

For many centuries, pilgrims believed that Manasarovar and Rakas Tal were connected by the Ganga *chu*. A *chu* in the Tibetan language is neither a stream nor a river, it is 'little water'. The Western world received contradictory data on the presence of water in the *chu*. It was no mean task to cross the Himalayas from the Indian subcontinent via high passes and surreptitiously survey southwestern Tibet. Several surveyors entered the area over time. Some explorers saw water in the *chu*, some heard from hearsay that there was water present in it, while others found it dry. So the answer to the question of the connection between the two lakes has remained an enigma for the last two-and-a-half centuries.

'One of the most widely held beliefs in Tibet is that when the waters between the two lakes are connected through the Ganga *chu*, it augurs well for the country.'

'Does it ever happen?'

'Well, once every few years.'

Apparently, in a year of exceptionally heavy rain, the *chu* is known to have water in it. One can safely conclude that in the last few centuries it was at least an ephemeral, if not a perennial, stream.

The Ganga *chu*, not seen by Dr. William Moorcroft and Hyder Jung Hearsey in 1812, does exist, even today. Their companion Harballabh, however, informed them that he had seen the channel with water in it sixteen years earlier, in 1796.

Moorcroft and Hearsey were colourful characters. They were the first British from across the Himalayas to survey this area. Moorcroft was a veterinary surgeon in search of high-quality studs to improve the stock of animals in the British army. He was last heard of and seen in Central Asia, where he went searching for the Farghana horse. He is believed to have been murdered there.

Hearsey was a mercenary of mixed Indian and English descent. He had surveying and cartographic skills and was the landlord of large estates in Dehradun Valley. He is said to have once owned the present Survey of India estate at Hathibarkala in Dehradun.

Their graphic record of the journey to Lake Manasarovar describes the terrible state of health suffered by Dr. Moorcroft, who assiduously surveyed the northwestern section of the lake, while suffering from what today can be diagnosed as HAS. Hearsey's days were comparatively less uncomfortable and he spent a day leisurely fishing and shooting ducks in the lake. But they did not find the opening to the Ganga *chu* that Harballabh had vouched seeing earlier. Their description of the northern shore is accurate and as such, one would assume that the mouth of the Ganga *chu* was then already blocked with sand.

Another reputed British surveyor, Henry Strachey, had seen the *chu* in 1846. In 1854, he wrote in his book, *Physical Geography of Western Tibet*, 'Its (Mapham's) [Manasarovar's] effluent runs through an opening in the hilly isthmus into the western lake: I found it a swift stream 100 feet broad and three feet deep in October; and its exit from the lake was seen by Mr. J.E. Winterbottom and my brother, Richard Strachey, from a height a few furlongs off; though Moorcroft crossed this very place without finding the stream, even in August, the time of highest flood — whether from its being then dry, or from its percolating through a bar of shingle close to the lake, as asserted by some of my native informants, is not apparent.'

In 1906, Charles Sherring wrote, 'It is a fact that at this present moment no water is actually flowing between the two lakes, the reason being that storms blowing from the east have thrown up sand at the mouth of the passage to a height of about four feet, but the best native information on the spot gives it as a fact that after heavy rains the water traverses the channel.'

'So it implies that the level of the lake rises after a season of heavy rainfall and this water flows into the Ganga *chu*,' concluded Anita.

'That seems logical. But consider the deep gullies that have formed by water erosion on the north side of the *chu*. This indicates that at least some of the water that causes flash floods is from sources other than the lake.' That was my view.

'In any case, it must be very exceptionally heavy rain for the lake to rise four or five feet!'

'Let's take readings on the GPS to check which way the water should flow in the channel.' Taking measurement with a scientific instrument (albeit not a very accurate one) added to our sense of exploration and adventure. We were not concerned with exact actual readings but relative positions and elevations, which would suffice for our immediate purpose.

The elevation reading on Rock's GPS receiver, taken at the two ends of the Ganga *chu*, was 15,072 feet at Manasarovar and 15,026 feet at Rakas Tal.

'So why does the water from the first not flow into the other?'

'God knows. It's a mystery to me.'

'The answer to the riddle of the connection between the two lakes is hidden within this *chu*.'

'He knows the answer,' said Anita.

'Who?'

'Padmasambhava. He's watching with his bulging large eyes from Chiu *gompa*.'

'The answer is not easily discernible to mere mortals like us. We've got to investigate.'

We planned an investigation of the Ganga *chu*. There may conceivably be a structural fault line along the *chu*. With a line of hot springs running from Gossul to Chiu, there was reason to believe that the western part of Manasarovar is geologically active. In fact, hot springs probably exist at the bottom of Manasarovar, which accounts for its ice melting earlier than Rakas Tal's. Over the decades, the water in Lake Manasarovar has definitely fallen in level. It probably does not rise to the point where it would flow into the Ganga *chu*. Indeed, it would need to rise at least four feet to be able to do that.

On our last expedition, in the rainy season of the year 2,000, I had observed that water did not flow from Manasarovar to Rakas Tal through the Ganga *chu*. Several explorers have suggested that there is a subsurface connection between Manasarovar and the Ganga *chu*. While this is within the realm of possibility, at present the manifestation of this subterranean connection is not seen anywhere on the land surface.

We visited the village adjacent to the hot springs on the Ganga *chu*. All the shacks were conspicuous by their remarkable architecture featuring rows of empty beer bottles arranged along the lintel just below the roof. Here we met a European couple living in the village. The young girl said, 'Hello. We are from Austria.'

This brings to mind *Seven Years In Tibet*, which recounts the story of the two Austrians, Heinrich Harrer and Peter Aufschnaiter, who escaped from a British prison in India. They reached Lhasa in 1946, fleeing across the Himalayas to Tibet. Harrer befriended the young Dalai Lama and lived for a long time in Lhasa. The film, based on his book, has enthused several Austrians to visit Tibet.

'Hello. We are from India and have just completed circling the lake.'

'We have been staying here in the village guesthouse for a few days.'

'Right next to the hot water baths? What a luxury!'

'Not really. I am worried because my friend is suffering from severe abdominal pain,' the girl volunteered. This was not the best place to be ill.

'There is a Tibetan medicine hospital at Darchen.'

'We should try and go there,' said the girl.

'We can help you get there,' we offered. 'I think there are a couple of Swiss doctors who visit the hospital regularly.'

'Thanks for the information. We should go there now.'

The villagers had covered the springs on the southern bank of the *chu* in a bathhouse partitioned into several cubicles. The sexes were seg-regated. A statuesquely built woman, Keeper of the Women's Section, who cleaned the bath, wordlessly instructed us on the operation of the plumbing. This involved removing a piece of rag that functioned as a stopper in the hot water pipe. While we soaked and warmed in the sulfuric waters, we looked up and saw the sky through the glass roof. After days of deprivation from baths, I was thoroughly enjoying the sensation of hot water on my skin.

Friends have asked, 'Do Tibetans ever bathe?'

My answer is, 'I am sure they do, but are not obsessive about it as some of us are.'

'You mean they do not bathe regularly.'

'They do not need to. Their climate is so dry that one does not perspire at all.'

'Even in summer?'

'Well, in spite of the hot days, it is quite possible to remain for days without bathing. And the winters are so severe and long that it would be sheer lunacy to even contemplate bathing.'

'Then why is it said that they smell?'

'That's true of some Tibetans. The ones who rub themselves with yak butter do give off a strong rancid stench!'

An investigation of the hot springs showed several points from which hot water was bubbling out, mainly on the northern side of the *chu*. Water collected in a large stagnant pool at the base of the village at the hot springs. There was a strong smell of sulphur in the water and many waterfowl swam in the pool, oblivious of the odour.

A stone dam, about a foot high, has been constructed right across the *chu* at the village and local people sat on the stones to fill their jerry cans with water. Although the banks were covered with sand, the village, like the outcrop on which Chiu *gompa* was perched, was built on highly metamorphosed igneous rocks. On the right bank of the Ganga *chu*, next to a massive crystalline quartz outcrop, one could hear the water boil and bubble away, almost as if a kettle was on the boil on a stove.

As I walked along the Ganga *chu* from the hot springs eastward to Manasarovar, I asked Pradip, 'Which way does the water flow?'

'From Manasarovar to the village,' he answered, bored, yawning.

'Look and tell. It's important for me to know.'

He looked. Then suddenly woke up and said. 'Why, it is flowing from the hot springs in the village towards Manasarovar.'

'And does it reach the lake?'

'No! It dries up at the base of Chiu *gompa*.' Pradip was surprised at his own discovery.

'Tsering, which way does the Ganga *chu* flow?'

He did not answer in words but smiled and showed me the direction of flow with his hand. The stream was no more than a few inches deep. From the base of Chiu *gompa* to the sand dunes and hills surrounding the lake was a distance of a couple of hundred metres. The channel was not clearly defined on the ground and was dry here.

Water from the hot springs also flowed westward from the village in a trickle through the Ganga *chu* to Rakas Tal. I dipped my walking stick to check the depth and direction of the flow of water. 'See, it's nowhere more than two or three inches deep!'

'But the valley is so well formed.'

'This only indicates that at one time there must have been substantial water flowing through this stream.'

'You would not imagine that looking at this small and insignificant stream.'

'It dries up in salt encrustation long before it reaches Rakas Tal.'

I would admit that I was not the first to note that water from the hot springs flowed west through the Ganga *chu* to Rakas Tal.

A century ago in 1904, Colonel C.H.D. Ryder stated that he could not find the Ganga *chu* outlet from Manasarovar. He 'struck the channel a mile below the outlet, a small stream only partly frozen over, and we followed this up and found that it did not flow from the lake but from the hot spring . . .' However, today it is the hot springs that are the chief source of water in the Ganga *chu*, something most travel books do not acknowledge and highlight.

It is my submission that while Lake Manasarovar is higher than Lake Rakas Tal, the hot springs are at a slightly higher elevation than Manasarovar. It is for this reason that the sulphuric waters from the hot springs at the village flow in the Ganga *chu* both in an easterly direction towards Manasarovar and a westerly direction towards Rakas Tal.

I asked, 'So if the traditional belief is that water flows from Manasarovar to Rakas Tal, should I discount it?'

'Yes. We can see it is just a myth,' said Medha.

'I say, no! It must have happened in earlier times when the level of the water was at least four feet higher in Manasarovar.'

'And how do you surmise this?'

'By looking at the width and depth of the tiny trickle of a misfit stream that flows in the fairly substantial valley of the Ganga *chu*. Such a valley could not have been carved out by a stream with as little water as it contains today.'

Anita agreed. 'This is a channel cut by a far more robust body of water that flowed in the past.'

I pointed to the beaches along the lakeshore. 'Can you see the raised beach along the northwestern circumference of the lake? Just beyond the marshy shore, where it forms an uninterrupted half moon?'

'Very clearly. What of it?'

'Can you see three levels? The highest is over four-and-a-half feet in relief, above the water level in June. This implies that the land has risen, while the water in the lake has also probably fallen because the climate may have become drier over the past centuries.'

Anita had studied geography and understood what I was driving at. 'It follows that the smaller streams, which earlier drained into the lake, have now dried up.'

'It is also the explanation for Pranavananda including Ponri (to the northeast of Sham Tso) as a *gompa* on the *kora* of Manasarovar. But the *gompa* is far away from this route today.'

'That is so. But Ponri would still be a *gompa* on the Manas *kora* for Tibetans.'

'Very likely. But that's not germane to the issue.'

'By the way, why would Ponri still be a *gompa* on the Manas *kora* for Tibetans?'

'I'm not sure. Perhaps it has something to do with the smaller lake to the northeast of Sham Tso, which is traditionally accepted as the bathing pond of the gods. Ponri is on its shores.'

Later that afternoon, I suggested, 'Let's drive around Rakas Tal.'

'No road around Rakas Tal,' stated Pema.

'But we can try and drive along part of the lake shore.'

'No. Tibet peoples no drive around Rakas Tal,' was Pema's response.

'Well, then let us drive up to it. At least see it.'

'*Nando*. Driver say, no.' The Tibetans were firm.

My repeated requests to drive me around Rakas Tal were met with the reply, 'Rakas Tal no good for religion (read: god-fearing) Tibet peoples.'

It seemed an impossible task to get the Tibetans to take me there, except, of course, by the standard means which works everywhere. A little conversation on the side and some trilingual convincing aroused interest. 'You give (additional) Yuan 4.50 per kilometre.' At the time of climbing into the Cruiser, I was informed that the driver's services were available at a revised rate of Yuan 5 because there was no road leading to Rakas Tal.

Buddhists and Hindus, Tibetans and Indians shun Rakas Tal equally. Our religions associate them with the *rakshasas* or demons. It is owing to this association that the lake has remained so isolated from the pilgrim circuit and off the beaten track of the casual visitor. The Rakas Tal is the most beautiful, serene sheet of water one can imagine, with the Gurla Mandhata towering over its southern shore. But it can be rough too and is frozen for a longer period than Lake Manasarovar in winter.

The only motorable road that approaches Rakas Tal is from the southeast, the same road that connects to Purang at the border with Nepal. There was no one else other than our small group at the lake. There was nothing eerie about the emptiness. It was the most perfect sight of a mountain lake with two large islands in it. A gravelly fan indicated that water had drained into the lake from the southeast. I counted twelve levels of raised beaches, some formed of large pebble, some coarse sand, some fine sand and some small round pebbles.

'This is the most spectacular beach that I have seen.'

'Resembles an enormous amphitheatre, doesn't it?'

'. . . with regular steps. How high do you think the steps are?'

'About a foot high, I'd say.'

'How well preserved the beaches are!'

In spite of the high overhead sun, I photographed this remarkable beach. Unlike the beaches of Manasarovar, these were in pristine and perfect condition, untrammelled by man or beast. There were no scattered remnants of human association or telltale signs of automotive wheels.

The driver absolutely refused to drive us around Rakas Tal and to show his displeasure went and peed into it. But a little further cajoling in the afternoon made him drive me to the northern part of the lake. This was at the foot of the Kailash range (Gang Te Se) and the Barkha plain that borders it immediately to the north. The northern part of the lake is smaller than the southern, and a narrow strait joins the two. Tibetans do not approach the Rakas Tal, which they say is 'Unlucky for Tibet Peoples'.

Medha, always ready for an adventure, accompanied me to survey this area. She took some photographs of the Kailash range and peak

Beach terraces of the Rakas Tal form an ever-expanding amphitheatre.

reflected in the waters of Rakas Tal. There was a very wide marsh as we approached the lake from the east — and there are no roads or tracks leading to this area. Many hares and bush-tailed fox scurried around on the tufts of short grass. At the edge of the lake were large Greylag geese and other waterfowl. I rather enjoyed watching the noisy party of eight heavy, well-fed, dark grey and black Greylag geese and amateurishly photographed them from a distance.

The birds were almost three feet in length and about a foot-and-a-half high. They were definitely unafraid of my presence. Although they did make loud ringing honks as I reached their marshy lair, they did not fly away. There were smaller, though numerous, silver-grey bar-headed geese too. As I approached them, I could hear them murmur. I believe these geese make a musical honking sound, but they only murmured all the while they were around me. I was also not blessed with the sight of the rare black S-necked swan. They are either a myth or extinct here.

On the shores of the lake run herds of musk deer. We saw a group of six. A seventh raced our Cruiser, overtook it and crossed it from the front. The Tibetan musk is of real high quality and in the past it was an important item of trade and was exported to India and China. We were simply lucky to see these graceful animals, bounding past, for only a few remain in this region now.

On reaching the point between the northern and southern side of the lake, we looked for signs of habitation.

'Are there no hamlets or huts here?'

'Seems like there are none.'

'See those four raised beaches on one side?'

'Yes. Anything significant?'

'Absolutely. Especially when seen in association with the strait, which is short and sharply defined. And both sides have identical sedimentary rocks, probably sandstone and conglomerate.'

'What's the implication?'

'I suspect that during a glacial age, ice sheets scoured many lakes, including Manasarovar and the northern and southern Rakas Tal. At a later date, the strait was formed, probably by subsidence of the area. The shear lines on either side even suggest a rift.'

'Really? Like a rift valley? Wouldn't it be great if we found a rift valley?'

'We probably have found one. Sand sheets and dunes now cover most of the older natural features. So we need geological confirmation.'

The two long exploratory trips to Rakas Tal were immensely satisfying from the investigative point of view. It also proved to be a bonding experience between the Tibetans, Nepalis and Yindu. So a gratuity to the driver was called for, for his fine services, over and above the call of duty. This had the salutary effect of changing his '*Nando*' (no) to '*Rha*' (yes) when broaching the subject of driving up to Dulchu *gompa*, to see the Lanchen Khambab. In fact, with much enthusiasm, a plan acceptable to all was chalked out.

Long after explorers had discovered the supposed outflow of the Sutlej from the northwestern corner of the Rakas Tal, Henry Strachey had noted in 1846 that the channel had dried up. He wrote about Rakas Tal in 1854, 'The effluence to the Langchen river is from the N. point, which I crossed, however in October, without finding any running stream, or any marked channel for one, though the flatness of the ground, its partial inundation in shallow pools, and obvious descent of the level towards the river, entirely corroborated the native accounts of an intermittent effluence in seasons of flood.'

Colonel C.H.D. Ryder corroborated this in 1904. He surveyed and drew a map of the area, but showed the connection between the lake and the river with a broken line because he did not see any water in the channel. He recorded, 'We went down the old channel from the Rakas Tal to the Sutlej and it was six miles before we saw any sign of water flowing. There may be an underground flow but not above ground.'

One must not discount the observations of the Swiss geologists, Heim and Gansser, made in 1938, regarding the northwestern corner of Rakas Tal. They wrote about the 'fathomless bogs' there: 'Here must once have been the outlet of the great lakes. Now the rivers flow in the opposite direction.' The truth is that Manasarovar and Rakas Tal are the lowest points in this region of Western Tibet and are centres of inland drainage. Streams from all around flow into these lakes.

'What a jest of nature! Rakas Tal, the Demon's Lake, is the prime recipient of the pure waters of Kailash.'

In a religiously charged area, Bons, Hindus, Buddhists and Jains all have one common belief: 'The clear and pure waters of Kailash flow into the Manasarovar, at its foot.'

But facts are very different. Waters from the Lah, Dzong, Selung and Darchen *chu* all spread over the Barkha plain in narrow, shallow braided channels, following the slope of the land. The streams merge and empty into northern Rakas Tal. Of these, the Darchen *chu* actually rises at the foot of the Mount Kailash peak. And why do the waters not flow into the Manasarovar? Because Manasarovar is girdled by low, sandy hills along its northern shores and only one small stream from the north debouches and drains into the Sham Tso lagoon, at Langbona (Elephant's Trunk) Monastery.

Should those who believe the Sutlej flows out of the Rakas Tal have had the advantage of seeing satellite images from different sources, their conclusions would be different. As mine were. Further on, I will elaborate on these in greater depth.

My friends said, 'I don't understand what you're trying to prove. Everyone knows that the source of the Sutlej is at Gunglung glacier.'

'Not everybody. Not the Tibetans, who think it is at Dulchu,' said I.

'Since the 20th century, the European geographers have been convinced that the genetic source of the Sutlej is at Gunglung glacier,' said Medha.

'What's all this? Tell me more,' asked Rock.

'It is simply this. Traditionally, the source of the Sutlej was known to be at Dulchu *gompa*, west of Rakas Tal. Since the 20th century, the British geographers believed the Sutlej from here is linked to the alternate source at Gunglung, approximately fifty kilometres further to the southeast.'

'And this is based on facts?'

'Partially. And partially conjecture.'

'But surely this area has been surveyed?'

'Not completely. And the British also based their opinion on the survey made by the Imperial Chinese lama-topographers of the 18th century.'

'And you do not think they were correct?'

'I'm not convinced.'

'Why?'

'Things change. It could have been in the early 20th century, but probably is not so today,' I said.

'And you have a basis for this view?'

'Certainly. At least we know that one link in the chain is broken today.'

'You mean the Ganga *chu*.'

'That we have seen ourselves. Water may flow from Gunglung glacier to Manasarovar, but not from Manasarovar to Rakas Tal.'

'So that's quite clear.'

'Yes, but the point is that I do not think the Sutlej is even connected between Rakas Tal and Dulchu *gompa*.'

'And why would you think so?'

'Several reasons. But the one I most object to is that there is a suggestion the link is maintained through an uncharted network of subterranean streams.'

'Sounds interesting!'

'It's an imagination grabber and the ultimate resort of those who have no other evidence to support their belief in the alternative source of the

Sutlej at Gunglung glacier'; I was as harsh as rash in my judgment.

Sven Hedin surmised that because Manasarovar and Rakas Tal were freshwater lakes, they would have outflows, either subterranean or on the surface. It was his opinion that the surface channels may have water in them ephemerally, only during a season of heavy rain and may be quite dry in other seasons and years. If this is accepted, then clearly, the Ganga *chu* and the 'dotted' outflow channel from northwestern Rakas Tal to the Sutlej at Dulchu, shown on Colonel Ryder's map, are all part of the Sutlej. His view was that the availability of water in these channels is a function of the amount of rainfall and snowfall, and therefore, the result of seasonal variations in precipitation. This explanation was accepted by Colonel Ryder, and later in 1908 by Colonel S.G. Burrard in his book, *A Sketch of the Geography and Geology of the Himalaya Mountains and Tibet.* Colonel Burrard used this explanation to assume the genetic source of the Sutlej to be the Gunglung glacier.

My own view in this matter is that if we take this basically sound argument to its logical end, then it is possible to understand this tantalising geographical conundrum of the link of the Sutlej to the lakes. Hedin's explanation based on seasonal change in precipitation can be extended to climatic (a few decades) changes. When the climate here was less arid, the Sutlej flowed uninterrupted from Rakas Tal to Dulchu *gompa*. But now there are many evidences of drying of the climate. We had seen that the water level in the lakes had fallen and impressive salt patches had appeared on the shores of Rakas Tal, where earlier the 'Sutlej' flowed in and out of the lake. Beaches and terraces were well established along both lakes. The conclusion was, with present low levels of precipitation and high evaporation, the surface channel of the Sutlej between the lakes and Dulchu *gompa* was always dry. The river had disappeared from this section.

'So you see, if the rainfall regime changes and there is marked increase in rainfall, then perhaps the Sutlej may once more be traced up to the Gunglung glacier.'

'But as of now you think, Lanchen Khambab is at Dulchu.'

'What else can I say? I've given you my reasons,' I said.

The geographical problem here was essentially a question of defining the catchment area of a river. In the case of the Sutlej, at the two lakes, it was a question of availability of adequate water for it to be continuous or discontinuous. Under the present circumstances, the catchment of the Sutlej from Dulchu westward is not connected to the watersheds of the Manasarovar and Rakas Tal. As a consequence, the two lakes cannot be considered a part of the Sutlej's catchment, The lakes Manasarovar and Rakas Tal are areas of inland drainage and the Gunglung glacier's melt waters form part of this catchment. The Sutlej catchment with its many watersheds, on the other hand, flows out into the Arabian Sea, after joining the Indus. Dulchu, then, laid claim to Lanchen Khambab.

Sutlej is perhaps the only long river in the world today (it cuts across three large countries, Tibet, India and Pakistan) whose source is not determined. Even modern maps indicate two alternate sources of the river. Observations clearly point to the tenuous and possibly evolving nature of the link between the places along the old stream channel.

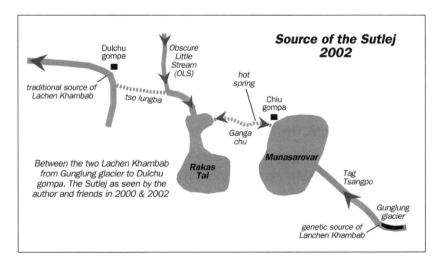

I told my friends that I thought there was a clear case for rewriting the story of the 'genetic' source of the Sutlej at the Gunglung glacier.

The chief character in this story is an Obscure Little Stream (OLS) that flows south across the Barkha plain. This OLS has little of interest to attract scientists to study it and relate it to the redesignation of the source of Sutlej from Gunglung glacier to Dulchu. So the survey of the OLS was the next important matter on my agenda to solve the problem of the alternate sources of the Sutlej. This was a rather complex matter of logistics in the absence of maps, paucity of information on local terrain, limited time and lukewarm interest of my companions. But I had a strong gut feeling it would be the proverbial cherry on the cake that I would savour long after the expedition was over!

7

PILGRIM'S TRAIL:
OUTER KORA OF MOUNT KAILASH

Mount Kailash is a name we have grown up with, a name which has been in our subconsciousness since early times. I was not the only one mystified and captivated by the illusion of the sacred mountain. Prana-vananda eulogised, 'The perpetual snowclad Peak of the Holy Kailash (styled Kang Rinpoche in the Tibetan language) of hoary antiquity and celebrity, the spotless design of nature's art, of most bewitching and overpowering beauty, has a vibration of the supreme order from the spiritual point of view.' Sven Hedin wrote in his three-volume *Trans-Himalayas*, Kailash was 'incomparably the most famous mountain in the world: Mount Everest and Mont Blanc cannot vie with it.'

Long before Hedin had set eyes on Kang Rinpoche, Desideri had written in his records, 'We left Cartoa (Gartok?) in the second-half of October, and arrived at the highest point reached during the whole journey in this desert, called Ngnari-Giongar, on the ninth of November. All these people, because of a certain Urghien, founder of the present Thibetan religion, hold it in much veneration. Close by is a mountain of excessive height and great circumference, always enveloped in cloud, covered with snow and ice, and most horrible, barren, steep, and bitterly cold (Mount Kailash). In a cave hollowed out of the live rock, the above named Urghien is said to have lived for some time in absolute solitude, self-mortification, and continual religious meditation. The cave is now a temple consecrated to him, with a rude, miserable monastery attached, where dwells a Lama with a few monks who serve the temple. Besides visiting the cave, to which they always bring offerings, the Thibetans walk most devoutly round the base of the mountain, which takes several days and they believe will procure them great indulgences.'

Well, it's a tradition that goes back to the 13th century!

Having reached the wonder after days of anticipation, the mystery faded and got replaced by practical concerns of survival and achieving the goal of completing the *kora*. An acquaintance had breezily stated, in a dismissive way, about this climb, 'Oh, its quite easy . . . no problem at all.'

I chose to remember this statement in preference to an American professor's admission that it was so tough that he did not have the strength to carry anything except his water bottle. This was one time in life when experience made all the difference between managing well and acute discomfort. We hoped that this time we were better fortified to climb up to Drolma La and complete the *kora* satisfactorily.

All arrangements had been made in advance for the *parikrama* of Mount Kailash. With the knowledge of experience, we knew that on this trek, Murphy's Law always prevailed. Many things would go wrong. When plains people start a trek at 15,000 feet to rise 3,600 feet in two days, it takes them to the limits of human endurance. While it is exciting to think one can, one must recognise that high-altitude trekking is largely a challenge to keep risks at bay.

In the year 2,000, I recall that when the first snowflakes fell and a sudden blizzard enveloped us as we stood on Drolma La (18,600 feet), Anita had suffered from serious HAS. She was low on energy, having thrown up innumerable times. Her lips and under eyes had turned blue. During descent, we took turns to hold her hand and guide her along narrow paths on steep slopes covered in loose gravel and over a glacier.

On reaching the valley, we found that the *yakpa* had gone several miles ahead, along with our tents and food. We caught up with them after seven kilometres, where camp was reachable only after crossing a fierce icy stream.

Next morning, Anita had neither any recollection of the swirling snow nor the walk over the glacier. But she had a faint memory of Tibetan pilgrims singing as they walked along the *kora*.

While still at the Chiu campsite, Pema said, 'I go Darchen.'

'But we are beginning the Kailash *kora* tomorrow. Why go today?'

'I take yak for tomorrow.' She planned to go to Darchen to arrange for yaks to carry tents, water and dry rations for the circumambulation. As she prepared to leave, we decided to meet next day at Tarpoche.

'That's a good plan! We can avoid Darchen and go straight to Tarpoche.'

'Okay. I get yak. We meet one o'clock,' confirmed Pema.

'And enjoy the evening with your friends at Darchen,' I said.

'I enjoy,' she said with the faintest suggestion of sullied virtue in her smile.

Pema then got into a Cruiser and drove off towards the bustling town. Pradip and Devi accompanied her to Darchen to buy vegetables and water for us to carry along. An extraordinarily large number of pilgrims had arrived at Kailash that year from all over Tibet and India in celebration of the Year of the Horse, after a span of twelve years. This had led to a dearth of those superb beasts of burden.

We had deliberately planned avoiding Darchen this time. The yaks would meet us at the same time as the truck, at the starting point of the *kora* at Tarpoche. The yaks would carry the tents and other supplies for the duration of the three nights and four days.

On the way, we had a short encounter with the Army at Barkha. All the soldiers manning the checkpoint were Chinese and young. They waved one red and another green flag for us to stop. At which point, one thought occurred to all of us: 'Our passports have been taken by Pema to the security office in Darchen.'

As a soldier walked up, we rolled down the windows and said, 'Good morning.'

'Good morning,' he replied. He examined our faces and then queried, 'Yindu?'

'Yes,' we smiled.

'Passport?' he asked.

'Darchen,' we answered in unison.

A serious look came over his face. The drivers disembarked and went across to the table, where the senior was sitting out in the open, next to the barrier. There was a conclave. Then the soldiers returned with the Group Visa document with our names listed on it and asked us to identify ourselves. Once this was accomplished to his satisfaction, the green flag was waved for us to continue to Tarpoche.

We reached Tarpoche on a clouded morning. Pradip arrived shortly after, bringing news from Darchen that Brazil would play Germany in the World Cup finals.

'Tarpoche' means a big flagstaff. The flagstaff was first erected here in 1681, to mark the victory of the Fifth Dalai Lama over the Ladakhi kings. After the military expeditions of 1679 to 1681, the three Ngnari *khorsum* (the three provinces of the west) finally came under the Dalai Lama's administration. This subdued the marauding Muslim warlords from the west and established the practice of their paying tribute to Lhasa. The same year the Fifth Dalai Lama died.

Saga Dawa had just been celebrated on the day of the full moon (May 25 that year). In India, we celebrate this day as Buddha Purnima, the day Sakyamuni was born and got enlightened. On this occasion, a new flagpole is erected here every year. Every twelfth year, it is rejoiced with special pomp. This was one such year. The flagpole was standing tall and upright. It was magnificent in its simplicity, wrapped around in yak hair and colourful prayer flags. From the pole, prayer flags were attached to the ground like the spines of tents. The flags had windhorses and prayers printed on them. It is believed that as the flags flutter, these prayers are carried directly to heaven.

*Tarpoche, the giant flagpole decorated with flags
at the start of the Kailash kora.*

Tarpoche marks the beginning of the Kailash *kora* and the first of several prostration points along the circuit. We watched as several Tibetan Buddhist pilgrims prostrated in veneration to Kailash here. If you are a pilgrim on this *kora*, Kailash is no mere mountain. It is the embodiment of divinity. It is Meru, the centre of the Universe, the abode of Lord Shiva and Demchhok, the place where the first Jain Tirthankara achieved Nirvana, and where Shenrab of the Bons descended from heaven to earth.

I had often wondered if Anita and Medha seriously believed that Shiva's abode was Kailash. But now I thought they did. It was Shiva's Kailash they had come to visit. Rock and I were also deeply interested in Kailash, but I doubt that either of us had the innate trust in the power of the mountain to influence our lives in the way Anita and Medha did. Naturally, we did not say so, for it would be disrespectful to their beliefs. But we could not deny being influenced by the faith of all our companions and other pilgrims that we met along the way. I admit the journey to Kailash has left a lasting impression on my mind, and it will remain till my dying day.

While we waited there, a Chinese television crew of two arrived in a jeep and interviewed us. The anchor asked me several questions in Chinese, possibly regarding travel and religion, which I answered knowledgeably.

'I think he is asking where we are from,' said Anita.

'That's easy. Lets say Yindu,' I said. Then I turned on a smile for the camera and repeated, 'Yindu.'

'We're circling the mountain,' I volunteered, not understanding the question and making a circle in clockwise direction with the index finger of my right hand.

One of the TV crew smiled and pointed to the flagpole.

'Yes, it's beautiful. But we do not understand what you say,' said Anita.

'Perhaps we can walk around the pole, and he can record it on the video,' I suggested to Anita.

Language has never been an insurmountable barrier, if one wants to communicate with gesticulations and expressions. Naturally, there was no way of knowing what we were asked, or for the TV crew to understand what I was saying.

'Maybe we can say, Atisha was from India,' I said.

The man with the camera picked up the word 'Atisha' and beamed at us, taking pictures frantically.

'Let's tell him the Dalai Lama lives in India.' The cameraman picked up the name of The Ocean of Wisdom and stopped taking pictures.

He said, 'Bye, bye,' in English.

We said, 'Bye, bye,' and began walking towards the entrance of the Lha *chu* Valley.

Mount Kailash is a massive block of conglomerate. The near perfect horizontal layers of the rocks can be seen distinctly from afar. The peak itself is instantly recognisable by its distinctive pyramidal shape, marked by a vertical cleft on the southern slope. It is the Kailash *shikhar* (peak), the concrete embodiment of the mythical home of Gods of several ancient religions. At 22,028 feet, it is not among the highest peaks in the world. Yet, to this day, no mountaineer's foot has touched its slopes and tip. So powerful is the belief in this abode of gods that it has become completely off-limits to humans. Hindus believe Lord Shiva lives in bliss with his consort Parvati there and similarly Tibetans believe that Demchhok lives there while his consort Dorje-Phangmo's abode is on an adjoining lesser peak.

Surrounding the Kailash peak is a ring of layered conglomerate fold mountains. Pilgrims follow a track around these outlying ranges of Mount Kailash, which is known as Kailash *Parvat* (mountain) between the rivers Lha *chu* in the west and Dzong *chu* in the east. Several of the peaks on these ranges have their own name and personality, like Nandi, named after Shiva's vehicle, the bull; and Tijung, the abode of Dorje-Phangmo.

The fifty-six kilometre *kora* would probably take three days of brisk walk.

Since part of the trail is very steep, most plains people plan to do it in four days and three nights. The Tibetans of the region often complete the *kora* in eighteen hours of non-stop walk, sometimes with packs of luggage and children tied to their backs.

The walk from Tarpoche is through a canyon, along the left bank of the Lha *chu* river. Bands of Tibetan pilgrims passed us by, some comprising as many as thirty persons. These included children carrying younger siblings on their backs. They walked rapidly, as though the burden they carried had no weight at all. Clearly, the elevation did not create the same level of stress in their systems as it did for us. The pilgrims went about shouting '*tashi dalek*' as they went by. Some little children politely stuck their tongues out in greeting, while a few very religious adults prostrated along the entire route without the slightest expression of discomfort.

At Chuku *gompa*, there was some special festival on. The traditional Tibetan suspension bridge was festooned with prayer flags. Groups of people were picnicking near the bridge and some were climbing the track up the incline to the *gompa*. We moved on. Every single Tibetan outwalked us with ease. They overtook us, smiled, waved and quickly disappeared.

A short trek was planned for the first day, not to exceed four hours. But our preference for the idyllic first night halt, planned from Delhi, had now been overrun by rock falls just short of the Kailash west face. Quite clearly this was truly a case of being wiped off from the face of the earth — and there was nothing nuclear about it! We looked around at the sheer mountain walls on the left and the right, and took some deep breaths. I knew I had made the right decision. I had come for the experience of this land again: its stupendous heights and sheer rock faces, its religious mystique, its faithful pilgrims, and its solitude. I had the courage of conviction that nothing would deter me from completing the *kora*. Here my mind was unfettered and none could interrupt my reverie. Through the uninterrupted hours of walk, my mind moved around the pieces of the Sutlej jigsaw, trying to conclusively solve the puzzle.

I walked on. I talked to myself and as I did, suddenly missed the com-

Entrance to Lha chu, the stream that pilgrims follow in their quest for solitude.

pany of Ayone and Ray, both of whom were with us on our earlier *kora* around Kailash. Ayone, normally confident and sometimes even brash in his dealings with others, was so affected on catching the first glimpse of the west face of Kailash that he sat quietly on a small rock and wept. Tears streamed down his face as he held the picture of his guru in his hands and said his *Gayatri Mantra*. This was such an unusual aspect of him that I could only guess at the powerful impact the pilgrimage had on him.

Ray, who had a rough couple of days earlier coping with HAS, walked slowly in a slightly disoriented and unbalanced manner. When he spoke, he said he missed his father, who had died some years back, and now felt close to him there. He knew he could communicate with his father as though they were in the same world. I recall telling him that I felt the same way about Joy, too.

A few Indians were circumambulating in a counterclockwise direction. A pilgrim holding a staff saluted us, '*Har Har Mahadev.*' He uttered '*Har Har*' like some fire was forcing itself out of the pit of his stomach. Delving into my sporadic experience in stage performance, I now responded dramatically with some semblance of fervour, '*Har Har Mahadev.*' Though feeling somewhat hypocritical, I was still pleased that I was able to give myself up to the spirit of the great pilgrimage to Shiva's abode.

'Why are you doing the *kora* in a counterclockwise direction?' I asked. Normally, it is the Bons who circumambulate in this way.

'Our travel agency allocated only one day for the *kora*. So we went up to view the west face of Kailash and are now retracing our steps,' informed a young girl.

'And several of us are not strong enough to climb over Drolma La,' said another in the group.

'So we decided to walk on this easy section,' said a third.

'Where are you from?' we asked. When travelling, it is the most frequently used opening gambit in a conversation. We were always interested in knowing where people had come from.

'From Mumbai. And you?' asked the young girl.

'You could say Delhi. Three of us are from Delhi.'

'We did not realise it was such a long *kora* around Kailash.'

'But you must be happy seeing the west face, at least.'

'Of course. But when you consider we have come from so far, we really should have been more prepared to complete the *kora*.' The girl was disappointed.

The sky was clear and we got a spectacular view of the west face of Kailash. It was a view the truly religious consider a blessing to see. There we waited for the yak train. Seated in the little temporary shop in the only hamlet on the way, I rested my legs. My eyes caught sight of the familiar royal blue, white and red cans in the corner. I marvelled at the shopkeepers 'foreign customer' focus, having brought these few cans for them from suppliers many, many miles away. I doubt there is a better example of Pepsi's exceptional market reach. I bought a can for Yuan 5, and enjoyed the homely comfort of the shop.

Tibetan nomadic traders are tremendously perceptive business people. Their tiny tents stock, albeit in small quantities, everything a pilgrim may want. The storekeeper was kneading dough. Her infant son was fast asleep on the mattress in one corner. The store was dark and cool, very inviting after five hours in the high-powered UV zone outside. Pilgrims dropped in to buy flasks of yellow yak butter tea, AO Deli and other local drinks and biscuits. The biscuits in all roadside stores in Tibet are very standard, circular with a hole in the centre, packed in transparent cellophane.

The yaks appeared shortly. The yak train arrived late because the supplies truck had reached Tarpoche well after the scheduled time. It took some more time to load the seven black and one white yak. I hoped my companions would not consider this unlucky, as only one white yak in a herd is believed to auger bad luck. There was also a horse along with the yaks, and Anita came riding it. It turned out that the horse belonged to the *yakpa*, whose vocabulary had a smattering of some Hindi words.

The *yakpa*'s forefathers had fought in the war against the valiant General Zorawar Singh and seen him being separated from his army by a cruel and long winter during his invasion of Tibet in 1841. His father had spoken of how Zorawar had been vanquished and as recognition of his valour, his flesh had been cut and distributed among the Tibetan soldiers. The *yakpa*'s little grandson, of about seven years, had also accompanied him. So we had three *yakpa* and the little child now as part of our team, while we were on the Kailash *kora*.

Rock went a little ahead, along with Pradip, to reconnoitre for a suitable camping site. We found our ideal little camp on a little island, about a foot above water level on the river Dunglung *chu*, just above the point of confluence with the Lha *chu*. The torrents of water did not engulf us that night, but we were blasted by cold winds. The camp was at over 16,000 feet and I slept fitfully through the night.

In the grey world, somewhere between wakefulness and sleep, inadequate oxygen began making its mark on my imagination. The first hallucinations began. Shiva spoke out of the picture frame in every Hindu's prayer niche at home. He was easily recognisable by his bare torso, plastered with ash, and the serpent wound around his head. He looked cheerful and was smiling. He shook his *damaru* and transformed to Nataraj, in the most elegant yet powerful dance pose, balancing on one foot with arms outstretched.

Shiva asked, 'What brings you here again?'

And I said to him, 'Why, I've come to meet you, like all other pilgrims.'

He quizzed me further, 'But why come to this remote corner of the earth? This desolate mountainside? The Meru of the Universe?'

'Because,' I said taking a deep breath, 'If the mountain does not come to Mohammed . . .'

'I see. So you came to the mountain. Isn't that reality reliving metaphor?'

I did not answer. Instead, I offered him a music CD and said, 'This music is for you to listen to.'

At which he was surprised and said, 'But I can hear it wherever you play it. Did you not learn in school that I am omnipresent?'

'Yes. But Joy is not. And he would also enjoy it. I also have a message for him.'

'A message for one who has crossed over to the other world?'

'Yes, Lord. Please tell him that I regret not bringing the music earlier.'

'Regret? In this world there is no regret,' Shiva gently reprimanded me. With this comforting thought, in the early hours of the morning I was seduced into slumber.

Morning was pretty as a picture, with yaks and *yakpa* wandering about the camp. I awoke to find two curious *yakpas* peeping into my tent. In another few seconds, a third face appeared. The *yakpas* had unzipped the tent and were intently checking out the person inside, namely myself. I indulged them for a few seconds and then suggested, *'Doh, doh. . .'* The message was well taken and they wandered off.

The little boy chattered away, hopping from stone to stone, and ran for his life when an older *yakpa*, his brother, tried to clean his face with a rag. This young man was the one with the habit of intently looking into our tents for many minutes at a time. I was at peace. The little boy ran up to the stream, lay flat on his stomach, and licked the running water. He reminded me of Pia at one-and-a-half. She would tilt the bowl of puffed rice onto the floor and lick at it like our two Lhasa Apsos. Pia was joining a new firm on July 1, in faraway Washington. I hoped that she would be content.

Late in the morning, we began trekking from camp and reached Dhiraphuk in three hours. It was an undemanding, though slightly uphill, walk. It was another clear day and just as we left camp, we saw the northwest face of Kailash. Several large hairy beaver-like animals scurried on the ridges. I remembered well this stretch of the trail from our previous trip. It had rained right through and I was soaking wet and shivering by the time we reached Dhiraphuk. I lay down in the sun to warm myself and fell asleep. Next morning, I could hardly walk and went a short distance on a yak. A Nepali Sherpa said, 'You've come so far from home. It's sad that you will not get any merit for the *kora.*'

'But why not?' I asked, surprised at his comment.

'Because a *kora* must be on feet only,' he said.

'So the yak will get the merit for this *kora*?' I asked mischievously.

'Of course,' he answered with conviction, matter-of-factly.

An agnostic, when it is convenient to be so, I remained perched on the animal till it was so unbearably uncomfortable that I decided to turn believer.

I liked the name Dhiraphuk. It evoked images of mysterious hide-and-seek games being played by *dakinis*, magical deities and Gotsankpa. The name means Cave of the Female Yak Horn. It is believed that the scholarly ascetic, Gotsankpa, instituted the Kailash *kora* in the 13th century. He found the labyrinthine route through the Lha *chu* Valley, and it was the supreme power of the deity Drolma which guided him by giving him clues to the path.

When he was led to the Cave of the Female Yak Horn, Drolma appeared in the form of a female yak and vanished into this cave, leaving behind hoof and horn marks. Here Gotsankpa meditated and was then revealed through a dream, the Drolma La Pass. This pass is the highest point on the present outer *kora* route, over which one crosses the Kailash range. It is this legend that gives the cave its singularly evocative name. There is a huge monastery at Dhiraphuk today, complete with a guesthouse and a glass house at its foot.

Across the river from the foot of the Dhiraphuk *gompa* is a small camp-site. There is a stone and wood bridge that makes it possible to move man and beast across the fast-flowing stream. You get an excellent view of the north face of Kailash from here. Devi had suggested that we eat a hot lunch on reaching the camp. We happily obliged and, after a short rest, prepared to explore the glacier that emanates from the northern flank of the Kailash mountain.

The glacier was a protruding tongue of ice with deep crevasses on its surface. From the edge we saw that it was about eight feet thick. Most of the crevasses were at the point where the glacier curved over a huge rock and then flowed down the valley, where there is a row of rooms that serves as the Indian guesthouse.

Pradip instructed us, 'Avoid crevasses and check the ice before walking over it. Knock on the ice with your stick before you step on it. And make sure you sit down immediately if you step into a crevasse.' As he was knocking on the ice with his stick, at a point where two crevices met, suddenly the triangle he was standing on collapsed. In a matter of seconds, Ramis was dragging him away, even before Pradip had time to sit down, as he had advised us to do should such a contingency occur.

We had not been so close to the peak ever before as when we moved up this glacier. It was quite amazing that this same peak, when covered with snow and seen in glossy pictures, appeared shining and white. At close quarters, the peak was dark in colour and the sedimentary strata were sharply defined. The denuded rocks and scree that come down from it were clearly mixed in nature.

Years ago, I had an excellent *Mastermoshai* (teacher), who had excited the imagination of generations of budding geomorphologists. I kicked myself for not giving full attention to the methods of physical identification of minerals and rocks taken by him back in the geolithology classes.

Two members of the group sponsored by the Government of India joined us on this exploration of the glacier. We got chatting on the way down. They informed us, 'Mr. Prabhu, who is accompanying us, is on his tenth visit.'

'He must love the place enough to bear the hardship ten times.'

'He'll probably be relieved of rebirth. Get Nirvana,' is a faintly guarded envious comment.

'Or at least be reborn a *bodhisattva*.'

Next morning, we planned an early start. There was excitement in the camp and most of us were up in the freezing sub-zero temperature well before we heard, 'Morning tea is ready' and 'Hot vasing vater.'

Medha left an hour before us, with her two Leki sticks, which drew much attention from the Tibetan pilgrims. For the first hour or so, the rise was moderate and many Indian *yatris* crossed us on yaks and on foot. These were surely not the 'shivering Indians' mentioned in the *Lonely Planet*, for they all appeared well equipped and prepared to brave the onslaught of the cold.

But I did miss the 'shivering *sadhus*' that we had met the last time. These *sadhus* were in rubber *chappal, dhoti, chadar* and 'monkey cap'. Openly smoking *charas* (marijuana) and stoned out of their minds, they walked ramrod straight. The *sadhus* were clad in thin cotton brown *dhotis*, but they did not shiver. There was a distinct unspoken suggestion of supernatural power to raise their body heat, something that is neither in question nor is it widely accepted today. Friendly and knowledgeable about the terrain, each one of them had walked over the high Himalayan passes several times.

We questioned, 'Are you not cold?'

They countered, 'Cold? What cold?'

We clarified the question, 'Your clothes are not adequate. You must be cold.'

One *sadhu* answered, 'Cold? No. It's all in the mind.' And there was no bravura in his expression.

It was fascinating that one could actually consider physical discomfort as an illusion, *maya*. I was reminded of Lawrence of Arabia, who had held his finger in the candle flame. His explanation for being able to bear the pain was in ignoring it. We had not seen even one such *sadhu* this year. The Chinese government had clamped down on pilgrims who, in the past, walked across the traditional routes of the porous border with Nepal and India.

The next hour was an easier climb while we passed through Shivathsal. These are actually two passes, easily identifiable by garments littered all over. It is here that the Buddhist pilgrims leave behind clothes or bits of cloth belonging to their departed loved ones. Sometimes a stone is dressed in a jumper and a cap. Some leave behind photographs.

Shivathsal is a dank and eerie spot. It sent a chill up my spine. I could almost sense the many spirits dancing, singing and flying around us, just beyond the zone of physical perception. They should be happy beings, simply moving from one life to another. But I could see all the images of formless beings lying dormant in my mind since childhood. I could recall the deep throbbing voice of the male singer describing a village completely destroyed by famine, hunger, disease and death. And then the unearthly beings had arrived in droves to celebrate death, *'Dakini, yogini, elo shata nagini, elo pishachi ra elo re. . .'* . (Sentient beings, hundreds of serpent maidens and the hideous ones all have come. . .)

The underlying threat in the words did not escape my young mind. These were not creatures of our living world, they were associated with death — the time that marked our passage to another world. I did not want to leave my parents and go with these formless beings. So, many years later, standing at Shivathsal, I could hear the gramophone spin out the song again. They were all there, for I could feel them, dancing and swaying, moaning and humming, waiting for life to move on from our world to another. For, they knew this was inevitable. For, in our journey through many lives, it was possible to spend many lifetimes in other worlds.

To us mere mortals, Shivathsal signified the end of a phase of life and a place to hope for the future. Instead of inspiring me to hope for a bright future, it weighed me down with thoughts of a past full of grief for the loss of loved ones. Anita placed some of Vir's belongings there, and we stood aside while she prayed. It was a poignant moment. I wondered if she felt a sense of detachment from life. Did she perhaps feel closer to him here just as Ray had to his father? But we did not discuss these matters. She then quietly climbed on a yak and rode up to Drolma La, awaiting our arrival.

As anyone who has been on a yak knows, they are the most uncomfortable animals to ride, particularly uphill. Yaks are primarily beasts of burden, so they are not fitted with comfortable riding saddles. More importantly, huge bags are hung on either side of their shoulders and the unfortunate human who may want a ride is left to slip off its sloping back behind the bags. As the animal climbs upwards, the slope on his back effectively increases and the rider slides back without the help of a saddle or stirrup. This gives the *yakpa* liberty to shove the human in a most crude manner, like pushing up a sack of potatoes. The unspoilt mountain man is most chivalrous in assisting the female of his species when opportunities like these arise.

The trail became difficult: rocky and steep. We were at 17,000 feet and had another 1,600 to go. This was among the steepest slopes I have ever climbed. I imagine we were now climbing more than one foot for every two or three steps. I blew out harder than I was breathing in and repeated in my mind, 'Yes, I can do it.'

The Tibetan pilgrims passed by singing and happy. Their songs reminded me of the Santhal singing in the sal forests at dusk. There was something so joyous in their undertaking the *kora*. Sometimes old women would sit down and smile at us, as though they understood that we needed to rest. I gave a Fox's sweet to a lady who pointed to her head and sighed. Then I walked along. Now I said to myself, 'Of course, you can do it,' although it got harder every minute. The old woman caught up shortly, took the sweet out of her mouth to show and her face wrinkled in smiles.

One person offered to hold my hand as I climbed. Three little girls in red blouses yanked me up from my rock, where I was resting, even though I could quite help myself. I think they were not used to visitors who liked sitting and watching as the great Year of the Horse *kora* moved by. There was a young man from Hong Kong, very well outfitted and attired. He said 'Hi'. A sprightly lama smiled and offered to hold my bottle of water. I was touched by these simple, spontaneous gestures from strangers.

For every peak I reached, there were a few more to go. But because of the gradient, it was always a surprise to see another peak rise behind the one just climbed. This year the *kora* was a procession of pilgrims and adventurers, the devout and the agnostic, in a celebration of the moment and reinforcement of the tradition.

One sees photographs in the newspapers of the Kumbh Mela, or processions on Francis Xavier's birth anniversary, and one marvels at the number of people who take part in these events. But far away from the eyes of journalists is this wondrous movement of people of different faiths, who move along a mountain trail and visit no shrine at all.

Short of breath but excited, when I reached the Drolma La Pass, I saw that there were many, many more prayer flags than before. Anita was waiting for us.

Anita had been there for more than an hour, having mounted on a very sure-footed and sedate yak. Many Buddhist pilgrims had gone by and so had Indian *yatris*. She said, 'I have been able to speak to Mr. Prabhu. He says that the Indian Ambassador to China is also undertaking the *kora*.' Prabhu had complained to the Ambassador about the impolite and 'bad' treatment the Chinese had meted out to the Indians.

The Indian *yatris* were unhappy about the unhygienic living conditions of the accommodation at Darchen. We sympathised with them. Tibetan guesthouses are still primitive and our preference was to camp in the open and live in tents. Anita asked Mr. Prabhu how the lottery system worked. How could one gentleman be selected ten times to travel to Kailash? The indefatigable Mr. Prabhu insisted, 'It's all in Lord Shiva's hands. I plan to do the *kora* once more.'

For those who find pleasure in storing trivia in their minds, there is one that only the most specialised quizzer would know. The boiling temperature of water at Drolma La is 81 degrees Fahrenheit, while it is 85 degrees Fahrenheit at Manasarovar. This is an observation made by S.R. Kashyap in the journals of the Asiatic Society of Bengal.

Drolma La was festive with the most colourful prayer flags, festooned on flagpoles. The Shaivites were ready to leave. They had danced with the *damaru* and said that they had brought enough *samagri* (worshipping material) to have a big *havan* (ritual fire) at Manasarovar. They left behind an ugly banner proclaiming to the world that a travel agency from some bustling city had reached Mount Kailash. I was appalled to see this and dismayed, imagining what a few more such pilgrims would do to this unspoilt mountainscape. This is a new manifestation of religion. For generations, indeed ages, men went for pilgrimages and left no vestige except donations for guesthouses and free meals for poor pilgrims. They certainly did not leave behind crude banners advertising travel services.

Then came along a Nepali family, a couple of Japanese, more Indians and many, many more Tibetans. There are many white tourists in Lhasa, but few came as far and as high as Kailash. There was much euphoria among those who reached Drolma La. Religion is part of the Tibetans' way of life. It is inseparably intermingled with the stones, streams, mountains and passes. Like us, they are also superstitious and believe in symbolic actions. The Tibetans threw to the sky bits of pink, blue and yellow pieces of paper with prayers printed on them. They unquestionably believed these prayers would be carried to the gods. These blew away like confetti in the blue sky. Some sang, folded their hands and prayed, then walked away after resting for a while.

I threw among the flags prayers written by friends and family, addressed to their gods. I also placed among the flags letters I had found in Ray's bag. I placed Joy's photograph here and prayed that he would be at peace forever. When I returned to see it again a few minutes later, it had blown away. A sense of panic came over me and I searched for the photograph among the bits of paper and flags. It was as if the wind was telling me that this was the final parting and I would not find him anymore, not until I reached the next world. This made me feel very sad and very alone.

Rock came, a little tired, having lost his fleece and one glove. This was in the nature of things, because Tibetans leave clothes behind on the *kora*. He accepted this unfortunate loss of his new fleece, bought in Kathmandu, with grace and equanimity. We moved on as he stayed back to meditate for a while.

Devi's lunch did not inspire anyone to eat it. In his fervour to protect us from HAS at 18,600 feet, he had flavoured all food with generous portions of garlic. I did not have the courage to open my lunch pack lest my stomach churn at the potent smell of the aromatic pods.

Before marching away from the highest point of our journey, I watched Medha arrive. She planned to climb down to the Gauri Kund and say a prayer on behalf of Ray, which he had planned for his father. This was very brave of her, because Medha did not find walking easy.

Gauri Kund is often known to be frozen. The story goes that once a woman with a baby tied to her back came to the pond. As she bent

Gauri Kund, seen from Drolma La.

over, the child fell into the lake and drowned. The gods, in their effort to avoid such occurrences ever again, froze the lake. As on our previous visit, we found the lake appear like a liquid jade green marble tabletop, with not a streak of snow or ice on it.

Sven Hedin talked of the two Tso Kapala lakes here. This is a pointer to the fact that he had not actually crossed Drolma La. It is impossible to miss Gauri Kund as one begins the descent. I am a great admirer of his adventurous spirit and his passion for documenting his travels. Thus I am loath to point out discrepancies in the details of his account, which I had noticed elsewhere too. I believe Hedin would have travelled directly from Dhiraphuk to the headwaters of Indus and so bypassed Drolma La, without actually having climbed up to the pass and then going downhill past Gauri Kund.

The descent from Drolma La was as treacherous as the ascent. It is a slope formed of loose surface rubble, where slipping is the norm. On the way down, we also crossed a glacier. It took us almost as much time, about two-and-a-half hours, to climb up the 1,500 feet, as it did to climb down. We were tired but reached our camp with a sense of satisfaction and relief that there had been no mishap. We were all a little anxious, in view of earlier health-related problems of members of our team. But the strange thing was that there really was no sense of achievement. It was a journey to be made and we had just recently passed through the most difficult section.

Our overnight camp was by the Dzong *chu*, at a point that was in spate. In spite of strict instructions to select a suitable camping site, Pema had decided that this was the best camping ground in a five-kilometre stretch to Zutrul Phuk. Having selected the spot a foot below the level of the river, she disappeared to enjoy the city lights of Darchen. By the time we arrived, the tents had been pitched. Shortly after, the water in the river rose surreptitiously and stealthily overflowed on to the banks. The unperturbed yaks were rounded up, brought reluctantly wading through the river. We passed the night expecting to run fast out of the tents, should the water inundate our sleeping bags. I kept my boots very close to my side, while sleep was nudged on by exhaustion.

The next morning, the little boy sat around a dying fire with his father, brother and the patriarch. They all looked subdued. Very soon the boy picked up my walking stick and, like all other little boys the world over, put it between his legs and rode it like a horse. We sat around the circular bamboo-leaf tray placed on the blue plastic drum, preparing for the day and eating breakfast. The session of planning with the *Sardar* was important because later that day we would move into fairly uncharted territory: the inner *kora* of Kailash.

Medha had already proclaimed in the morning that she was planning to undertake the inner *kora* wholly on foot. Pradip's information from Darchen and other Tibetan pilgrims on the outer *kora* indicated that it was an eighteen-hour trek for them. That would translate to four days for us — whereas we had set aside only one day for it. This was a point we needed to talk about and work out a plan, by means of which we would undertake at least a part of the trek.

Medha had said earlier, 'I will do only what pleases me and only for myself.' In theory, this was probably a sign of self-confidence, but in practice it was becoming worrisome. Determination is no guarantee for success in such ventures.

An eminently doable twelve- to fifteen-kilometre trek to Darchen lay ahead that morning. Lost in my thoughts, I walked along the Dzong *chu*, finding my way through big boulders and a marshy valley floor. It was monotonous. I caught a short but clear glimpse of an extended arm of the east face of Kailash.

Walking on Kailash is an intensely personal persuasion. It needs conviction in one's ability to remain constant to the idea. For, once you begin you must reach the end. Everyone who begins this walk, must complete every inch of the course. It has been so from time immemorial and it is so today. If someone has not completed it on his feet, horse or yak, then he has remained on the trail, to be reborn or relieved from rebirth. If one breathes one's last on Kailash, Hindus consider it a special dispensation of Lord Shiva. That year, several people had already been so dispensed.

At Zutrul Phuk I got a can of cold drink for Yuan 5 after bargaining with the shopkeeper. More than the drink, I was interested in spending a few minutes in his stone-walled shop, which was lit by a low wattage bulb, connected to a blue rectangular photovoltaic cell being charged in the sunlight outside. He told me Kailash was just behind, but you could not see it till you climbed the high range in front.

I had climbed up to Milarepa's cave at Zutrul Phuk. It was sombre with soot and smelt strongly of yak butter, which devotees poured into lamps. It was said to be a very old temple, built around a cave in which he had lived and meditated in the mid-8th century. Milarepa, the Buddhist ascetic with supernatural powers, is said to have travelled on a beam of light to the crest of the Kailash peak. Milarepa's reputation is so stupendous that the mystic is said to have visited and meditated in just about every cave you see. This is similar to the belief of every villager on the Indian side of the Himalayas that the Pandavas have visited their village during the fourteen years of banishment from their kingdom.

A very young girl and an older couple with weather-beaten faces came and sat by me. We shared the almonds and raisins in my backpack. The little girl picked up bits of *reshmi* (silken) glass bangles, perhaps broken during some Indian woman's *parikrama*, and placed it admiringly on her wrist. I displayed my wrists for her to see that I, regrettably, had none. Every once in a while I heard the birds chirp.

'Did you hear that?'

'Hear what?'

'Why, birds? I heard birds chirp.'

'Are you sure?'

'Yes. But I do not see any birds,' I admitted.

'Oh. They are mountain mouse. They sound like birds,' explained Pradip.

While I sat on the grass and wrote my journal, the younger *yakpa* kept watching me write. His gaze was intent on the scrawl being created by an inexpensive plastic ADD Gel pen. I made a mental note to give him a pen when we parted company in a couple of days.

On approaching the final bend of the *kora*, I had an uninterrupted view of Rakas Tal. It was positioned picture perfect between the two spurs of the mountains on either side of the Dzong *chu*. The pass here was marked by prayer flags. 'I wonder how it is possible to tie flags on the two sides of a deep gorge like this,' I spoke aloud.

The Sherpas had an answer. 'One end of the flag is firmly placed on the ground and kept in place by a rock. The other end is tied to an arrow and sent across to the opposite hillside to remain as long as the arrow is firmly impaled into the ground.'

'Well, I am glad to hear this. I am happy to note that archery is still practised in this country.'

'I have not seen any bows and arrows in shops, though the motif is often embroidered on the *dukpa's* tent.'

'I have read about and seen pictures of archery contests during Tibetan picnics and celebrations.'

'And in blood sport. Like in hunting wild yaks in the past, before the advent of the shotgun.'

'Now we see a very practical use of this traditional skill.'

We walked steadily towards Darchen along the right bank of the Dzong *chu*. It was a downhill constitutional compared to the demands on body and mind in the earlier part of the *kora*. All along, this fast-flowing stream appeared as a sliver of silver, as the sunlight bounced off its surface.

We walked up to the final rise of the ridges encircling the Kailash peak, and immediately descended through a flurry of green and brown stones to the Darchen plains. Manasarovar was hidden away from sight from everywhere on the Kailash *kora*. The beautiful serene picture of Rakas Tal, spread across the horizon, was the first sight of the plains from the mountains. It also happens to be the first of the two lakes to be seen by Indian pilgrims when they follow the road from the international border at Purang.

Ahead lay the ambitious programme of undertaking the inner *kora* of Kailash. We were all walking into the mysterious world of the poorly documented and less frequented core of the mountain and, according to some, the centre of the Universe. Were there trees in Shiva's abode that Kalidasa wrote about? Was Nandi truly golden? Would ice falls and sudden blizzards prevail over our devotion to undertake the inner *kora*? Right then, we had so little information that we felt justified in feeling like pioneers.

8

THE HIDDEN PATH:
INNER KORA OF KAILASH

Deep in the womb of the mountain is a path hidden from most men and women. The Tibetans know it as the inner *kora* of Kailash. Only the most committed and spirited ambulists, who undertake thirteen outer *kora*s of Kailash, are deemed fit to walk on the inner *kora*. So strong is the belief that dangers would befall those who have not met the minimum requirement for this *kora*, that all pilgrims give themselves up to self-regulation. There is no official to whom one declares the number of outer *kora* undertaken.

We had worked out a devious way to overcome this problem of numbers. An outer *kora*, every twelve years, in the Year of the Horse, is so meritorious that it is considered equivalent to twelve *kora* of other years. This was a Year of the Horse. So we counted our previous *kora* as one and the present as twelve to add to thirteen.

Now, barring Rock, we were all eligible to perform the inner *kora*. This mathematics held great significance to Medha and Anita, who planned to reach nearest to Shiva's abode through the inner *kora*. It was equally important to Rock, who did not plan to attempt it, and to me, as an example of the supreme power of the mind, a belief that could shape one's destiny. I did, though, believe that actually undertaking thirteen outer *kora* would make one more psychologically and physically prepared for the inner *kora*, which was not to be the case for us.

Our overnight camp by the Dzong *chu* was left behind and we shortly reached Darchen. The little town had become uglier and dirtier, if either were possible. Under normal circumstances, the town is no more than a few stone huts, which function as homes and guesthouses for pilgrims going up to Kailash in the summer. But this year, there were a very large number of pilgrims and an entire tented suburb had mushroomed around the town.

As modern water supply, garbage and sewage disposals are unknown here, it was but natural that mounds of garbage had accumulated in huge dumps. In time, it would all disperse in the wind and rain and disintegrate. But now it was revolting to smell and see.

I suppose even 'bad' has some 'good' hidden somewhere, if we look hard enough for it. So, it was a pleasant surprise when we saw a solitary feathered figure sitting on an enormous garbage dump. It was the scarce lammergeier that inhabits high mountain ranges, known to be addicted to scavenging on garbage dumps. The rare bearded vulture was perched atop the dump, monarch of all it surveyed. It was close enough for us to see the tufts of hair over its bill and its round bulging eyes. But before we could get our cameras out, it shook itself, spread its enormous wings and flew away in a huge swerve over Darchen. It was so big that it was a wonder it could fly. It flew over the mountain ranges and we watched it till it became an unrecognisable speck and faded into the cloudless sky.

At Darchen, Kuman picked up some World Sports News. He told us that Brazil had won the World Cup. But the *Sardar* had heard in the bazaar that the President of Senegal had gone to Korea to welcome his team back home. Ignoring the improbability of the occurrence, we were just a little uncertain if it was Brazil or Senegal that had earned the highest honour.

Darchen's satellite connectivity to the world came in useful once again. I called up my daughter, Radha, in Delhi on her mobile phone. The line was crystal clear and she gave me all the information about my older daughter, Pia. 'Ma, Didi now has an apartment in Washington. She begins work tomorrow.'

'I feel bad that I'm not there to help her settle in.'

'It's cool. She'll manage.'

'What are your plans?'

'I have decided to go back to college in January. I've sent an email and informed my college. Are all of you all right?'

'Yes. We're okay. Have you spoken to Ray?'

'No. Both he and Soma are out of town.'

'How's Redd?'

'I think he misses you.'

'Take good care of him and yourself,' the mother instructed.

After several 'love you', 'miss you' and 'come back safe and soon' messages, I put the phone down. I sighed and conceded failure in disassociating with worldly matters.

Would the girls ever understand why one must travel? Could they imagine the rush of adrenaline associated with suddenly approaching the expanse of Far West Tibet, after a gruelling four-day drive over the plateau and precipitous hairpin bends of mountain ranges? As Kipling had said, there were those who stayed at home and there were those who did not. Perhaps, there is a third in-between category. Those who travel away from home, yet whose thoughts of home recur and memories of family and friends keep wafting back.

Just outside the telephone office, we came across engaging Tibetan women who sell ornamental artifacts and turquoise jewellery. We recognised one vivacious, chattering lady who insisted on charging outrageously high prices and settled for much less. The most popular word spoken in English was 'I'm sorry', with the most sophisticated intonation. Suddenly, there were so many lively Tibetan women, dressed in the traditional long dress with a striped apron tied around the waist, insisting that they apologise. We quickly realised that they were greeting us with the only English they knew. There was much friendly banter, with them asking us to pay exorbitant sums of money for little trinkets, because they mistook us for Americans travelling in Land Cruisers. We explained we were Yindu and were thus quoted more appropriate prices. I selected a beautiful dagger with a carved handle, the silver sheath set with coloured stones. Our *yakpa*, who wore a small dagger on his waist tied to his belt, examined my dagger and nodded in approval. Each of us picked up small trinkets to carry back home as souvenirs.

The Indian group of pilgrims, who had come through the Government of India, had a free day and were using it to exercise a bit. We walked together for a while. The filth and squalor of Darchen had clearly disappointed several of them. The toilets were unusable and the entire guesthouse yard was unhygienic. The Darchen river was used for washing and locally as a sewer. But on the way to the Kailash *kora*, Darchen was an essential stop to call family and friends. It has the best telecommunication facility for hundreds of miles around. Besides, one must complete travel formalities with the police there and stock up from the many small shops that sell goods for travellers, essentials like torches and batteries.

We were full of admiration for the sixty-year-old Jain lady who walked barefoot and ate only fruit. For a vegetarian, it was difficult to sustain oneself in an area where there were no vegetables or fruit. We marvelled at her energy and enthusiasm.

Some of the Indian pilgrims were keen to see the *Ashtapada*, the foot of Kailash, sacred to the Jains. This was where Adinatha Vrishabhadeva, the first Tirthankara of the Jains, attained Nirvana. We showed them our map and the way to Selung from where they could get a glimpse of it. The barefoot lady did not finally make the Kailash *kora*.

Pema appeared for a few moments and begged leave, claiming she was suffering from a cold. This was fairly standard practice and expected behaviour. I, for one, would have been surprised if she had volunteered to accompany us on this hard trek.

From Darchen to Selung *gompa* was an uphill trek for about three hours along the Darchen *chu*. The yaks were loaded with tents, water and dry rations bought at Darchen. The excitement was now palpable, but breathing was difficult.

The entrance to the valley was akin to stepping into a cavernous tunnel that led to the bowels of the earth. In spite of the high sun, the narrow valley was in the shadow of the parallel ridges on both sides of the Darchen *chu*. Except for the singleminded purpose of following the route to the navel of the universe, all other thoughts had been shut out. We had entered a very sacred space, seldom touched by foreign footsteps.

On the way, we lingered and stood about idly. Anita, who was unhappy, as Shiva had not heard her prayers, admitted that she now felt more 'accepting' of circumstances. She was reconciled to the inevitability of life and death. Several dusty young children passed by carrying bundles of dry stems and roots of shrubs from the hillsides. I do not think these children had the luxury of going to school.

The plan was to camp at Selung and on the next day walk up to Serdung Chuksum, the Thirteen Chortens, built on a ledge on the southern foot of Kailash. The Tibetan word *ser* means yellow, *dung* is a *chorten* and *chuksum* was the number thirteen. The approach to the Serdung Chuksum is from the west tributary of the Darchen *chu*, named Selung *chu* after the monastery on its right bank. On moving past the Nandi massif, on the southern foot of the Kailash peak, pilgrims turn east, go over the 19,500-foot Chaksama La Pass (almost 1,000 feet higher than Drolma La) and then come down to the eastern tributary of the Darchen *chu*. From the confluence of the two tributaries, the pilgrim's route follows the left bank of the river and ends opposite the Selung Monastery.

Just off the *kora* route are two lakes, the Kapala *tso*, which are considered auspicious. It is difficult to imagine today that these two lakes above the tree line were once actually under a sea. This was where fossils were excavated from the lakes, indicating that at one time it was part of the seabed, possibly under the waters of the Tethys.

Later, we walked up to Selung *gompa*, where Sven Hedin had stayed overnight. It was situated on a ridge that formed the outer ring of Kailash. The central prayer hall of the *gompa* was on the first floor, and the climb up and down the staircase was enough to cause vertigo to the unsuspecting visitor. Several metallic implements that looked like iron tridents, blades, axes, horseshoes and arrows to my untrained eyes, decorated the altar.

Pradip, who had been there with a German team earlier, had photographed the Head Lama. He was carrying the Lama's photograph now. But the Lama had been transferred to Ganden, and his picture was left with the inmates with instructions to forward it.

Between the *gompa* and Tarpoche was a sky burial site, a charnel. Dead bodies with severed limbs were left here for animals and vultures to devour. That, of course, was a disgusting sight, but a very ecologically sound custom in a land where there is neither enough earth to waste for graveyards nor firewood to cremate the dead body. The skulls and bones of limbs are also used for ritual worship in monasteries where *tantric* Hindu practices have influenced Buddhism and in the Bon shrines as well.

Back at the camp, Rock was unwell. He had not eaten all day and lay in the sun without protecting his head. Hot soup, Electral water and paracetamol were all sent to his tent with dire threats that if he did not follow our path of treatment, he would be sent to the Tibetan hospital at Darchen next morning, while we continued on the inner *kora*.

Devi excelled himself that evening. 'What's for dinner tonight, Devi?'

'Mixed vegetable soup. . .'

'You have fresh vegetables?'

'From a packet.'

'Didn't get any at Darchen?'

'No fresh vegetables in Darchen shops.'

'What else?'

'Momos and noodles. You like momos?'

'I love momos. That's a feast. But don't put garlic.'

'But garlic important for *kora*.'

'All right then. Just a little.'

'And I also make rice and fried sardines for dinner,' he gave the radiant smile of one who had just pulled out a live rabbit from the hat!

'Perhaps you can cook the sardines after the *kora*.'

As *yatris* we were abstaining from fish and meat till the *kora* was over. For several days now we had not eaten fresh vegetables. Even as he called out the menu, I could not but smile at the combination of eatables being served. But these were a luxury here, very far from where the produce came from. Cooking a hot meal consisting of cereals was commendable at this elevation, for the boiling point of water here was low enough for us to dip our hands into without damage.

Devi volunteered, 'For tomorrow's trek, I give pack lunch.'

'Don't bother to cook, Devi,' I suggested, hoping this would ensure garlic-free food.

'Okay, I give popcorn, yak cheese, biscuit and fruit.'

'Right. That sounds good. And easy to carry too. Thanks.'

'No problem,' said Devi.

It was drizzling and the smell of the damp earth rose up from the ground all around. The little boy had tied his legs in a red cloth and was jumping about pretending to be an animal, and in the process had become quite an expert in some form of children's race. The sky had a bright arch of colour streaked across it. Nature had painted the sky with all the innocence of a child using bright crayons on a freshly wiped slate.

The rainbow was a link to my innocent young years left far behind. I had been an enthusiastic learner at four and knew my colours well. Red, blue, yellow and green. I proudly recognised the colours and joyfully uttered their names while I drew lines and shapes with stained chalk on my slate. I learned the coloured lines in the sky were called a 'rainbow'. Sometimes I would see one after a shower. My cousin said that if I were good, one day I would climb onto a rainbow and be taken to heaven's door. There, I would be welcomed into a paradise full of chocolates and yellow butterflies.

The purity of the environment was stark and truly awesome. The existence of the tiny local populace was fragile and at the mercy of the powerful elements. There were a few shepherds with small herds of sheep. The animals nibbled away at tiny tufts of vegetation by the stream, while the men sat around wood fires and sipped tea.

I could foresee that if too many sheep were brought here to graze, then there would be a real possibility that the loose rocks on the slopes would slip down in huge avalanches and completely bury our camp. From where I stood, our tents looked like tiny blue specks on the brown valley floor and did not in any way interfere with the grandeur of the mountains. I did not see any birds at all. Not even vultures that I expected would swoop down onto the sky burial site on the ridge just behind our camp.

We were camped at 16,500 feet. When the sun set and the moon rose above the ridge tops, it illuminated the nocturne. The high peak was clearly outlined against the sky and the entire valley lay in the shadows of the encircling ridges. It was the first night that I had disturbed sleep. I awoke at the jingling of the horse's bell, and slept fitfully. I thought that it was a symptom of HAS. I had dreams haunting me through the night. The forms and expressions of people and places were so vivid that I believed they were real.

Shiva asked me, 'Why are you here?'

It was something I had asked myself repeatedly and failed at a satisfactory one-line answer. I said simply, 'I have come to see you.'

At this he smiled and his face was surely that of Joy's.

He said to me, 'You have come a long way'.

'Aren't you cold?' I asked. I was shivering but he was sitting calmly on snowcapped Mount Kailash in his cotton bush shirt. He was smoking a pipe. I gave him his tobacco and he smiled and said, 'Ah, its Dunhill's My Mixture 965.'

'Isn't it what you smoked in the old days?'

'Yes, but now I like *ganja* . . .'

'Don't fool me. You are not Shiva.'

I woke up and heard gentle snores and light coughing from the neighbouring tent. A swig of water and my mind calmed for a while. But the hallucinations began again.

Shiva was sitting bare-bodied, crosslegged on Mount Kailash. He had a deerskin loincloth; his matted coils piled high on his head and a fierce serpent wound around his neck. It was a cobra with a white spectacle marked on its hood.

Shiva asked once more, 'Why are you here?'

And I answered, 'To tell you that I know your secret.'

'And that is?'

'Your snake is not real.'

Shiva was startled. In an eternity, this was the first instance when an *atithi* to his abode had broken the rules of divine etiquette and questioned the authenticity of his pet serpent. 'My *Naag*? The world trembles at my sight and you think *Naag* is costume jewellery?'

'I have walked for miles in your land, and trekked through remote mountains and valleys. There are no serpents in your land.'

Now Shiva sighed in resignation. 'That is true. . .'

I said to him confidentially, 'But I promise your secret is well kept with me.'

'That is so clever. So I will grant you a wish, and you will keep this secret.'

'My Lord, I cannot claim to be an ardent follower. But I hear you can be compassionate, even if you are the Lord of destruction and death. Can you show me compassion?'

'What do you want *vats*?' He imitated, with great aplomb, the Bollywood actors who imitated him on screen.

'Lord, you have a consort for eternity. Can I have mine for my life-time?'

At this he was angry, and thundered, 'You ignorant woman, you are a mere mortal. Mortals must die.' At which he stretched out his hand in the most regal style and struck lightning. And I woke up, quite short of breath.

The next morning, we began the inner *kora* from Selung *gompa* to the base of Kailash. Medha had left at seven in the morning with a Sherpa. Rock wanted to lie around and read. Anita and I negotiated with the *yakpa* to take yak rides for an hour to save time before we caught up with Medha beside Nandi. The *yakpa*, an astute businessman, settled for a hefty amount for providing two yaks. But the two yaks refused to budge unless the other yaks accompanied them. 'Herd mentality,' I muttered under my breath. The *yakpa* let us have the companionship of the other yaks for a charge equal to that of the two we would ride on. Finally, we came to a compromise, where the *yakpa* was clearly the winner.

I was overcome by fear that the yak would climb down the precipitous cliff with me on pillion. I held on to its small wooden saddle precariously while it bumped along with several other similar shaggy ones, moving in a herd, seemingly with no clear direction in mind. Finally, we dismounted and decided to walk, which was less frightening and certainly more within one's control. We were terrible trekkers that day. Our ankles twisted as we walked on the sharp-edged scree.

On the way, as we trudged along towards the peak, I said lightheartedly, 'Come on, Mountain, come nearer.'

Medha said sharply, 'No, don't say that.'

'Why not?' I demanded.

Medha said in a mysterious way, 'Shiva is calling. We are going to the Mountain.'

'Of course, we are. But he can help by making it come closer.' This climb was proving to be tougher than all our previous treks, in terms of the roughness of the ground, the steepness of the slopes and difficulty in breathing.

Anita said slowly and softly, 'I want to turn away from this mountain.'

'No, you don't. We've not come so far to turn away,' I reminded Anita.

'I am afraid of it,' said Anita.

I'm afraid that I might just trip and become part of the local folklore about incompetent dead trekkers,' I said.

'These dark rocks and black clouds are sinister,' said Anita.

Perception of one's surrounding varies so much from person to person, I thought. Here was Anita, who saw the Kailash peak as sinister, and there were legions of others who were ecstatic just thinking about the mystical crystal mountain. I was silenced by what I considered overly irrational responses to a harmless string of words. Between the two women, I walked silently.

Anita laughed, but she was tense. 'What are three middle-aged women doing at the base of Kailash?'

'Fulfilling their life's desire.'

'Pretending to be modern Sven Hedin?'

How could she have read my mind? But I was enjoying every bit of the landscape and the sight of Nandi, a rectangular massif that was almost flat, except for remnants of a horizontal layer of rock on top. From the perspective of landforms, Nandi was a butte: a hill that rose abruptly from its surroundings and had a flat top. When you looked at its southern wall from Selung, it looked as if some ancient civilization had carved eight columns on it. Perhaps this had something to do with the Jain's *Ashtapada*, where the first Tirthankara had attained Nirvana. When the sun struck it at an angle, its western face turned golden yellow.

Kailash, on the other hand, is a massive outcrop of dark conglomerate, always topped with white shining snow, a four-sided pyramid. Sometimes, I imagined it as a chocolate cake with cream layers and white icing. Some supernatural being had passed a knife along the southern edge to leave behind its remarkable cleft.

Between these two is a narrow valley, joined by the high pass, Chaksuma La. This valley and pass formed part of the inner *kora*. And both these were girdled by enormous chains of mountains of conglomerate. The outer *kora* of the pilgrims was beyond these encircling ranges.

The Tibetans, Nepalis and Indians all stopped and prayed. Everyone was terribly serious in demeanour and in a state just short of 'surrender'. I was aware of the spiritual magnetism of the place, although I was amused when reading Pranavananda's description of it.

Medha reminded us that ultimately it was we, the three women who had technically undertaken thirteen *kora*, who had reached the foot of Kailash without a mishap, so far. She held the belief that any attempt to undertake the inner *kora* without complying to the rule of thirteen would end in disaster.

I tried very much to remember and recite Shiva *shlokas* but none came to my mind. I could only recall a childish irreverent rhyme:

> *Brishti pare tapur tupur, nade elo baan*
> *Shib thakurer biye holo, tin kanya daan.*

> (It rains pitter-patter, the streams are in spate
> Lord Shiva weds three maidens.)

I requested Shiva to forgive me, for these were the only words that came to my mind.

And the rhyme ended thus:

> *Ek kanya randhe-bare, ek kanya khan*
> *Ek Kanya gosha kare, baper bari jaan.*

> (One bride cooks and serves, another enjoys the meals
> The third leaves for her father's home in a huff.)

There were black clouds all around, engulfing Kailash and the top of Nandi. We had no clear and detailed mission for the day. This trek was not mentioned in the *Lonely Planet*, our bible for the trip. Some claimed the trek to the Thirteen Chortens and back would take seven to eight hours. Others said the Tibetans took eighteen hours, past the Thirteen Chortens, over the high Chaksuma La Pass, past the two lakes and back to Selung. After an hour on yak-back and another hour and a half of trudging, we crossed the Selung *chu* and reached the foot of Mount Kailash, just short of the Thirteen Chortens.

I cannot imagine why anyone should want to build a *chorten* so high up and at such an inaccessible place. The *chorten* were built by the ancients in a horizontal crag on the vertical southern face of the Kailash peak. Pranavananda saw eighteen small and large *chorten* there. The *yakpa*, on seeing them through the field glasses, dashed off to them, completely unmindful of the yaks. He had never been there before and this would probably be his most pious pilgrimage ever. In the meantime, low, dark menacing clouds swirled around Kailash and enveloped all mountains, peaks and valleys. It began raining and snowflakes, like Aladdin's magic carpet, floated in the air. Large chilly drops stung our faces while snow swirls reduced visibility appreciably.

Medha declared, 'I will complete the *kora* with Pradip and Ramis.'

Anita and I decided against continuing in view of inclement weather. 'We'll return to camp with Kumar.'

I picked up a piece of ochre 'golden' rock from Nandi and a piece of quartz from the base of Kailash. Medha's decision did not surprise us at all, but we were worried that no specific preparation had been made for it. Ramis had inadequate warm clothes and there was not enough food for the full *kora* for the three of them. As the party left, Medha suddenly turned around and shouted, 'Want your blessings, guys.'

I reciprocated, 'You have all my blessings. But please do not do anything foolhardy.'

'I'll be careful,' she said, but she did not convince me. She was much too determined to go over the Chaksuma La Pass to dispassionately consider the dangers associated with crossing it. And to my mind, being aware of dangers was a way of protecting oneself from them.

'You are not aiming for the Book of Records. All the best and come back by nightfall,' I told Medha. Actually, Medha did deserve recognition for her painstaking *kora* — all done for the sake of Shiva. She was an outrageously slow walker but very persistent.

Medha is among the few people that I have met whom I always imagine as a character in a book. When Medha spoke, others listened. When she had an idea, she enunciated it clearly and embellished each little thought with the perfect phrase. She did things others would not consider attempting. When she found a cause, she stood committed to it. And once she set a goal, she devised all the means and actively put all her energies to generate the resources necessary to reach her goal. I think it could be safely said that some enjoyed her eccentricities while others found her annoying. I once asked her what drove her to these long treks. She said, 'I do not know. I just do it. It's the power of the Mountain.'

The sky was overcast and the atmosphere became incredibly terrifying and sombre. An avalanche came hurtling down and snow slipped down the central cleft on the southern face of the Kailash peak. This fell on the dome-shaped conical hill at its base. Like Nandi, this dome is not seen from the outer *kora*, nor had I ever seen any pictures of it before.

We watched like passive spectators of a film while we saw nature unfold its many forms in the natural world. Right in front of our eyes, the snow melted to become water that flowed by the western tributary of the Se-lung *chu*, to join the Darchen *chu*, that flowed to the Barkha plain. Then there was brilliant sunshine for a few minutes. Mount Kailash glowed in fresh snow and the strong wind atop stirred up a storm around the peak. The snow swirled around like a hula hoop till it was spent and lay suspended, like a wispy smoke ring at the tip of a cigar. The luminescent pyramid ringed by a white halo, embossed in the bluest of earthly skies, was imprinted forever in my memory.

I cannot think of a soul-stirring awareness of nature that is more stupendous and captivating than what we had just experienced. The nearest would perhaps be my early awareness of the first monsoon rains — the heavy shadowy stillness followed by the sudden, violent downpour that hails the beginning of the season along coastal Bengal. Dazzling flashes of light and eardrum-shattering thunderclaps accompany a seemingly impenetrable curtain of large heavy drops from the sky.

Standing at Kailash, we watched the sky turn ominously dark. The black clouds descended between mountains and enclosed them within its cold dampness. We knew it would rain. The atmosphere was threatening, but unlike in the monsoons at home, there was no blanket of four walls and a roof to protect us from the stinging chilly sprays of water and the blustering wind.

Were I asked about my experience at the foot of Kailash, I would say it was an awakening. It was an awakening to the awareness of the power and transience of nature. The impact was so lasting that I can relive it by the second, again and again, in my mind. Every time I think of it, I am amazed at the rapidity with which the events took place like a well-rehearsed drama of nature, where the Kailash peak and Nandi hill formed the most imposing props in a stage, enclosed not by screens but walls of mountains. Like some giant stage performance, the sequence of events unfolded in front of us on cue.

The light that had focused on the yellow stones of Nandi, setting off golden inflections, suddenly appeared to have been eclipsed by a throbbing, vibrating darkness. The golden mountain was now dark grey and all attention was riveted on the white storm on the pinnacle of Kailash. The spiraling white crystals formed a garland around the tip of the cone. It seemed to hang there interminably while a light blanket of snow covered everything around. It amassed layer by layer on the slopes of the Kailash peak, like a fresh rendering of a picture on a computer's monitor. And then theatrically, with a bang (which Anita said I imagined), the snow came hurtling down the southern cleft in a weighty mass of an avalanche, with billowing snow escaping all around.

The avalanche slipped and fell along the Kailash cleft on a petite hillock at its base. And suddenly all attention was on this inconsequential little mound, which cannot be seen from the outer *kora* of Kailash, and whose picture I had not seen earlier. While the rain subsided and the wind dropped, the snow piled on the dwarf mount. The white powder changed form and became liquid aqua. Drop by drop, it fell into zigzagging rills at its foot and then joined to become the beginning of a tiny brook. As if an invisible hand had used a heavenly crow quill to finely etch a line on the ground to ensure that the clear drops of water were restricted only to that channel. The heavenly craftsman had already preordained the brook would then flow by our camp and be known as the Darchen *chu* for all who cared to call it by a name.

Of the many magical moments I experienced on the journey to Tibet, the hours at the foot of the Kailash peak were most stunning. Later, I wondered if my response to the changing elements was similar to that of the ancients, who would have shuddered in awe at sudden natural happenings and prayed to the gods to protect them from nature. Sudden snowstorms and avalanches are directly associated with destruction and death, unlike solar or lunar eclipses, which they associated with good or bad events. I am sure that my experience at the foot of Kailash will be more lasting than my wonder at living through many eclipses. At Kailash, at one plane, I felt small and ineffectual, at the mercy of nature; and yet on another, I felt I was privy to nature's grandest show. A blessing, which could be compared to no other.

On the way back, the clouds lifted. There was a general stark theatrical quality about this hidden valley to the south of the Kailash peak, enclosed within the ring of Kailash mountain. It was a pristine landscape bereft of telltale signs of man; no bridges or culverts, trails or paths, hamlets or shops. A group of monks stopped and asked for a roll of film for their camera. They offered us money but we did not have spare film.

The monks showed us the aromatic herbs with tiny round leaves that they were gathering for incense, with the same degree of attention that tea pickers collect a flush of bud and two leaves. Sitting on the rocks, we enjoyed the serenity and the clear air. We spied bhurel, the blue mountain sheep that were almost completely camouflaged by the barren rocks. The most intent scanning of the ridges showed them up on the ridge tops, somewhere about 17,500 feet.

While we rested on the rocks, I recounted my strange dreams to Anita. She diagnosed them as a symptom of HAS.

'Strange how the same idioms were repeated.'

'That's because it was in your subconscious. I had hallucinations too.'

'Really?'

'I was awake last night thinking that my tent's ground sheet was placed on a mountain mouse's burrow.'

'They're safe.'

'I sat up all night, looking out for the mouse. I must have been awake for hours looking at their burrows near the tent's opening in the dim light,' said Anita.

'Not really?'

'What if a mouse was inside? I did not want to share my tent with the mouse. Now I cannot tell if it was real or hallucination.'

'I am reminded of an essay I had once read about James Bond.'

'What nonsense are you talking?'

'I can't help it. Listen to this. When 007's two-hour-old bride was exterminated violently by enemies, the poor broken man sat looking at ants and pondering on their existence. For some unexplained reason, this thought has now come to my mind.'

'His mind was numbed by shock. He wasn't suffering from dearth of oxygen.'

'I cannot rationally see any parallel situations, but the thought did come to mind.'

Anita was wary of Kailash. She was afraid of it and saw it as representing doom and death. Last time when we were at Kailash, she had prayed for Vir's health. In a few months he was gone. And yet she had made every effort to return here. I had not come with any overt religious or spiritual feeling. However, as the days went by, I was beginning to be aware of a fading away of sorrow that had become a part of my being. I felt a sense of peace.

Rock was disappointed that he had not felt the deep spiritualism mentioned by so many different travellers and writers. I thought that he had prepared himself for an intellectual approach and response to Tibet, but it was the physical aspect of the country that was most powerfully felt by a short-term visitor. He said he could better experience spiritualism through meditation anywhere. And I thought he couldn't have got a better place to do that.

Our *yakpa* caught up after having visited the Thirteen Chortens. He was at a loss for words to describe the sublime sight, but we had seen arguably the best pictures of the Thirteen Chortens, photographed by Dev Mukherjee. We declined riding the animals back and walked into camp several hours later in a cold drizzle. We related our experience at the foot of Mount Kailash to Rock. It was the day of the most wondrous experience of nature in its utmost dynamic and yet changeless form.

Over hot soup and dinner, we discussed the state of the world, especially South Asia. We were concerned over South Asian peace, General Parvez Musharraf's folly, HIV, migrants from Bangladesh to India, Line of Control in Kashmir, etc., etc. We talked of everything we had come here to be away from.

Medha had not returned well past sunset. The short dusk was now definitely over for the day. Devi had sent out Kumar with a flask of hot *chia* and food. Later he realised that Kumar was not equipped with a torch and sent Kuman with one hands-free kind, fixed to his forehead. By eleven o'clock, Devi himself had set off with another torch, with a sense of foreboding and the *yakpa* for company. He was worried beyond measure. He had recently suffered the loss of a nephew, later diagnosed with pulmonary oedema related to HAS. I could hear Rock cursing outside and Anita asking him to stay in his tent. It was a cold night and the wind was howling, as it could only at Kailash.

At midnight Medha, Pradip and Ramis returned. They were not able to move beyond the barrier of icefalls at the Thirteen Chortens. But they were so exhausted that they just wanted to worm into their warm tents and speak later. Kuman, Kumar and Devi all arrived shortly after, followed by the *yakpa*. Apparently, on seeing the lights at the camp, they telepathically knew all was well.

Next morning, without the slightest hint of dishonourable machinations, we suggested to Medha we would not proceed to Chung Tung from Tsaparang, but find our way back to Kathmandu from there. We were certain that she should not have put the lives of the Sherpas at risk by her unprepared decision to conquer the inner *kora*. Besides, she had caused a great deal of stress and anxiety to us. Having informed her of this, and suitably purging ourselves of our tensions and anger of the evening before, we felt more suited to cope with the remaining days.

Medha said breezily, 'Hey guys, sorry to have caused you worry last evening. I was given to understand that we were not expected before midnight.' This, from someone who had earlier taken two people up to 19,500 feet on an unknown route, without sufficient warm clothes, food or light or camping gear!

The decision to discontinue with the Chung Tung expedition was based on the party beginning to show signs of exhaustion and word-of-mouth reports that herds of wild yaks could no longer be seen along the highway. The northern Chung Tung plateau was truly desolate, while the southwestern Tibet plateau was somewhat less desolate by comparison. Desolation was no longer attractive to us. The decision was taken while Medha, who was keen to drive through the heart of wild west Tibet, was away. I was party to the decision, and it made me feel less honourable than was expected of pilgrims and explorers.

It was, however, on this aborted inner *kora* that Medha had gathered valuable information from a Swiss couple who for several months lived in Darchen. She had met them at the Thirteen Chortens, which they were helping rebuild. Medha herself was too exhausted to climb up to the *chorten*, and was dragged up by Pradip. The Swiss had stated that the complete inner *kora* was only for the fittest and those with mountaineering skills. The pass was very difficult to cross. Icefalls were treacherous and ubiquitous. The two lakes beyond were exquisite, but a few kilometres away from the regular *kora* route. Some of this we had surmised from various sources earlier. But the personal account of the Swiss, who had experience of the route, confirmed our view that fairly rigorous training was necessary before undertaking this section of the inner *kora*.

Mount Kailash with the Nandi butte in the foreground.

Many months later, I read that circling Kailash or Manasarovar 'during the *Ta-lo* was considered as virtuous as thirteen rounds made during other years.' So wrote Pranavananda. My first reaction on reading that a *kora* in the *Ta-lo* year was equal to thirteen and not twelve rounds of other years was that we had made an appalling mistake. This error had debarred Rock from walking up to the Thirteen Chortens. Perhaps Medha and Anita were correct after all. The mountain must call.

Quite unperturbed by the previous day's events, the Sherpa went about packing tents and the *yakpa* loading them on the yak. I sat on a boulder by the pure cold waters of the Darchen *chu* and watched the shepherds on the other bank. They had lit a small fire and were making tea in a large kettle. Their sheep and yak were wandering around, while they exchanged gossip and turned prayer wheels.

This was the last picture of pastoral harmony in the foreground of the Nandi and Kailash peak that returned with me. And just then I knew where the clever and gifted photographer Kami Tshering Sherpa had stood to take the 3D picture of Kailash for the poster we had seen in Kathmandu. It was right there on the outer ring of ranges that surrounded these two mountains, from the high ridge across from Selung *gompa*, on the other side of Darchen *chu*. That was one mystery solved beyond doubt, almost!

9

HOT SPRINGS AND MUD FORTS

At this point in our journey, an overwhelming sense of anticlimax prevailed among us. We had 'done' Manasarovar, Outer Kailash and Inner Kailash. Surely no other corner of Far West Tibet could compare to these significant places in our minds. All other places we now planned to visit would necessarily be trivial in comparison. Were we justified in our view? In another few days, we would know.

Next on our itinerary were visits to the three Ts, Tirthapuri, Tsaparang and Toling. While traditionally many pilgrims visit Tirthapuri after the *kora* of Manasarovar and Kailash, Tsaparang and Toling are now sought after by only a few. At that time, the three Ts did not generate the excitement that a journey so far and away from home, further into the heart of Far West Tibet, should rightly have. The remaining journey would need to be undertaken because one could scarcely deviate from an assigned tour route in Chinese Tibet.

On reaching Darchen, we dismissed our *yakpa* and bade them farewell. The *yakpa* were fully aware of their enormous significance to foreigners from the plains in these extreme conditions. They could be suitably opportunistic in driving hard bargains for carrying baggage and providing information on the terrain. We were aware of this and had, on several occasions, experienced the futility of bargaining prices with them. However, we were grateful to the *yakpa* for their constant and excellent service. A few plastic ballpoint pens, presented as token parting gifts, were greatly appreciated by them.

My mind was once more on the Sutlej. I meant to explore the north-western corner of Rakas Tal and follow the 'outflow' stream up to Dulchu *gompa*. However, there was powerful resistance to this suggestion from Rock and Anita. I was faced with the real possibility that the journey to Tibet might end without completing my exploration to 'discover' the headwaters of the Sutlej. I was determined to accomplish the mission. Finally, it was agreed that this would be done on the return journey from Tirthapuri, Tsaparang and Toling, when we planned to spend some time by the lakes.

The nature of relationships within a group changes subtly under the pressure of living closely together, particularly when there are limited interactions with people outside the group. It was for this reason that we had carefully considered every request to be a part of our team on this five-week expedition. However, now the first signs of stress were beginning to tell. Insignificant issues often led to discordance among the tiny group of four. On several occasions, I remembered Mandy's apprehension about group dynamics, which she cited as the chief reason for discontinuing the journey after Ray was forced to retreat to Kathmandu.

The forty-kilometre drive from Darchen to Tirthapuri was fairly un-eventful. We were in an area that was uncharted for all practical pur-poses, for we had no reliable maps to consult. Driving at an altitude of 15,000 feet, we followed wheel marks over undulating gravelly plains on the right bank of the Sutlej. There were some nomadic settlements and many sheep wandered in large herds, unmindful of us as we drove by.

Several narrow deep streams flowed from the Gang Te Se range on our right, cut across our route and joined the Sutlej on our left. These were the remarkable Chukta, Goyak, Trokposhar, Trokponup and other tributaries of the Sutlej. The streams were truly remarkable for they appeared to be short and insignificant in size, but were fast flowing and deep on the ground. Once again we entered the heart of the Sutlej Valley. I heard the ripple of water on the soft contours of a wide green valley that had been carved out many thousand centuries earlier on to a surface formed of glacial till. As elsewhere in much of Far West Tibet, broad well-defined terraces enclose the valley on either side. Three levels of terraces were clearly identifiable here, each easily five to six feet higher than the one below.

Traditionally, conservative Hindus and Buddhists complete their pilgrimage to Kailash and Manasarovar with a visit to Tirthapuri.

'Why is Tirthapuri a part of our itinerary?' asked Rock.

'To rest and recover from the treks,' patiently reminded Medha.

'Shouldn't we go directly to Tsaparang and Toling?' I asked.

'No. We finish *kora* first,' said Pema.

'Another *kora*?' I was surprised.

'Not big. Only small,' consoled Pema.

'Where's that?'

'We go to Retapuri,' informed Pema.

'Where's Retapuri now?' I was getting worried that we were to waste time on a *kora* that was not part of our plan.

'It same Tirthapuri,' clarified Pema.

Tibetans call Tirthapuri, literally meaning in Indian languages a place of pilgrimage, Retapuri. And though Retapuri meant 'place of demons', it is derived from Pretapuri, a name given to this place by early Indian pilgrims. *Pret* refers to beings from the other world and *puri* is a settlement or habitation. Legend has it that Bhasmasura, the demon, prayed and undertook penance here. Satisfied with his penance, Lord Shiva granted him a boon, which he injudiciously used against the Lord himself. This enraged Shiva enough to trick the luckless demon to turn himself to *bhasma,* or ashes. The whitish calcium deposits at Tirthapuri are said to be the ashes so produced.

The Sutlej flows in large meanders here. The ancient Tirthapuri Monastery on the right bank of the river is about twenty kilometres further downriver from Dulchu. Immediately above this point, alongside the Tirthapuri Monastery, it passes through a narrow gorge. We camped at about 14,000 feet, at least 3,000 feet lower than on the last several nights. The sky was overcast with black clouds, surely from across the Himalayas, but there was not a drop of rain. Billowing clouds constantly transformed to new shapes and then drifted away to the east.

Just outside the Tirthapuri Monastery gate, there was a camping ground by the river. We could see the hemispherical tents of the visiting monk from New Zealand there. While we waited for the monk to appear, Rock said, 'I saw an informative documentary about practising Buddhists in New Zealand.'

'I recall seeing it too. Wasn't it about a Tibetan family who fled the country and settled in New Zealand?'

'I think so. It was very interesting. Besides the freedom of worship in New Zealand, the lama said that the mountains reminded him of his homeland.'

Anita was intrigued by the ethnicity of the monk in the camp. 'Is he Tibetan or White?' she wondered aloud. We never saw him.

There was no Hindu temple anywhere in sight. There was an 8th century Buddhist monastery and an important Bon worshipping site along the short *kora* around the Tirthapuri hill. Behind the monastery was the Bonpa shrine, where stacks of horns and carcasses of yak could be seen piled up in heaps.

It called for tremendous restraint on my part to hold myself from telling my companions how Tibetans killed their animals for sacrifice. I had learnt that they plunge a knife or spear through the left shoulder of the animal, then pass the hand through this rupture and extract the still palpitating heart. This live heart was then given in offering to the deities. I never did get around to finding out if the method was still employed in killing animals for sacrifice.

An interesting account of Tirthapuri is found in Ekai Kawaguchi's *Three Years in Tibet*. Of the great explorers of western Tibet, one who for many years was not widely acknowledged for his contribution to the knowledge of the country was this Japanese priest. Kawaguchi planned well before travelling to Tibet. He spent time at the Tibetan School in Darjeeling, where Sarat Chandra Das was the Principal. Here he learnt

Idyllic Tirthapuri on the banks of the Sutlej and a trader's tent pitched there.

to speak Tibetan, before entering the country disguised as a Chinese lama. Trekking between the Dhaulagiri and the Annapurna peaks of the Himalayas, he reached Lo in Mustang, Nepal, and lived there for a year. Here, he prepared for his journey through Tibet to collect Buddhist scriptures. Kawaguchi would exercise carrying weights, running up and down hillslopes with stones in his backpack. Villagers thought this was a form of self-mortification being practised by the 'Chinese' priest. He entered Tibet through Mustang in the year 1900, and spent the next three years travelling on the plateau.

Kawaguchi gave a detailed account of his journey through hail, rain, deep snow, blizzards, starvation, burglary and spells of writing poetry. Living amongst *dukpa* (nomads) in Far West Tibet, he reached as far as 'Retapuri', before turning east. He wrote about the influence of the Hemis Monastery of Ladakh and noted that many times invading marauders had plundered it. This seemed to be the fate of many of the monasteries in western Tibet and the PLA's vicious attacks were only the most recent examples of a violent past.

When we reached the monastery, we saw that the older buildings of the complex were cut into the rocks and were both under and above ground. Inside the temple was a cave. The resident monk took great pains to inform us that it was there that Urghien had meditated with his Tibetan consort.

'Why is Padmasambhava called Urghien?' asked someone. At that time none of us had an answer. But later I understood that since he was from Udiyana, which was also known as Urghiyana, by association he became Urghien.

The long lines of *mani-walls* were the most significant architectural feature of the temple and monastery complex. These same *mani-walls* had reminded Ekai Kawaguchi of 'railway cars'. In his account, Kawaguchi wrote on seeing *mani-steps* at the temple: 'The sight was a grand one, with its *mani-steps* of stone, which looked, at a distance, like a long train of railway cars. . . . I should add that in that mighty range of sky reaching mountains, there lives a species of strange birds, whose note is exactly like the whistle of a railway engine. The *mani-steps* looking like a train before me made me think of the whistle of these birds, and I felt as if I had arrived once more in a civilized country.'

I beg to suggest that there are no high 'mighty range of sky-reaching mountains' at Tirthapuri. In fact, this is a gently undulating country and the birds he spoke of were possibly partridges and Tibetan snowcock. But this is the charm of Kawaguchi; he goes in the wrong direction, gets drowned, is engulfed in snowstorm, almost freezes in the cold, is lost and burgled, and then composes a poem!

That he did not actually think of this little town as a civilized place is evident from his rather critical statements: 'The place was called Retapuri (town of hungry devils), a name which *Paldan* (Father) Atisha gave to the place when he arrived here from India on his mission of evangelisation. The name is not inapplicable to the Tibetans. The Tibetans may indeed be regarded as devils that live on dung, being the filthiest race of all the people I have ever seen or heard of. They must have presented a similarly filthy appearance at the time of the visit of Atisha, who, therefore, gave to the place the not-so-inappropriate title of Pretapuri. The Tibetans, thanks to their ignorance of Sanskrit, are rather proud of the name.' One hundred years after this was written, we, however, found a very small population at Retapuri and it was fairly clean.

In the cave temple was a rock that was held in high esteem, as it was believed to have the imprint of the feet of Guru Rinpoche. In this respect, the Tibetans are very much like people of many other old cultures. We love attributing supernatural explanations to natural occurrences. But the devout, and not a little bigoted, Buddhist monk Kawaguchi was enraged to find Sakyamuni and Guru Rinpoche being worshipped in the same temple. And this is what he had to say about the latter:

'To this Lobon (Guru Rinpoche) are attached many strange legends and traditions, such as would startle even the most degenerate of Japanese priests. I already knew the strange history of the founder of this Tibetan sect, and so a sensation of nausea came over me. It was really blasphemy against Buddha, for Lobon was in practice a devil, and behaved as if he had been born for the very purpose of corrupting and preventing the spread of the holy doctrines of Buddha.'

Kawaguchi's comments on Padmasambhava (Guru Rinpoche) seemed rather bizarre and extreme. They also appeared at variance to my information on the Guru, on reading commentaries and speaking to the Tibetans amongst us. I had read a short story about Padmasambhava on a website, which went somewhat like this:

'A goddess stole some celestial flowers and because of this bad karma, she was reborn as a woman on earth. Here she commissioned a magnificent stupa at Baudhanath near Kathmandu, but died before it was completed. Her four sons completed the construction and prayed to be reborn as a Dharma king, a *khenpo*, a *tantric* master and a messenger, who would bring the other three together. A wise donkey standing nearby, which had carried huge burdens during the construction, was privy to this prayer. He was angered that they did not remember him in their prayers and vowed to spoil the fruits of their prayers.

In their next lives, the four brothers were reborn as King Trisong Deutsen, the 38th king of Tibet; *khenpo* Shantarakshita, the *tantric* guru Padmasambhava and the messenger who was sent by the king to bring the *khenpo* and *tantric* master to Samye, where the first great monastery was built. Here the first seven monks were given vows and many Buddhist texts were translated into Tibetan. Thus Dharma was established in Tibet. And the donkey almost succeeded in dislodging Buddhism from Tibet, for he was reborn as Langdarma.'

That was a legend, but history also records that in the 8th century, King Trisong Deutsen heard of the 'Lotus-born' guru from Urghiyana, known to Indians as Padmasambhava. He sent the monk Shantarakshita to Swat to invite him to Tibet. At that time, Bonism, a form of Buddhism which had greatly absorbed its shamanistic rituals, was practised in Tibet. Langdarma, the pro-Bon 41st king of Tibet, who was later murdered, initiated many actions that went against Buddhism.

Along with Urghien Guru Rinpoche also came other teachers. Since translation of scriptures was an important goal of his work in Tibet, knowledge of both Sanskrit and Tibetan were essential. Thus several *pandits* came from Ladakh, where Buddhism was well established. Among them the most outstanding scholar was Ananta, who was

Shantarakshita's interpreter. The latter was not proficient in Tibetan, the language into which the texts were translated from Sanskrit.

In the book *Buddhist Savants of Kashmir: Their Contributions Abroad*, Advaitavadini Kaul provides a comprehensive review of the contribution of Kashmiri scholars who worked in Tibet. It was at this time that many religious texts, particularly the *Khanjur* and *Tanjur*, were transcribed into Tibetan by translators, many of whom had been trained in Kashmir.

My understanding was that Padmasambhava, a *tantric* Buddhist, reached Tibet with the intent of 'subduing evil spirits' and reforming a religion strongly influenced by shamanism. Then I read Desideri's comment on Urghien, recorded in several chapters of his book. It must be remembered that Desideri was writing in the early 18th century, but had access to Buddhist texts and scholars because he had spent time at Tibetan universities and three years at the monastery at Sera.

Desideri spoke of Urghien's influence on the King, about how he enhanced the palaces and grand monastery of Samye and built a large network of monasteries in remote places. The practice of hermits meditating in isolation in remote caves was rampant. He wrote that the princesses once watched through the cracks in a door as Urghien undertook his *tantric* rituals with blood and skulls. They were frightened, but the king was the ally of the powerful Guru and later even succumbed to his machinations. The implication was that Padmasambhava, a *tantric*, was a fervent ascetic and practised black magic.

Kawaguchi, who also spent time at the Sera Monastery, must surely have referred to this in his book. Besides, Kawagachi was a puritanical celibate Zen monk. It was quite possible that he disapproved of monks and laymen praying to a Guru who had several consorts and even meditated along with one.

Tibetans are great believers in the healing properties of various natural elements. They have a rich tradition of using herbs for curing ailments. Much of the knowledge of centuries of experience in using medicinal herbs was documented and kept in the scrolls at the Tibet Medicine

School opposite the Potala Palace, which was completely destroyed after the Chinese occupation. But there was also a great deal of unsubstantiated belief in the use of earths, rocks and minerals as medicines.

Along the *kora* route in Tirthapuri, our drivers and guide dug into the ground with their fingernails. The coloured soil was then wrapped and packed away in bits of plastic and stored away to be used as medicine to cure a wide range of ailments. This yellow earth was probably a weathered form of calcium carbonate, which is widely found here.

Maya had mentioned an interesting feature of Tirthapuri, while we chatted on the shores of Manasarovar. She said that the local women sift the sands along the banks of the Sutlej and sometimes find pearls! This, to my mind, was far-fetched, as there were no oyster beds for pearl culture. It was conceivable that they were formed in the past in a lake that was now dry. But the little white nodules that the local women sift out of the soil, in fact, turned out to be limestone and not pearls. These too the local people believe have supernatural curative properties!

'A whole habitation's populace cannot suffer from pika, can they?'

'Of course not. They could have iodine deficiency, being a land far from the sea. . . But calcium carbonate? Unlikely.'

'Anyway, there does not seem any iodine deficiency like you see in the Himalayan villages at times. The rainfall is too low to cause iodine leaching from the soil.'

'That's the point. How does one explain their swallowing calcium carbonate nodules as a pastime?'

'People here really do believe the lime pellets cure a wide range of diseases. Only I don't seem to get them to say which.'

A short visit to the monastery was followed by a long, hot natural shower at the waterfalls from the spring. I was told that this was once a geyser, spurting out jets of water. The thick white calcium deposit over the area does indicate that, at one time, there must have been a great deal of water gushing out of the ground to leave behind so much deposit. In fact, the hot spring water flows over the edge of the calcium deposits to form the famous bathing hot waterfalls of Tirthapuri.

It had been a cold and windy afternoon. Sometimes the sun dazzled for a few minutes from behind the cloud screen and disappeared with great alacrity. Hardly the perfect day to bathe out in the open. But Rock ventured to the Hot Springs and came back with flushed glowing cheeks, saying, 'Most invigorating. I strongly recommend a bath.' Throwing all modesty to the wind, Anita and I washed and scrubbed in abandon. Scantily clad, we frolicked in the waterfall, hastily darting out of its reach when the sulphuric waters scalded, springing right back under the deluge when the body noted the first signs of cooling.

There is something special about bathing in hot naturally flowing water. It is more than a sensual experience. The water seeks every nook and corner deep inside you, searches out all the knotted worries, dissolves every bit of tension, and washes it away. When we stepped out of the water, we were light enough to walk on waves. When we stripped off the steaming few wraps, we could not care less that Tsering, the driver, was having a good view from the local trader's tent.

As I rubbed shampoo into my hair, I passed my hand through the foam and made a mental note of the fact that the manufacturers deserved a commendation for creating a product that lathered so easily in hard water. We debated on what could make good copy for an advertisement, perhaps something like, 'Washes hair under the most difficult conditions'. This could be with a picture of a yak being shampooed by a stream. Perhaps the copy should have read, 'Used at Heaven's Door . . . Kailash, 18,600 feet, endorsed by yak and *yatri*.' Or perhaps, picture us (alas, somewhat thick in the waist) under the waterfall, conspicuously displaying the label on the shampoo sachet, too tiny to actually appear in any photograph. Through all this, I was aware of the shaggy yak across the river, staring at us morosely between nibbles of grass. Probably contemplating human follies and absurdities.

Standing by the Cruiser, Tsering was in conversation with the Keeper of the Hot Springs, negotiating a waiver of our bathing fee of Yuan 10 each. The man, who looked like the wanderer of the Hindi films of the 1950s, let us leave with good grace. While we combed our hair and drank tea at the camp, he appeared again along with a young man. The youth spoke in Hindi and demanded money on behalf of the Keeper of the HS. We paid up sheepishly. Tsering lost face.

Our first relaxed evening after days of hard treks was celebrated with Lhasa Beer, prawn crackers and Maharashtrian *chewra*. Dinner was laid out in style in the dining tent, where the staff had produced a spotless white tablecloth for the folding table. Spring rolls, mushroom soup and vegetable noodles were rounded off with a dessert of Kiwi fruit, straight out of the tin. This had been the trend of our dining experience. We never tired of discussing the cook Devi's rare gift in producing high-altitude meals.

'Devi is an enigma.'

"Why do you say that? He's quite predictable.'

'He produces barely edible *roti* and *dal-bhat* for several days . . .'

'True.'

'And then surprises us with a multi-course culinary indulgence.'

When dinner was over, Devi sent Kuman over with a special treat. 'Do you like to have cake?' he asked.

'Sure. Let's give it a try.' Medha and Anita politely nibbled at Devi's steamed cake.

I eyed it with distaste. 'Please excuse, Kuman. I am through. I'll try it to-morrow,' I said, hoping there would be none left over for the next day.

'The orange chocolate cake at Kilroy's is what we will eat when we reach Kathmandu.' We got vicarious pleasure in just imagining what that would do to our taste buds. I appreciated Devi's effort, but could not stomach his steamed cake.

My head was lightweight after the exhilarating shower. Sitting at the opening of my tent, I wrote notes on the possibility of the area being seismically active. What were the pointers? Geysers, springs and even what looked like volcanic craters in the area.

My mind wandered. I was enjoying the sheer simple luxury of breathing easily. As twilight settled in and the clouds covered the sky, there was a dreamlike quality to the picturesque valley, so different from the harsh scree slopes and craggy ridges of Kailash. I still could not recollect the Tibetan word for snakes. Was it benign dragon or gentle dragon, or friendly dragon, or had it anything to do with dragons at all?

Morning broke gently in the upper Sutlej Valley. We began our movement further west, in an area seldom visited by foreigners. On reaching the complex of single-storey huts, the important crossroads of the west, Moncier (Mansi of the past), we drove north along the Tasam Highway, today's Southern Route. Then we turned west onto tracks between limitless open fields. We aimed to reach the ruins of Tsaparang and the nearby monastery of Toling in the town Zada, on the Sutlej, close to the Indian border. This area was off the beaten track and among the most difficult to reach. We drove through the stupendous heights and vibrant hues of the landscape.

It was a mountainscape born in the mind of a wild painter. The artist had dipped his brush in all the colours of his palette. Lilac, mauve, purple, grey, rust and burnt sienna mountain slopes spread across the land. Stark and dry as it was, it was captivatingly beautiful. For a few moments, I felt a mounting excitement in the pit of my stomach and awaited the free fall of the Land Cruiser, as I anticipated it dropping off the face of the earth. I was stunned into pointing at nothingness and could only say, 'Look!'

Rock looked and without any emotion said, 'Void.' At this point in the journey, we should have tumbled and crashed straight into a valley below, just a few metres ahead. Instead, an unending vista emerged.

Imagine, the ground beneath your feet and yet you are looking down on the highest peaks on earth. Was this grey-blue mirage at the edge of the earth . . . the Himalayas? I had never conjectured this was possible. A spectacular girdle of mountain ranges formed a semicircle on the south and west, with clusters of clearly recognisable peaks covered in snow. There was something wondrously unreal about gazing on them from above. I had always been fascinated watching eagles and vultures fly in the valleys, as I watched from higher ridges and peaks. But to see the majestic Himalayas from above, while still on the ground, was a sight worth cherishing forever. With hindsight, I can say that if the highest point of the expedition was finding the source of the Sutlej, then this was a vision of the highest points!

'The view is breathtaking!'

'Yes. The very thought of looking down on the high Himalayan peaks is mind blowing!'

'What could that group of mountains be?' one asked, pointing west.

'Almost certainly the K2 group of peaks. . .'

Awestruck, I heard someone say, 'No! Surely not K2, the second highest peak on earth?'

And the answer came, 'If not, then the Karakoram cluster.'

'Seems much too close for that. But the direction is correct.'

'The guide does not seem to know what the other high peak is.'

'The nearer one is probably Kunjur.'

The sheer magnitude of the upward warp of the earth's surface forming the Tibet plateau left one surprised, while inspecting the silhouette of the high peaks under one's nose. For the moment, we were not considering physics and the role of the curvature of the earth in this amazing illusion. A few hours drive further south and a magnificent peak dominated the horizon, its shoulders far above the Himalayan range.

'It's positively Kamet. It rises above all other peaks.'

Following another change in direction, we saw the twin peaks of Nanda Devi rising high. There was agreement among all on this one.

Once, several years ago, I was on a flight from eastern India to Delhi. There is a point where you can see the Himalayas quite clearly, and I looked out of the window to catch a glimpse. What I saw then in the sky was as magical as what I saw that day from the high plains of western

Vista on the way to Toling from Tirthapuri.

Tibet. There was a completely circular rainbow in the sky, and within it was the shadow of the airplane that we were travelling in.

It was as if a fairy had swished her wand to draw the image on the clouds. For many years later, I could see in my mind's eye the shadow of the plane on the clouds, encircled by the rainbow, moving along with the plane. These are lumieres of physics that we never learn of in our school texts. Standing on the plateau and scanning the high peaks below had exactly the same feel as of living in a fairytale world, where you could levitate above the highest mountains!

We entwined and wound around several tributaries of the Sutlej, through the loneliest country imaginable. Suddenly, we approached an unbelievably arid clay and sand landscape formed of wind action, but strangely, sculpted superficially by rills of water that were probably the result of occasional storms and flash floods. It seemed to have been chiselled out of light clay by some superhuman craftsmen.

The rock strata were clear and conspicuous. Layers of fine clay in shades of grey and white lay horizontally one over the other. Their textures varied from very fine to coarse. The bands were well formed and each reflected the climatic conditions under which it was deposited under water, probably the prehistoric Tethys Sea. Later, vertical movements of the earth's crust raised the compacted sediments. This resulted in the horizontal bands of the landscape. Deep gullies were carved in, leaving behind the impression of a monstrous ghost city, once carved out by man and long abandoned.

Not able to sight any water, we drove for miles looking for a suitable campsite. Finally, it was the little truck driver, Jaunty in the Red Cap, who drove us to a secluded green patch in the middle of this surreal wilderness. I never really felt the urge to remember his name, because he was Jaunty in the Red Cap. Later, the Nepali boys told us that he had suffered a severe nervous attack at a hairpin bend, where his truck had unexpectedly approached a 2,000-foot precipitous drop, his front wheels about a foot from the edge. The reason for this rather unusual nervous attack was the sight of a crumpled truck, lying twisted and mangled on the slopes.

We camped at this water hole. It was a microcosm of a plant and animal world, independent of the regional setting, and a relief to have finally reach. The small brook that passed through the centre of this oasis watered all the coarse grass, shrubs and small trees. But we saw no animals or people. This little ephemeral stream was a tributary of the Sutlej, which joined the river on the opposite bank from Toling. On all sides were high walls of grey-white clay, the impenetrable ramparts of a natural fortress, built around an abandoned fairyland.

It was Pema's birthday and we felt a celebration was called for. We cooled tins of beer in a drum of cold water from the tiny brook passing by the camp. Pradip and Ramis went to Toling to buy provisions and returned disappointed, as they found neither fresh chicken nor sheep. The table was set in the middle of the clay and sandstone fortress. We opened a bottle of Glen Morangie and had generous portions of the manna. Regrettably, the Tibetans and Nepalis diluted it with their *chia*.

Medha danced while the younger Sherpas sang their folk songs. She tied a scarf around her waist and stretched out her arms and moved grace-fully with the music. Her face reflected her complete absorption in the sounds reaching her brain. Anita kept herself aloof and at a distance. She was thinking of things far away and was the only one who did not sing or dance. I was so acutely aware of her personal loss that I always imagined she was pondering on the past. But she too slowly gave herself up to the mood of the evening.

Anita appropriated the bottle of Scotch and asked me to put it away in my tent. In no time, Rock demanded the bottle back and poured a round of drinks. After the hard treks to Kailash, Manasarovar, and the base of Mount Kailash, this was the most convivial evening in a long time. The Nepali Sherpas and the Tibetans were now happily drinking barley beer.

'What's that?'

'*Chhang*! Do you like to have some Tibetan beer?' offered Kuman.

Medha danced with abandon and was annoyed when others stopped. The boys laughed and she responded, 'Who cares?' to no one in particular. She repeated it several times, almost as though she were convincing herself. Anita was now relaxed. Rock, who was reserved by nature and did not exhibit his emotions wildly ever, poured another round of generous drinks. I found myself clapping and tapping to the rhythm of the music.

The Sherpas sang melodious songs of love, unrequited love, separation, angst and the mountains. Medha swayed along, claiming, 'I have the power of Lord Shiva,' and a little later, more theatrically, 'I am [goddess] Devi.' By now the only purpose the empty bottle of Glen Morangie served was to mark the centre of the circle around which we all marched. All of us moved in a circle clockwise and when that became repetitive, we were creative enough to turn anticlockwise! That marked the end of festivities for the evening. Devi predictably produced on order what we knew he cooked best: *dal-bhat* and tinned vegetables. All this he served with pickles and relishes of various kinds, including *kasundi*, the sour mangoes in mustard.

Around this time, most of us retired to our tents. I heard for a while a profound and protracted discussion on Buddhism between Medha and the others in the kitchen tent. She was referring to herself as Tara and expressing her views on *tantric* Buddhism to an utterly uncomprehending but captive audience. Naturally, she could not remember any of her discussion points next morning.

I slept well and had gentle dreams of the mud castles around us changing form. At times the ramparts appeared as the old mud-walled city of Kashgarh and at others they metamorphosed to form the faces of the four Presidents of America, sculpted in rock on Mount Rushmore. I have never seen these masks of rock except as a child in my View Master. The clay towers and turrets all appeared with prayer flags hoisted on them. The flags fluttered and the windhorses printed on them whispered our deepest thoughts to the spirits, demons and deities in the sky.

The three drivers and Pema danced around a fire they had lit. The five Sherpas formed a circle around them and moved to their own mountain music. The Yindu danced to the music of timeless Vedic chants. All the dead monks who had lived in the caves of the soft ash-coloured ridges around the oasis stepped out to watch. They were no more in their meditative mood and openly expressed their desire to participate in this conviviality.

The travellers sang, 'Yo ho ho, the lamas go to Mustang.'

Ghostly voices reverberated across the oasis, 'Yo ho ho, and a bottle of *chhang*.'

The Sherpas shouted, 'Yo ho ho, tomorrow we go to Zarang.'

And the plangent voices of the long dead, loudly repeated the refrain, 'Yo ho ho, and a bottle of *chhang*.'

When all the *chhang* had been drunk and daylight enveloped their caves, the shadowy figures disappeared, awaiting the next convivial evening.

I woke up in the middle of the night and realised I had been dreaming. There were no monks in the caves and there was deep silence in the ravines. Even the insects of the Guge Kingdom had faded noiselessly into the night.

I drifted back to sleep, my mind lazily wondering what remnants of this lost kingdom awaited us the next day. How would this long ride to the extreme Far West end? Were we in for disappointment or a dazzling experience of the remnants of the kingdom at the Tsaparang citadel and Toling Monastery? We had heard of widespread destruction of monuments and irreparable damage to exquisite murals and idols. So, would we just be witnesses to this wanton destruction, or would we find hidden treasures in the ruins?

In the midst of desolate Guge, a lost kingdom of yesteryear.

10

IN LOST GUGE KINGDOM

There is a rather otherworldly ring to the phrase 'Lost Guge Kingdom.' The kingdom that is unknown, except perhaps to the very few specialists on Himalayan and Tibetan civilizations. Its once famous capital, Tsaparang, on the trade route between Ladakh and the lands of eastern Tibet, is in picturesque ruins; a citadel on the southern bank of the Sutlej.

I had not heard of the Guge Kingdom till I began reading about Far West Tibet and its history. And then, unexpectedly, a wonderful lost world of flourishing trade, benevolent kings, free religious debate, the synthesis of art and culture, all seemed to converge and blend for a few centuries at the temple town of Toling and Tsaparang, its capital. The kingdom had a short life, but it was then the centre of Tibet, marked by royal patronage of arts, craft, trade and religion. It was caught in the crossfire between the indigenous Bonpo and foreign Buddhist rituals and thoughts, Christian evangelism and marauding Muslim warriors from Ladakh.

The rise and eminence of Toling is associated with the revival of Tibetan Buddhism in the 11th century. Later, Guge became the victim of intrigue and jealousy of other kingdoms. Its decline began with the death of the young king of Tsaparang at the hands of bloodthirsty mercenaries, and the end of the kingdom followed shortly thereafter.

The Guge Kingdom comprised three *khorsum*s (provinces) of Ngnari (Western Tibet). These were Purang, Guge and Mangyul. In the 10th century, Nyima Gon, a Buddhist descendant of the Bon King Langdarma, surveyed Ngari *khorsum* to identify a suitable place to settle his fleeing army and establish his kingdom.

According to Tibetan texts, this is what they had to report about Purang: 'The land looks like the carcass of a slaughtered horse surrounded by snow mountains. The people resemble demons.' About Guge they said, 'The land looks like the white carcass of a fish surrounded by barren canyons. The people resemble sheep.' Of Mangyul they commented, as mentioned earlier, 'The territory looks like a hollow land filled with lakes and surrounded by snow mountains. The people resemble frogs.' As far as description of the morphology went, although their descriptions were in profoundly metaphorical terms, the comments were quite indicative of the nature of the lands.

Guge was a narrow tract in the northern foothills of the Himalayas, along the river Sutlej, stretching till Purang further east. It included the areas earlier covered by the ancient pre-Bon and pre-Buddhist kingdom of Shang Shung, also in the upper Sutlej Valley, with its capital at Kyun-glung, twenty-five kilometres southwest of Tirthapuri. To the north, it did not extend beyond one day's horse ride and the Ladakh range of the Himalayas marked the western fringe. Its trade links were stronger with Leh, Zhanskar and Spiti in the west than with the commercial capitals of Shigatse and Lhasa in the east, which were long distances away.

It is doubtful if the Guge Kingdom could ever have been very large, either in terms of numbers or extent. This was principally because it was located in one of the driest places on earth, with the possibility of agriculture limited to valley floors. As the annual rainfall was very low, farming was completely dependent on river water. The oasis that we had camped in occupied one such valley floor of a small tributary of the Sutlej.

Just as we moved a few hundred metres away from the water channel, everything was in a haze of bright light and grey-white rocks carved into columns by wind carrying abrasive sand. Most of the common people had probably lived in large communes of caves dug into these horizontally-layered soft rocks along the river. Many such sites have been found and documented along the upper Sutlej.

But Guge had the advantage of its strategic position along the trade route between First and Second Tibet in the west and the kingdoms of central and eastern Tibet in the east. The Sutlej Valley was an important trade route before the roads along the Indus were constructed. And its fame was not for its military might but for the initiatives in the revival of Buddhist religion, art and architecture. However, it was this same position along the easy access route from the west that led to the temples, palaces and monasteries of the realm being plundered and destroyed several times over in history.

In its heyday between the 10th and 16th century, Guge flourished in the upper Sutlej Valley. Except for a short while, it was a vassal of the Kingdom of Ladakh, which was for long the strongest of the western Tibet monarchies. By the mid-15th century, to keep the powerful kings of Leh happy, Guge sent large tributes in the form of gold, turquoise, corals, yaks, horses, saddles, sheep and weapons. 'All these weapons had appropriate names, and the most striking among them were the resplendent 'devil-coat-of-mail', the coat of mail 'devil-darkness', the sword 'licking blood off the sky', the sword 'wild yak, long point,' the sword 'killer of the red lightning flame.' The list was long.

The worst attack finally came to the monasteries and palaces in modern times, from the east by the means of the Cultural Revolution (1966-1976). Inventories of murals, statues and religious paraphernalia kept regularly in Toling showed records for the year 1841, when General Zorawar Singh had reached the temple town. Later, paintings and valuables were painstakingly documented in 1933, by Guiseppe Tucci and his photographer Ghersi, and translated and published in *Secrets of Tibet*. A comparison of these inventories with present cultural treasures indicates that they have all but disappeared.

Tsaparang and Toling are well away from the tourist circuit. These are places of interest to the student of Buddhist art and paintings and for one with enough enthusiasm to journey across a distance of 1,500 kilometres from Lhasa over poor and nonexistent roads for four to five days. It is so off the beaten track that when the Jesuit priest Ippolito Desideri came to Ngnari from Leh in 1715, specifically with a view to visit Tsaparang, there was no road leading to Guge, nor any pilgrims headed towards Toling. He missed the road to his goal and continued east to finally reach Lhasa. There is only one approach by road to the capital of the lost Guge Kingdom. This is through the town of Zada (Tsamda) at the Sutlej gorge.

Zada is situated on a high terrace on the south bank of the Sutlej. When you approach from the north, before crossing the Sutlej bridge there, you can see a perfectly levelled high plain with poplars and modern buildings. From afar, it looked like an architect's model constructed for making a presentation. There was frenzied development activity on. Tubewells have been dug on the low-lying riverbanks to tap groundwater.

The river has cut deep into the loess, the fine windblown sand deposits, and the valley is verdant green with crops. To the geographer, it is evident that the valley slopes are almost vertical because the climate is extremely dry and the surrounding rocks soft. Small boulder dams have been constructed across the tributary streams. It was the only place in Western Tibet where we saw well-fed large cows, sitting by the road, calmly chewing the cud. But where were the yaks? The symbol of Far West Tibet was absent. In fact, there were no animals at all on the plateau here, except in the valleys.

From our camp we drove for about half an hour and crossed over the Sutlej bridge at Zada, at a narrow gorge. This perhaps is a reinforced and renovated structure that was photographed by Capt. C.G. Rawlings in 1904. The photograph of the earlier iron chain bridge is presently in the repository of the Royal Geographic Society. We were dismayed to see the river had been dammed behind a new barrage and a hydroelectric power station was being constructed there.

'The site is perfect for it at the gorge.'

'Yes. But water will collect behind the dam and much less will flow downstream.'

'That is the purpose . . . and it will be served well.'

The snow-fed tributaries above Toling gorge brought a vast volume of water to the Sutlej. The blocking of the river here implied that this water would now be released for consumption downstream in a regulated manner. This thought agitated us all considerably.

'My concern is the impact this concrete structure will shortly have on restricting the flow of water to the lower reaches of the river.'

'I guess it's good for the people here, but bad for those in the valley in India.'

'I doubt if anyone in India is aware of it.'

Zada is a town for the Chinese in Tibet. It is of strategic significance, and military presence was seen and felt everywhere. The high-street was being paved and ugly structures being built. Rows of trees have been planted along the main thoroughfare. It was mushrooming with symbols of Han and military presence.

The Toling Tourist Office, under the Seal of Ngari district official, exhorted tourists to visit the 'Places of Travails': Toling Monastery for Yuan 80 and Ruins of Tsaparang for Yuan 105. Trade was flourishing and restaurants with exotic names, like 'Androsia Trattoria' dotted the main thoroughfare. The food was not quite what an unsuspecting tourist might have expected of an eatery thus named.

Nyima Gon's famous descendant Lha Lama Yeshe-O, popularly known as Yeshe-O, a devout Buddhist, became the benevolent and undisputed ruler of Tibet. He founded the monastery at Toling (sometimes also spelt Tholing), twenty-six kilometres from the capital, in today's town of Zada.

Toling, meaning 'the lofty place', was established about the year 996 A.D. Yeshe-O's rule was probably prosperous and had the support of the lamas, for he supported the construction of palaces and monasteries. He was able to achieve this ambitious plan by demanding rich gold mines as compensation from a vassal state, where one of his senior administrators had been murdered. Toling was the mother temple and several important satellite monasteries with beautiful temples had been built in the kingdom.

In this theocratic state, 'eminent attention was paid to Tholing and its support', wrote Roberto Vitali in *The Kingdoms of Gu.ge Pu.hrang*. 'To provide supplies for the monks, farmers were required to give to the monasteries, and in particular to Tholing, the main temple, a piece of land that needed a specified weight of seeds to be cultivated. The nomads of the country had to provide various types of their produce equivalent to such a piece of land.'

With full administrative support, Toling became the nerve centre of western Tibet, and the capital, which had earlier been at Purang, moved to Toling during Yeshe-O's reign. The famous scholar-translator, Rinchen Zhangpo, was the abbot of Toling Monastery at that time. Yeshe-O invited great Buddhist teachers and scholars to his kingdom from Kashmir, Bengal and Bihar. Thus it was that Atisha arrived in 1042 A.D, from the Vikramshila Monastery in present-day Bihar, and thereby began the Second Diffusion of Buddhism in Tibet.

At the time of our visit, Toling Monastery was operational and there were six resident monks. The buildings were devastated by both time and man. On several ruined walls, there were impressions of large statues, now removed. Some destruction may have taken place before the irreparable damage wrought during the Cultural Revolution, perhaps during some earlier Islamic incursions.

The extent of recent injuries to the monastery can be judged when compared with the reconstruction of the complex illustrated in the *Records of Tho.ling* by Vitali and his team. This outstanding piece of research, 'Literary and Visual Reconstructions' of Toling was made from ancient texts, temple inventories and oral records from elder monks who had lived there. In the *lakhang* (chapel), murals survive in gloomy vaults and next to these exquisite old paintings are garish renovations, lustrous with recent oil paint. When you flash torchlight on the walls, you see vibrant colours.

'Don't these forms remind you of Indian-style miniature painting?' we asked one other.

'They do. They were commissioned by the monastery from Kashmiri and Kangra craftsmen, who were brought here from Ladakh.'

There has been some rather crude and amateurish renovation. So the grotesque travesty and the sublime original lie side by side. Whatever has remained untouched is still worth taking a long ride to Far West Tibet to see and savour.

This is the destination for the voyeur of Buddhist paintings. Even though I don't claim to be one, I was entranced by their flowing lines, colours, themes and excellence. It was a close peep into the world of 11th and 12th century monastic life and beliefs.

The *Du-kang* (Red Chapel) and the corridor of the *Lakhang Karpo* (White Chapel) were in better condition than the other dilapidated buildings in the complex. The forty-two original wooden pillars still remained in the *Lakhang Karpo*. The roof, lintels and walls were replete with motifs picked from the Buddhist texts and Indian myths. Dancing *apsaras* with round bosoms and pronounced abdomen, strong muscular men carrying heavy weights, people celebrating in gardens, a burial site with corpses and funeral pyres, hermits in prayer, musicians; nothing was omitted.

Detail and intricacy were the hallmark of these fine paintings. Ornaments worn by the dancers included anklets and armlets, necklaces, tiaras, earrings, bracelets and mob-chains going down to the shins. Birds, fish, lions and flowers embellished wooden frames. On one wall were images from the life of Sakyamuni Buddha and another had an almost perfect mural of Atisha.

'Do you know that Atisha did not wish to come to Tibet?'

'And yet he spent so many years of his life travelling and living here?'

'There is a lovely story about King Yeshe-O. He lost in war against a king, probably of Garhwal, and was imprisoned in a bid to collect a large ransom. When a ransom equal to his weight in gold was demanded for his release, Yeshe-O informed his nephew that he would rather the gold was used to invite the great Buddhist teacher Atisha to his land and build monasteries. Atisha, who had refused to go to other empires and great monasteries, recanted and arrived in Tsaparang when he heard this tale.'

'So that is how he arrived at the Toling Monastery and Buddhism further entrenched its roots in Tibet.'

I wondered how Atisha would have viewed his newly adopted home and prepared for adjustments. Bengal is less than twenty feet above sea level, thickly populated, lush and green. It has moderate temperatures throughout the year and has a heavy rainy season. In every possible way, this place was the opposite. Bengalis relish eating rice and fish and the Tibetan staple is meat and *sampa*!

The monastery shop had closed early because it was a weekend. But someone offered to call the Chinese official from the town. We sat by the ruins of an enormous denuded *chorten* in the courtyard and breathed in the aura of the past. I wondered if one of the reasons for the shift of power of the Tibetan kingdoms from the west to central Tibet had to do with the introduction of the practice of sending novices to central Tibet early in the 14th century.

A.H. Francke wrote, 'This arrangement was not only a death-blow to the Bonreligion [sic] of Ladakh, which probably had lingered on down to that time; it also meant the end of the ancient forms of Indian Buddhism, which had had their principal seats in the grand monasteries erected by the Kashmir emigrants. Individuality was stamped out, and Lhasa became the literary centre.' Could this perhaps also partly account for the waning influence of Toling?

The government caretaker arrived on his bicycle and graciously opened the shop. We were thus able to purchase copies of the Toling book, beautifully illustrated, but poorly written. The Tsaparang book was out of stock. I made a mental note to consult the Tsaparang and Toling section of the *Footprint: Tibet Handbook*, which, I understood from Medha, is detailed and reliable. Also, many overseas Tibetans consider it among the most authentic travel guides on the country.

The road stops at Tsaparang. Beyond are the Himalayas, less than forty kilometres away. The ghost city loomed up on the whitish grey horizon, a city of caves, carved out of a clay hill. The entire habitation was built around a peak, from the base to the pinnacle, with public and private rooms dug in. Steep staircases connected these. Even today, several of these rooms, constructed into the hillside, survive.

Within the apparently sombre empty enclosures, the warm colours of the wall paintings suddenly became visible in the flashlight. The contrast between the hot whitish world of the outside and the cool darkness of the inside was striking. Though well publicised, it still came as a surprise and left us astonished. The paintings on the walls of the chapels were in fairly good condition though statues had been wilfully and maliciously destroyed. The looters were more interested in the jewels and precious stones, which were stored in the core of the idols. Mercifully, the vibrant murals, made of natural dyes from minerals and vegetables, remain a valuable part of the cultural heritage of Tibet. As in Toling, the floral and animal motifs and the human forms had a strong resemblance to Kashmiri paintings.

As one looked around the quiet and unpopulated lands surrounding us, it was difficult to imagine that at one time this was the centre of the Guge kingdom, its capital city.

'It's so peaceful. Seems so unlikely that royalty, lay persons, monks and warriors lived here for centuries.'

'And that bloody massacres have taken place right at this site.'

There were no signs of the turbulent past. The Sutlej flowed gently in its deep valley and the citadel leaned peacefully on the grey peak, standing like a humungous anthill. A few huts at the foot of the hill had neat, fenced little orchards and gardens around them, giving the area a pastoral serenity quite unknown in this part of the world. Neither was there any trace of the Jesuit church that was built there by the Portuguese priest, Father Antonio del Andrade, and his companion, Brother Manuel Marques, who had arrived from Goa and established a mission in 1625.

It appears that the King of Guge, though initially displeased that mere mortals, not hardy traders or mendicants, had breached the protection of the Himalayas, was later willing to give them audience. Andrade and Marques had, in fact, undertaken a remarkable exploratory journey and stepped where no European had before them. They had approached the mountains from Haridwar in the summer of 1624, to cross the Himalayas over the Mana Pass at 18,390 feet, and approached Tsaparang along the banks of the Sutlej in August of the same year. They had travelled disguised as pilgrims.

A devout Buddhist and practising the religious tenets of debate, the King was glad to discuss Christianity with Andrade. He was impressed enough by the priest to give him protection and to permit him to evangelise in his kingdom. Andrade returned at the end of 1624, to Agra, along with two Tibetan boys. Andrade was probably an exceptional man, for he was given the following document by the King:

'We, the King of the Kingdoms of Potente [Butan: Tibet], rejoicing at the arrival in our lands of Padre Antonio Franguim to teach us a holy law, take him for our Chief Lama and give him full authority to teach the holy law to our people. We shall not allow that anyone molest him in this, and we shall issue orders that he be given a site and all the help needed to build a house of prayer. Moreover, we shall give no credence to any malicious accusations of the Moors against Padres, because we know that, as they have no law [religion] they oppose those who follow the truth. We earnestly desire the great Padre [the Provincial of Goa] to send us at once the said Padre Antonio that he may be of assistance to our peoples.

'Given at Chaparangue [Tsaparang], etc.'

At the end of 1625, Andrade returned once more to Tsaparang, over the Himalayas, having won support from his superiors in his efforts

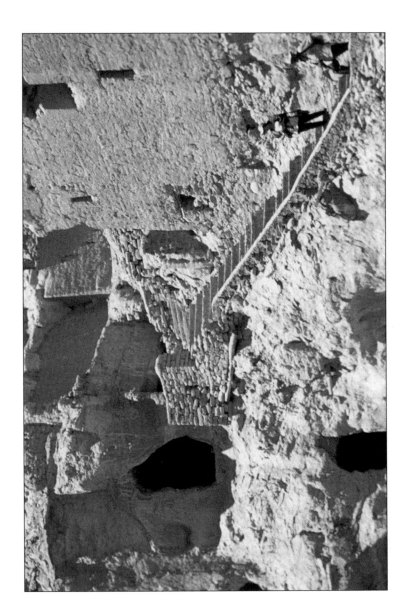

Tsaparang, a deserted city on an isolated bill, on the southern bank of tbe Sutlej.

to establish a mission at Tsaparang. He was sent three missionaries at Tsaparang the following year. A church, complete with altar, bell and wooden cross, was constructed at the foot of the fortress. On Easter Day in 1626, the King himself founded the first Christian church in Tibet.

Although Andrade's work brought fame and he was invited to meet the Kings of Ladakh and Utsang, he did not similarly succeed in conversions. By the end of 1627, he had only twelve baptisms. Andrade left four years later, called back to Goa to a higher position around 1630, leaving Marques to run the mission.

The King's support of the Christians did not please his subjects, while his brother, the Head Lama, spearheaded a revolt against him at the end of 1630 for openly encouraging the Jesuits to preach and collect their 'harvest of heathens'. Describing the revolt, Andrade wrote from Goa in 1633, 'the storm broke out during a protracted illness of the king'. First some vassals rose in revolt, then powerful military commanders rebelled with the support of the King of Ladakh. The hapless king, after being under siege for a month, was tricked into surrender. He was imprisoned and carried off to Leh. The Muslim military commander appointed by Leh was particularly ill-disposed towards the four missionaries there at the time of the revolt. The church and mission building were ransacked.

In 1635, six missionaries were sent to Tsaparang from Goa, under Father Coresma, to see the condition of the mission. Of the journey, Coresma later reported: 'Of my six companions, only one reached Chaparangue [Tsaparang] with me. Two died on the way, and the other three became so ill that it would have been inhuman to have taken them further. . .' Of Tsaparang he wrote, 'Trees are entirely wanting, not only fruit trees, but even trees for firewood. There are no herbs to serve as food, only a little barley and corn. Supplies from Hindustan or Srinagar could only be obtained at prohibitive cost; the carriage of a quantity of rice bought for one rupee at Srinagar is ten or twelve rupees, as everything has to be carried along the passes.'

Though Coresma was not popular with the Church for having disbanded the Tsaparang mission in May 1636, his letters were an interesting window to life in Tsaparang. About population and conscription he wrote, 'The population is very small... It is impossible to assemble 2,000 warriors, though all are obliged to serve from their eighteenth to their eightieth year. The others are lamas... In this town, the residence of the king, the mercantile emporium for the whole country, it is impossible to count up more than 500 inhabitants, of whom a hundred are slaves of the rajahs . . . they are very poor and uncivilized . . . There is not a shadow of any religious sense; they only frequent their temples to eat and drink.'

Once more we debated amongst ourselves at length about the possibility of Shangri-La having been somewhere in the vicinity. Each of us had a view on the matter based on which books we had read.

'Have you read Charles Allen's *A Mountain in Tibet?*' asked Anita of Rock.

'No. Is the 'mountain' Tsaparang or Kailash?' he enquired.

'Obviously Kailash. But the book has an account of Tsaparang,' answered Anita.

'In *The-Search for Shangri-La*, Allen describes the upper Sutlej Valley and also the Lost Guge Kingdom,' commented Medha.

'Does he find Shangri-La?'

'Almost. He thinks he reached within a day's walk, but had to return after running out of time and money.'

'That book was my first introduction to the Guge Kingdom and Tsaparang!' I admitted.

'It's no help that I cannot read Tibetan. . .' rued Anita.

'But there are many English works of early travellers, like G.M. Young's "Tsaparang and Toling,"' I added.

'True, but their perspective is Western,' pointed Anita.

The Sutlej flows quietly at the foot of the hill and the only remnants of the past are the few *lakhang*, the Winter Palace, several almost vertical flights of stairs and some empty chambers. Lama Govinda and Li Gotami had catalogued the murals of the *lakhang* of Tsaparang in 1949-50. But several have since been destroyed.

The notice 'No Photo', prominently displayed, was easily ignored. The restriction was ignored quite simply by the easiest means known: illegal gratification. This was the most rapid-fire bribing operation ever conducted in two different languages, with little intervention by the translator. It began by a pretty straightforward offer from the caretaker for us to consider. He offered, 'You can take photographs for $20 per camera for five minutes.'

'He no look five minute,' Pema clarified.

Counter offer was made, '$10 per camera.'

'*Nando*,' he said, very firmly. He made a fresh offer, 'Total $40 for all cameras. Time 15-minute.'

We accepted conditionally. 'Okay. Provided all *lakhang* are included.'

'No, impossible,' said the caretaker. 'Cannot take photo of all chapel. School children coming soon for excursion. Only one chapel.'

'Okay, then $30 for all cameras and one chapel only.'

'Okay,' he said. But we were routinely being outperformed in bargaining. 'Hurry, children climbing stairs and here in minutes.'

The guide was engaged in conversation outside with the caretaker, while we photographed *Lakhang Karpo*, the White Chapel. There were two enormous protector deities on either side of the entrance, inside the chapel. These beautiful figures with wrathful scowls and horrendous fangs have been broken and the treasures from within stolen.

All the walls and roofs have beautiful murals in the *tantric* Buddhist style. But very few paintings were, in fact, photographed because one required a flashlight to see the paintings in this unlit gloom. Besides, more than photographing, one really wanted to soak in the ambience of the *Lakhang* and enjoy the beauty of the paintings on all the four walls and also on the roof above. The room was small enough for one to feel

A mural seen inside Tsaparang cave.

confined but the motifs on the walls were gorgeously extravagant. The trees in the paintings were heavy with leaves and flowers and the women are distinctly Indian with voluptuous full figures.

Just when we thought our feet must now give up climbing and rest, or that it was pointless to climb against gravity higher and higher to see more wall paintings of similar genre, we reached a tunnel cut through the clay mountain. This was the magical moment. Beyond the tunnel lay the hidden fresh water springs, secret hiding places and the path that connected to the king's protected Winter Palace at the pinnacle of the seemingly impregnable fortress. Part of the palace was dug into the mountain to protect it from chilly winter winds.

'It is where the last king remained barricaded from the Muslim mercenaries from Baltistan sent by the King of Ladakh.'

'He was besieged for more than a month.'

'Till they were all killed.'

'But I thought there were secret escape tunnels. . .'

'And also regular supply of drinking water from hidden springs?'

'Regrettably, the invaders decided to kill fifty citizens a day outside the gates of the fortress if the young king did not surrender. So he asked to be exiled.'

'This was a ploy beyond his imagination. When he appeared with his queen and supporters to surrender, they were all beheaded and killed.'

'That is one version of the happenings. The other was that the king was imprisoned and taken to Leh. It's not clear what happened to the warriors and other supporters.'

'You see those caves?' asked the guide.

'Yes. But why are they at an angle?'

'These were prisons. One for men, one for women,' said the guide. 'You can see skeletons without heads inside.'

All the king's nobility and glory was not enough to ensure the perpetual rule of the kingdom, which is now lost in the annals of Tibetan history. As we walked down the stairs, we passed the school children climbing up, seemingly not subject to the laws of gravity. They were full of energy and jumped up the steps.

The caretaker informed us that the book on Tsaparang, a government publication, was out of stock, but we would find it in Toling. In the meantime, he offered us some ghastly lurid *tankha* painted by himself, conspicuously featuring deities and mandala.

Tsaparang and Toling may someday become thriving tourist destinations, if they are connected by air to Lhasa, Kathmandu and Leh. It can be said with certainty the world would delight in the distinctiveness of their landscape and the history of their old civilization. But now the difficulty of approaching this remote place discourages tourists who visit more accessible areas of Tibet. Very few people get to see this heritage, quite distinct from the monasteries further east.

Tsaparang and Toling are the symbols of the Buddhist past of Western Tibet: one the political capital of a flourishing kingdom and the other a centre of religious revivalism in Tibet. Yet, on that date, July 6, the Dalai Lama's birthday, no one mentioned his name there. Tibetans all over the world sent greetings to His Holiness. There was widespread celebration and on that occasion He freely met visitors. But there was no celebration among the Buddhists in Tibet that day. The Dalai Lama, the 74th incarnation of Avalokeshavara and the 14th God-King of Tibet, was all but forgotten in the places of prayer and religion in the land of his birth.

We were advised by Pema not to be politically incorrect and put the Tibetans amongst us in trouble. It was as if the Dalai Lama had been erased from the firmament of Tibet's complex religious and cultural system. No one mentioned him, even when they knew that we were all ethnic Indians and that He had chosen to live in our midst. It was something the monks of Toling would not acknowledge. The fear of authority is deep-seated in the Tibetan psyche. We were mute observers to this in several monasteries on our journey through the land, starting from Lhasa in the east, traversing the Roof of the World and now having reached the westernmost part of the Tibet Autonomous Region.

I plucked leaves from three young trees planted along the road outside the monastery and put them inside my diary. When I look at them now, they are faded ash-green in colour. I feel that all our experiences in Tibet had been like the now-vanished Guge Kingdom — transient and faded. The impact of the harsh environment, the desolate countryside and brilliant colours within the chapels had a powerful sensory impact then.

Today, far away from it all, my memories as a traveller are softer and the outlines of the monastery and citadel are less sharp. But for those Tibetans who have left behind a home, a country and a way of life, these images must live on forever.

'So, do you think Tsaparang was Shangri-La?' asked Medha.

'Why do you ask? I thought we settled this earlier,' I answered.

'In favour of Tsaparang or old Khyunglung in the Garuda Valley?'

'I'll settle for near Tsaparang, not Tsaparang. . .' I said.

Vitali wrote in his scholarly work on Toling under the section, 'In the Surroundings of Tho.ling,' that several destroyed temples, in later times, were located 'on the slopes of the conglomerate Shing.sgra hill, which stands to the southwest of Tho.ling dgon.pa at a distance of a short horse ride.'

This was the same hill on which stood Nyima Gon's palace in the long past. From the hill, roads lead in the four directions. Later, according to historical texts, in the 11th century, a golden *chorten* was built on the hill and so was a new chapel, while at the foot of the hill was built Toling Monastery. Could this Shing.sgra hill then have been Shangri-La? It was not my intent to particularly solve this mystery of where Shangri-La could have been, but the thought was interesting. I smiled because I thought we had just left Shangri-La behind.

Back at our idyllic oasis at the centre of the clay and sandstone fortress, we prepared to bathe. The pool in the stream, identified by Rock on the previous day for bathing 'dusky maidens,' had dried. The water had disappeared into the rocky bed of the brook. Finally, we cooled ourselves in the shower tent, with cold water stored in a drum. The same drum in which the cans of beer were cooling.

Rock and I went off to explore the microenvironment of the oasis and the surrounding cliffs and hills. We had not seen the bearded vulture again, but we did see imprints of some large bird's foot in the mud by the stream. The microcosm of life in this treeless oasis was composed of grass — short and fecund by the brook, tall and coarse elsewhere, a few herbaceous plants, some birds, insects and rodents, but no people. We were intruders there. We saw some temporary shepherd's huts, although we saw no shepherd, yak or sheep. It was possible that the animals were kept in these huts during the long, cold winter months.

Anita and Medha, in the meantime, relaxed and gave themselves manicures. The nature walk ended in a minor tragedy. Rock tripped while crossing a ravine and his favourite Nikon camera fell and its lens cracked. He had another camera to take him through the journey, but he was heartbroken by the loss of his favourite apparatus.

It was now time to retrace our steps back home. We began our return journey. Looking back as we drove higher and away from Toling, I saw the textbook perfect levels of mud terraces. This area, clearly formed under the sea, would have seen at least five different phases of uplift. Mesas and buttes abounded, as did neatly stacked rock strata of loam, clay and conglomerate.

In some places, the clay was so fine that when the truck moved, it sent up clouds from its wheels before settling into a foot of superfine powder. Where the powdery clay had mixed with drops of rainwater and settled on darker soil, it formed a fine thin coating, with typical cracks of baked clay.

Change is slow in Far West Tibet. There is really little difference since the time, a century ago, when Sven Hedin had travelled on this high plain. The land and climate are so severe that there is not much that man can do to put it to productive use — except in small pockets, like the towns along the old Tasam Highway and the new military stations.

There are fewer shepherds here than further east. They must cover greater territories to feed their animals, making full use of the summer months. By the time we arrived, they had already visited and moved on. The nomads surely had sheep, as could be seen from the temporary structures along the valley floors and the droppings on the grassy patches. But we saw no sheep. Even in the markets of Zada, scoured by Pradip and Devi for fresh mutton, there was none for sale. We did, however, see small Rhode Island hens in a basket outside a grocery shop.

'Are there no yaks here?' I enquired.

'Too cold, too long. Too dry. No grass for many months,' explained Pema.

'There is just not enough to feed herds,' noted Rock.

'And they cannot transmigrate over long distances like the sheep, I guess.'

'Did you know that yaks are left outside even in the coldest months?' Pradip informed us. He added, 'If the snow is very deep, they cannot reach even dry grass to nibble at.'

'No wonder so many die.'

There was much mention of the black tents of nomads, but we only saw the white tents with royal blue appliqué designs. I understand the white tents are used in summer. It was in the southwestern parts of the country that we finally came across the black tents, from which the *dukpa* have got their name. And *dukpa* literally means dweller of a black tent, i.e., a shepherd.

At a nomad's tent, we stopped for lunch. Tsering wished to buy a sheep, but the deal fell through because the shepherd would not consider selling at less than Yuan 350. He had a big herd of sheep and goat, and a few yaks. We sat down for lunch, with the two sheep dogs watching.

An old lady brought a huge aluminum pan, a *degchi*, of curds and refused to take money for it. We appreciated the family's hospitality and were shown the shepherd's tiny grandchild, who was a few weeks old. The proud young mother brought the infant out for us to inspect. Children are very precious because infant mortality is high. It is not so much disease as the many months of cold, the rare atmosphere, and poor nutritional standards which are the real killers.

The young mother and I did not exchange words, but her eyes spoke to me. They said, 'This is the life that I have brought into this world. I am the mother and this is my child and between us is a very special bond.'

I looked at her and thought of my children when they were tiny. They were contented babies, soft to the touch and beautiful to watch. Their grandmother would suggest, 'Bring the children,' and then proceed to display them proudly to the visitors. She would always say, 'See, baby, your grandmother loves you most.' It became her greeting to the children. And I never had the courage to say, 'Baby, your mother loves you too!'

From the depth of my heart I wished this young woman would enjoy the natural rights of a mother, while the grandparents too would share in the bundle of joy. The meeting with the shepherd's family opened up a raw wound of many years. A wound which had healed over time as I had reconciled myself to others' idiosyncrasies.

The shepherd's wife had lined up about forty sheep for milking. They were tied flank to flank, in two rows, facing each other. I had never before seen this method of milking animals anywhere else. The animals stood absolutely still, anticipating the routine. The woman began milking at one end of the line, reaching out to the udder from the hind legs. She was through with one sheep in about a minute and immediately moved to the next. The process was very efficient. When travelling past nomads' camps, we saw lines of animals, still as statues, waiting to be milked.

Very high up in the sky was a lone vulture. It hovered above us for a long time and then disappeared. One of the dogs was old and limping. He kept himself at a distance from the herd. The younger dog, like most of the other sheep dogs we saw, had bountiful energy and matted hair. He displayed strong herding instincts by barking at the sheep that were wandering off from the camp. But these sheep dogs were a far cry from the ones that you see on farms in Western films. The old dog chewed at the food we gave him and watched the younger one listlessly.

Anita and I have pet dogs. We take pleasure in narrating the escapades of our dogs. Anita has two ancient Lhasa Apsos. They are shaggy and nervous little canines, ready to snap at your ankles if disturbed unexpectedly. She showers them with affection, and as far as I can remember, whenever I have visited her, I found them sitting on floor cushions in the sitting room. These are Anita's Koko and Kyushu.

I adopted Redd, a strapping muscular Boxer, when he was six-months-old. He immediately became popular with the neighbours and was an obsessive ball player. When he came to us, his name was Dredd. Shortly after he became one of our family, I returned home from work and found the house staff, who do not speak English, command him in the Queen's tongue, 'Dead Shit' (Dredd, sit).

The dog immediately obeyed, sat down on his hind legs and began drooling with an eye on the biscuit. With no time to lose, I rechristened him to the more pronounceable 'Redd.' We asked for the names of the shepherd dogs, but Tsering, after confirming with the shepherd, informed us that they had no names.

All the Points of Interest on our itinerary, except for Chung Tung, had now been visited. My companions seemed quite gratified that they had embarked on this expedition. But my personal mission was incomplete. The old 'outflow channel of the Sutlej' on the northwestern corner of Rakas Tal remained to be explored. What facts the survey of the area would reveal were still in the realms of the unknown. Could it perhaps throw up new problems? Would there be a logical explanation for what now appeared a reversed flow of the river there? The evidence together would provide a reasonable pointer to which of the alternate sources of the river could be the true source of the river Sutlej. Or would there always be two Lanchen Khambab?

11

SUTLEJ REVISITED

As we retraced our steps eastward, the Himalayas in the south were on our right and the Gang Te Se in the north to our left. Once more, we drove over enormous rolling plains, perhaps the most extensive high plain of golden yellow drying grass in the world. These we saw as far as our eyes went…. And that was very far indeed in such clear air. At the centre of the meadows of eternity was a signpost:

This was black humour, for there was no road, surfaced or otherwise. There were tyre marks encircling the signpost. I could imagine a sequence of events happening here. A strong wind blows, the post falls, someone fixes it again. Pointing incorrectly, of course.

We moved generally in the direction of Manasarovar, past the turn to Dunkar, an uninhabited town of caves, long since abandoned and forgotten by the world. Once again we met the solitary hitchhiker, whom we had seen earlier at Mayum La. He was the quintessential Johnny Walker who would keep walking. This time we stopped and spoke to him. He had been travelling from Harbin in Manchuria since 1998, and planned to continue to travel all over China till 2008.

The hitchhiker carried with him his 'Impossible Dream' album of pictures and showed us photographs of himself in Macau, Hong Kong, at the Potala and a sky burial site. He showed us the only photograph that I have ever seen of a vulture at very close quarters, in a spread-eagle disposition. It looked like a Himalayan Griffon vulture that inhabits the high mountains and plateaus. This photograph was probably taken at a charnel. Some beer and chocolates were passed on to the hitchhiker. Then we wished him good luck and moved on. This also happened to be the place where someone took the trick photograph that shows Dorji with three hands. This was unintentional, but the result turned out to be amusing.

A while later, as I was dozing off in the Cruiser, I had a vision. I saw a line of five men walking on air, each horizontally balancing in his hands a log about ten feet long. The men walked gracefully in a column, floating on air. When I focused my eyes on the apparition, I saw clearly that the men were gliding on an unseen surface, as if practising a balancing act on the high trapezium.

How effortlessly they carried their weight! Their hands were the fulcrum on which the heavy dead wood was balanced, so the kilos were spread equally and they felt no weight at all. I sat up straight and watched more intently. By now the column of men had come closer and I saw that they were indeed holding long tree trunks horizontally in their hands, but their feet were on the ground. A log would careen and dangerously tilt to one side even if a little bird sat on it. This was an unexpected sight, for there were no trees in that area and certainly there was no habitation.

From my position on the seat, I had not been able to see the men's legs earlier. The men were carrying tree trunks for telephone poles. We were familiar with metal telephone poles along roads at home. So I was surprised to see the telephone poles made of tree trunks. Through

Chinese initiative, the telephone network today is widespread. We noticed telephone lines laid across long distances. It is impressive that the remote corners of such a vast country have been wired up.

I had a plan. The plan was to reconnoitre the area between Dulchu *gompa* and the Rakas Tal. We drove along the left bank of the Sutlej. There was some disagreement among the Yindu regarding the prospective survey of this area. Everyone was exhausted and some were beginning to show signs of annoyance at the smallest instance. After having visited all the important places of 'tourist' and '*yatri*' interest, there was no excitement in seeing a few bogs.

There was no interest in any more places after the experience of Lhasa, Kailash, Manasarovar and Tsaparang. But my mind's canvas had yet to get the most important part of the painting tinged with colour. Pema was not pleased with my decision to drive up to Dulchu. Her chief concern was that the Chinese authorities would object, as it was not specifically mentioned in our Group Visa.

'Remember, we now have to drive up to Dulchu,' I reminded my companions.

'Chinese police say no,' said Pema.

'When did you ask them?' I asked, surprised.

'No, she did not ask. She means they will say no, if asked,' explained Medha.

'So let's not ask and go,' I said.

Rock and Anita tried to persuade me to navigate straight to camp.

'You've confirmed that water flows to Manasarovar from the hot springs at Chiu. We've seen it does not flow from Manas to Rakas Tal. So now there is no need to investigate further.'

'Let's go straight to camp,' suggested Rock.

But if we were to return to Delhi without seeing the Dulchu area, it would be an unmitigated disaster for me. I felt betrayed. I could not possibly return to Delhi without seeing this section of the Sutlej, surveying the Obscure Little Stream (OLS) and the confluence of the two.

Determining the true source of the river, the present Lanchen Khambab, was the underlying *raison d'etre* of my visit to Tibet. How could I return without even reasonably exploring the relevant areas for the purpose?

It was one thing to admire the basic tenets of the Middle Path that inspires one to reconcile to disappointments, sufferings and disasters in life; it was altogether another to actually practice it. I was ready to sit down and cry at the poignancy of the situation. I was so close to the goal and yet so far. It was Medha who understood that I would be devastated, if I were to return to Delhi without having the opportunity to personally check out the environs of Dulchu *gompa* and the streams nearby.

'Look, I'm more than prepared to accompany you. We'll take a Cruiser and go. Rock and Anita can take the other Cruiser to camp,' intervened Medha.

But Anita said, 'We can't separate and each go our own way!'

'So come.'

We drove through a narrow rapidly flowing stream for a short distance. Later, on reading a map of the area, I realised this was the Sutlej, just below the Dulchu *gompa*. The stream had cut a deep trench into the glacial till on the extreme south of the Barkha plain, south of the Kailash range. A group of five kiangs (wild asses) leapt past, as we forded the river and drove up the steep slope. Here we reached the most spectacularly beautiful rolling plain of moraine deposits. And somewhat by chance, came upon Lanchen Khambab, the *chu* and the rocky outcrop near it.

Dulchu *gompa* (14,820 feet), which was at the Lanchen Khambab, was not in operation. It had fallen into disuse. The Hindi-speaking monk, who had lived there for fifteen years, said that there was water in the stream all the year round though it froze in winter. The local boys, who helpfully identified the Lanchen Khambab and the *gompa* for me, corroborated this. The monastery had only a couple of monks and no prayer was held inside. There were no idols and images within the

A prayer flag marks Lanchen Khambab at Dulchu, the Tibetan people's traditional source of the Sutlej.

gompa, although we saw books of scriptures stored in cubbyholes along the walls. Carpenters were at work renovating the *gompa*.

The Lanchen Khambab was actually several slim water channels here and occupied an elongated depression between the hills. Glaciers probably formed this valley in the remote past. This shallow valley stood out in the landscape by its colour; an extravagant stroke of green on a grey-brown background. Clearly, the water from the surrounding areas collected here and the water table was very close to the surface.

The local people have encircled with boulders the point they consider is the source of the Sutlej and also marked it with a pole tied with a prayer flag on top. They accept this point as the true and traditional Lanchen Khambab, or source of the Elephant river. But if you look upstream from this point, you can clearly see that the stream's origin is further to the south, in the same valley.

We did not see any other rivers flow into the valley occupied by the Lanchen Khambab. So, the claim that the Lanchen Khambab here is connected to the Rakas Tal is incorrect. However, there was evidence of a dry streambed from the east, from the general direction of Rakas Tal. The monk said that this dry riverbed joined another stream that flowed from the Barkha plains into the northwest corner of Rakas Tal. This was just the kind of apparently inconsequential anecdotal evidence that I was looking for.

'I think I've found what I was looking for. Let's drive by this dry riverbed as far east towards Rakas Tal as possible,' I suggested.

'If you've found what you were looking for, why drive along this godforsaken dry riverbed? Look how full of pebbles this is,' said Anita.

'That's just the point. The river is dry at present but the round pebbles indicate they have been deposited here by a stream with substantial water in the past.'

'So?'

'This may have been the bed of the Sutlej, now dry and with no vegetation at all. The section that was once the *tso-lungba*,' I explained.

'Where did you get that?' asked Medha.

'One phrase hidden away in Pranavananda's book.'

'Wow! Let's go.'

'*Tso* is lake and *lungba* is a valley. So it was the valley connecting to the lake,' I surmised.

From Dulchu in the west, we drove by the dry river channel eastward. Then we reached the confluence with an OLS from the north on its north bank. I suspected this north-south OLS carried the round pebbles to the dry riverbed here, when it flowed westward into Lanchen Khambab. That was before it flowed eastward and into the Rakas Tal, as it does now. But more of that later.

We turned north along this OLS. Interestingly, this stream had a trickle flowing through it. The flow of the water was north to south and then the stream swerved eastwards and disappeared from our sight. We continued along the OLS northward, but we lost our way after a few kilometres.

We stopped at a tiny hamlet, Kore, to the northwest of Rakas Tal. There was a central *chorten* at the hamlet. Three young men came out to speak to us, but could not help on directions, for they were recent immigrants from Shigatse. They had come seeking employment at a monastery to carve wood. So we continued northward through the north-south riverbed till we could detect wheel marks on the Barkha plain. Here we turned east.

With renewed vigour, I launched upon the reconstruction of the whole sequence of natural events, which may have taken place leading up to the disruption of the flow of water from Rakas Tal to Lanchen Khambab at Dulchu *gompa*. The testimony was consistent. I indulged in a few moments of delicious fantasy of presenting my findings at the now famous Tuesday afternoon meetings of the Royal Geographic Society, just as Sven Hedin had. I even dreamt of informing the Asiatic Society in Kolkata about my 'discovery'. I pondered if people were still interested in mountains, rivers and lakes in remote lands. I wondered if uncompromising and inaccessible lands still lured men and women who were prepared to die, just to reach them.

Where does the Lanchen Khambab derive its waters from? Clearly not from Rakas Tal or Manasarovar, even though there was reason to believe that it may have in the past. So what were the sources of water for the Sutlej? I tend to select two important sources. The first would be the perennial springs on the mountains on the west of Rakas Tal. The waters from here flow down a broad though shallow channel right through the year. It is a wide grassy patch with a very high water table. Yak and sheep graze in this shallow trough. By this channel is Dulchu *gompa*. The source of the Sutlej is marked by a prayer flag in the centre of a garland of stones. Several narrow channels flow from here in the western direction and join to form a well-established riverbed, marking the southern limit of the Barkha plain. This is the Sutlej.

Another source of water is from the Gang Te Se (Kailash) range, to the west of Lha *chu*. By the time the Sutlej reaches Tirthapuri, several small and large streams bring water to it from the Kailash range. These are well-watered deep rivers fed by glaciers. These include the Chukta, Goyak, Trokposhar and Trokponup. Regrettably, I did not write down the names of all the other impressive rivers, although a teashop owner did mention them.

But the greatest volume of water comes from the Sutlej's tributary, the Lanchen Tsangpo. The confluence of this river with the Sutlej is a few kilometres below Tirthapuri. It is, in turn, fed by Himalayan glacial waters. Its many tributaries, including the Darma Yankti and Guni Yankti, bring a vast quantity of water to the river. In fact, the ancient Sanskrit name for the Sutlej, the Satadru, implied a river with a hundred streams. It probably referred to the numerous tributaries from the Himalayas; the section Indian pilgrims were most familiar with.

So, in the end, if evidence and logic were the main ingredients for scientific reasoning, then, I believe, most would root for the Dulchu channel to be awarded the 'Lanchen Khambab' status. But the source would not be at the shallow spring at the foot of Dulchu *gompa* marked by the flag, but a few kilometres further to the south along the same broad shallow valley. This valley is clearly recognisable.

But if someone were to propose that the Darma Yankti stream be given the honour of being the Lanchen Khambab, I would say that it could be considered, if volume was the only consideration. But as length of the primary headwater is also a criterion for award of this honour, it is my suggestion we go along with the traditional source. There can be no merit in adding further confusion to a complex situation.

Scientific discovery must be partial to evidence and logic, although it may pick up ideas from traditional belief. This was the principle I followed in tracing the source of the Sutlej.

Moorcroft and Hearsey, Gansser, Burrard, Hedin, Pranavananda and other eminent explorers, geologists and surveyors had all been read (Chapter 6) and their views on the source of this river were thoroughly studied.

Unfortunately, Strachey's map has not been seen. Using two reliable instruments, a magnetic compass and a wristwatch, he surveyed this area in 1846. Those were the best instruments he could inconspicuously carry north of the Himalayas and into the region of the lakes. He further refined maps of the area that were earlier surveyed and formed a part of the Indian Atlas. This map forms the source material, among others, for a compiled map of the area that is now a 'restricted' map in the possession of the Survey of India. I have not been successful in persuading my friends in the organisation to show it to me.

My conclusions were based on the observations that I have made in the field. No effort has been spared in following as much of the river as was possible. In the event, I am a little dismayed that inaccuracies have been recorded widely regarding the source of this river. It is astonishing that in this day and age, the source of a large river has proved to be so tantalising. Satellite images show riverbeds, but they cannot explain why a section of the river flows in the opposite direction to the traditionally accepted view. This is the case with the Sutlej.

S.R. Kashyap, who made geographical observations, wrote in 1929, 'Sir Sydney Burrard, considering the evidence available up to 1907, decided that year to include the lake basin of Manasarovar in the catchment area of the Sutlej. The evidence available since that date, . . . certainly confirms his conclusion.' I am convinced that this is not so today.

Today, the Ganga *chu* stream has little water and its link between the two lakes is tenuous. A marshy shore more than twenty-five metres wide along the lakefront and an outer pebbly beach of another twenty-five metres width blocks the confluence of Ganga *chu* with Manasarovar. The beach is approximately five feet high.

One could argue that subsoil water would seep into the Ganga *chu* from Manasarovar beyond this point. But there is no definitive proof to that effect. I have visited the Ganga *chu* on at least ten different occasions in the rainy period of July-August 2000, and the dry period of June-July 2002, to search for any signs of water in the shallow gravely channel between the Chiu *gompa* outcrop and Manasarovar, and found it dry.

Now to return to the river Sutlej. The traditionally accepted outflow from the northwest of Rakas Tal has long since dried up and any empirical evidence of the Sutlej flowing from there was not seen. But this river is marked on the northwest corner of Rakas Tal in many maps even today. This can only be the result of a myth perpetuated long enough to be accepted as reality. This outflow channel has been recorded as dry for at least a century and a half; certainly by Hearsey (1812), Ryder (1904), Hedin (1906-1908) and Pranavananda (1949), who have made detailed observations of the area, as mentioned in the Chapter Six, 'The Sutlej Conundrum.'

My own observations have indicated the presence of marshes and salt flats along the shores of the lake here, with some pools of water in the sand flats. In fact, the slope of the land and riverbed indicate the water along this channel should flow towards Rakas Tal from the northwest, as noticed by the Swiss geologist August Gansser years ago in 1938.

As field study ultimately confirmed, truth is indeed stranger than fiction. Irrespective of all the mystery invested by legend and tradition in the belief that Ganga *chu* connected the waters of Manasarovar to Rakas Tal, and that at one time these same waters flowed into the Sutlej, I know it is not so at present. I am certain of this on the basis of numerous and repeated empirical observations and logical reasoning. I have described the Ganga *chu* in detail earlier, but here I must document the most dramatic feature of the hydrography relating to the source of the Sutlej.

There was once upon a time a channel joining the northwest corner of Rakas Tal to Dulchu. Since the water level in the lake was higher than it is today, the water flowed along this artery westward from the lake to Dulchu *gompa*. As the water level of the Manasarovar too was higher than the Rakas Tal, the Ganga *chu* carried fresh water from the former to the latter. Along the way, tributaries from the north bore water and debris from the Kailash range into these two channels.

In time, the climate became drier, as evidenced by the shrinking of the surface of so many lakes and complete drying up of previously ephemeral streams. At the same time, the Himalayan range rose slowly but surely, including the areas immediately bordering its northern limits. This was also associated with the fall in the level of the water in the lakes.

'So is the source of the river at Gunglung glacier or Dulchu?' asked Rock.

'Dulchu, now.' I said, with confidence. 'I have a theory about the reversal of the flow of water in the *tso-lungba*.'

'And that is?'

'I'll explain it to you simply by drawing a series of diagrams on the sand. But till I go back and check those satellite images from ISRO (Indian Space Research Organisation), I cannot hold out the clinching evidence for the world to see.'

'Okay. I believe you have the clinching evidence. Just explain the reversal theory. It gets curiouser and curiouser.'

'I call the stream flowing south over the Barkha plain (west of Kore), the OLS.'

'What's that? What are you talking about?'

'Have patience. The OLS is the most important piece in this story. It is the Obscure Little Stream, linchpin in my theory.' I drew a line. 'This is figure one — the east-west *tso-lungba* channel and we are on its northern bank.'

'Go on.'

I drew a line perpendicular to the *tso-lungba*, 'This is the OLS. It joins the east-west *tso-lungba* channel on its northern bank.'

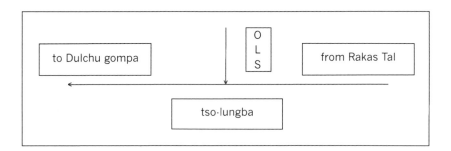

'How do you know?'

'We drove through both, remember?'

'If you say so,' Medha said, doubtfully. 'Go on.'

'Now, an important point is that the *tso-lungba* flowed from east to west, fed by waters from Rakas Tal, flowing to Dulchu.'

'I'll note that.'

'This OLS has deposited a substantial fan of gravel at the confluence with the *tso-lungba*.'

'Quite. We saw that too.'

'At some point in time, this little north-south OLS choked the east-west channel with gravel and sand. So, *tso-lungba* could not carry its waters to Dulchu anymore.' I separated the west arm of the inverted T and showed a dotted line for the dry west arm of the *tso-lungba*.

'This is figure three. The western part of *tso-lungba* is disconnected from the rest of the stream. East of the confluence, its flow is reversed and the waters go straight into Rakas Tal.' I drew an L-shaped line here.

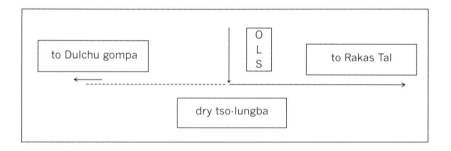

'Is it possible?'

'Has happened. The *tso-lungba* is beheaded now. Its head now flows eastwards to the Rakas Tal and is fed by waters of the OLS. From the point below the confluence with the OLS, the stream flowing west up to Dulchu has no water. It is biologically dead'

'Can a little rivulet sever and turn the flow of another river?'

'Well, it got a fair bit of help from the lowering of the level of the lake.'

The pirated stream now forms the lower reaches of the stream that flows into Rakas Tal from the northwest. It was the same stream that travellers claimed carried water out of Rakas Tal into the Sutlej, but August Gansser saw it flow into the lake.

'This form of piracy has been recorded for other rivers in some other parts of the world, you know. Because of the remoteness of Tibet and the sheer difficulty of accessing this particular point even by Tibet's notorious access standards, this exciting and unexpected event in geological history has remained unexplored and unrecorded. Now we have investigated it and I am almost certain the events happened as I explained them to you.'

If it were not for the fact that two completely different sets of headwaters were marked as the alternate sources of the Sutlej on a map, my curiosity about the more probable source of the river would never have awakened. Perhaps there was a divine hand in guiding me to this particular map, for without that happening, my long adventure in tracing the source of the Sutlej would not have begun.

ISRO had contributed two satellite images towards the study of the sources of the Sutlej. The particular image of interest is Path 99, Row 49 of July 21, 2001. One look at it later was enough to clearly show the east-west *tso-lungba* riverbed joining northwest Rakas Tal and the Lanchen Khambab at Dulchu *gompa*.

A huge gravel fan had formed at the confluence of the north-south stream (the OLS) and the *tso-lungba*. Another striking feature was the character of the east-west stream. To the west of the fan it was dry, while to the east it showed signs of surface water, as did the OLS. These points were critically important in supporting my understanding of the nature of surface hydrography in this area and identifying the true source of the Sutlej.

This was my 'vision of visions that heals the blindness of the sight'. No other words could better express my feelings than this line from Anthony Powell's *Dance to the Music of Time*. The evidence struck my confused mind with electrifying clarity. I saw the landscape and streams of the area with new eyes. At least for the moment, I had the answer to the mystery of the two sources of the Sutlej. I had a logical, reasonable explanation for the complex ground situation. The very next minute I was mortified that some upstart graduate researcher would disprove my theory. I said, 'So be it, but let the world know of my explanation too.'

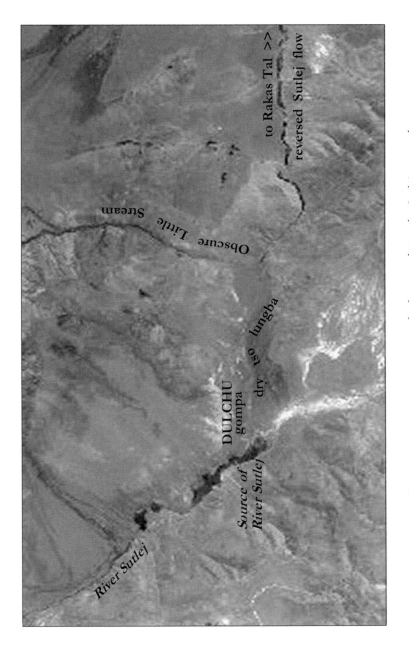

This satellite image, courtesy ISRO, was the key to solving the Sutlej conundrum.

I would have considered this theory suggested by anyone else as wild and unreliable. It would not have occurred to me had I not visited the spot and also pondered on several facts for two years. First, the stream northwest of Rakas Tal (shown on some maps as the Sutlej) was mostly dry and actually trickled into the Rakas Tal when it did have water. Next, there was a wide dry stream from the bend of this river to the Dulchu *gompa*, but this river had no water. Further, Rakas Tal and Manasarovar were areas of inland drainage in an arid area. They formed the lowest points on the land's surface for great distances around. It was far easier to accept streams flowing into them than propound theories of mysterious unseen subterranean connections between the lakes and the river, to fall in line with accepted belief.

One may well ask, why did the stream flowing in from the north not join the Sutlej and remain as an ephemeral tributary, bringing waters from the Barkha plain? Why did it end up cutting the east-west Sutlej channel into two parts and completely reverse and divert the eastern shorter section?

Here one must take into consideration the changing nature of the physical world. This is a geologically active area as indicated by thermal springs and earthquakes. The rise of the Himalayas, documented and accepted, has also affected the rivers in its proximity — certainly the Sutlej. Deposition of impressive amounts of moraine and sand has interfered with natural flows and new channels have been established. Raised beaches, incised meanders, and paired terraces of banks on the sides of entrenched streams tell a story of adjustments to rising land.

Climatic changes too are taking place. On the whole, it appears that there is a phase of 'drying' presently on. Water levels in the large lakes are lower, and many little streams appear to occupy unnaturally large valleys. Several streams have disappeared permanently or dried temporarily in sections.

Burrard's conclusion that the alternate source of the Sutlej could be traced to the southeast of Manasarovar at Ganglung glacier was probably unquestionable in 1908. But the geomorphology of the area has changed considerably since. Today, it is very unlikely that the waters flowing from the Gunglung glacier and from the Gurla Mandhata to Manasarovar, reach beyond the lake.

There is a view that every few years, new discoveries enable extension of knowledge. My understanding is that in the case of the Manasarovar region, this happens every half-a-century. Take the example of the last two centuries. Burrard wrote, 'The Manasarovar lake was surveyed by Henry Strachey in 1853, and his maps proved of great use for half-a-century until they were superseded by Colonel Ryder's admirable survey of 1904.'

By 1949, Swami Pranavananda had published his seminal work, *Kailas-Manasarovar*, which greatly added to factual information on the area. Another half-a-century and our group of inexpert but dedicated 'explorers' have contributed to the understanding of the source of the Sutlej.

In the end, one must accept that there is one eternal and universal truth of nature: it is that change is constant. The physical environment is as adept at changing as we are. It throws up mysteries for us to solve and we can only surmise with some level of uncertainty that we have answers to the questions nature proposes. All the necessary measurements of height, depth, geoid, position and flow can best be used to establish benchmarks for comparison over space and time — but what of explanations of how and why changes happen?

That fortunately is left to our ability to interpret facts, our understanding and our imagination. The adventure was in finding new answers to old questions; of seeing stones, rocks and mountains living their legends in the tradition of ancient religions. The fun was in peeling off some of these myths to delve into prosaic reality. The years of filling up 'white patches' on maps are clearly over, but there are still many phenomena in the filled patches that are yet to be explained.

In my heart, I now know that pilgrimages are not made to places. Pilgrimages are made to ideas about places. You think about them, mull over them, toss them over in your mind, and after a long, long while you reach your destination. The spiritual upliftment occurs from coming face to face with the notion in your mind and the excitement of discovering, determining and knowing. Perhaps that was one way to feel the essence of *Om mani padme hum*, the crystal clear jewel (insight) in the many-faceted lotus (environment) that holds our world together.

I bent over rucksacks, windcheaters, water bottles and other sundry travel equipment piled high on the seat of the Land Cruiser to catch a last glimpse of the Lanchen Khambab watershed. Some of the most exciting bits of evidence supporting my theory were being left behind there. Who knows, in time, I may be back to study them again.

But for now, we must return home to consolidate all the data and document the findings. With a sense of satisfaction, I breathed in deep and long, filling my lungs with all the air that the thin atmosphere could spare and reluctantly blew out the rare commodity. Satisfied with my findings, I looked forward to the eastward journey across the Tibetan highlands to the plains of Nepal.

12

RETURN JOURNEY

There are so many layers of the past that one experiences on a journey across Tibet. There is the recent past in the memory of adults, a complex of harsh and traumatic events in the background of a dull slow attrition of a way of life under foreign occupation. The world got a glimpse into this reality through books written by Tibetans, like Palden Gyatso, who had personally experienced that life.

This period was preceded by the documented history of the country, reconstructed from texts, monuments, sculptures and paintings, the result of the perceptive work of scholars over the last many centuries. As one goes back in time, the factual content of that history is replaced by stories. From there on, till time immemorial is the history of imagination, derived from the oral transmission of legends and myths. But all that is predated by the most amazing geological past.

Tibet was born under a sea, the Tethys, at a time when the continents, as we know them today, did not exist. Later movements on the crust of the earth resulted in the formation of the Himalayas and the uplifting of the Tibetan plateau. These must have happened by slow evolution over long phases and catastrophic events in short phases. Through geological eons, many plants and animals would have flourished and become extinct.

But dig into the soil and rocks, and all the evidence is around for scientists to unearth the stories of the past. And as the hand of time moves on, it leaves little marks and scratches on the land. Sometimes they create patterns and we can make some sense of them. Sometimes, we are blind to them ... These were some stray thoughts that often came to my mind as we left Guge behind and traversed the plateau moving east.

The supplies truck was waiting at Darchen. People flocked around the filthy courtyards and dingy guesthouses, happily exchanging information on friends, who had passed through and the status of various trucks, which may have broken down on the plateau. It was a major restocking point for water and victuals. It was almost nine o'clock in the evening by the time we connected at the Barkha checkpoint, after fording several fast-flowing streams crisscrossing across the Barkha plain. When we reached the southwest corner of Rakas Tal, our destination for camp, the last rays of sunlight fell over the lake and long shadows followed as we walked along the beach.

Rock espied the carcass of a yak and was quite certain the Tibetans would refuse to camp there. As it happened, they did not see the carcass, hidden away from sight in the darkness, but they were very reluctant to camp there overnight. Rock suggested we consider another site for camp.

'It's too late. It is after sunset already. We'll camp here,' Medha insisted.

'You were very adamant about staying by Rakas Tal,' I commented later.

'I was only promoting variety in the choice of camping sites, because we had camped on the shores of Manasarovar on several occasions before,' was Medha's explanation.

'That's not how we deciphered your words. We thought you specifically wanted to be here.'

Night had descended on the lake by the time the kitchen tent was secured to the ground. The wind was strong and gusty, at times almost carrying us off our feet. It turned cold quickly and the wind bit into our faces. Pradip and Kumar marched off to the lake over a pebbly beach, about half a kilometre from the campsite, to collect water. The remaining staff set about pitching tents. The Yindu sat in the Cruiser, huddled and sipping brandy.

Rock had bought a bottle of Courvoisier at the Duty Free shop at Delhi airport — his contribution to the Group. All the others had made more down-market gifts of *achar*s, relishes, *poova*s, chocolates, dry fruit, etc., which we knew from past experience we would miss, as the meals became progressively monotonous and Spartan.

We had jealously guarded the bottle for the post-*kora* celebration. It had been protected by layers of clothes in my rucksack stored in the truck and bumped over hundreds of miles of dusty surface that went by the name of road, till we uncorked it on that last day by the lakes. We passed it around and sipped straight from the bottle to keep warm.

In the meantime, Rock went for a stroll around the camp, investigating the level of preparedness for dinner. He came back and said, 'I have news for you. Pema is blowing up a life-supporting oxygen pillow with her mouth, probably to rest her head on it for the night.'

This bit of news did not in the least agitate me. 'This has been my suspicion from the beginning.' I conjectured bicycle pumps had been put to action to inflate the oxygen pillows, in the first place.

Devi cooked some soup. But it smelt distinctly of petrol. This was probably the result of petrol leaking and spilling out of the drums stored in the truck and finding its way into a food bag. He discarded the soup and set about cooking some more. We waited hungrily and partook generously from the warm liquid in the bottle.

'You know, I think Lola would have truly enjoyed being at Tsaparang and Toling. She has such a feel for design, colour and form,' I commented to Anita.

'Yes, she would surely have appreciated the art. And so would have Mandy.'

'I had not seen pictures of those murals earlier. Perhaps Mandy and Lola had not either.'

'The murals do seem to be the best kept secret from tourists.'

'Not really. The works of Tucci, Gotami and Lama Govinda, documenting them, are well known. All the lovers of Buddhist art know of these works. Of course, they are not widely available.'

'What a pity!'

The night was chilly and the cutting wind made it worse. But the sky was brilliant. The Milky Way was suspended enticingly above our heads and it seemed all we needed to do to touch it was to stretch out our hands. It never stopped amazing me that 15,000 feet could make so much of a difference to the astronomical glitter. The stars had never twinkled quite so alluringly. My childhood memories prompted, 'Catch a falling star and put it in your pocket . . .'

In this wonderfully light and magnanimous state of mind, we shared popcorn and hot vegetable soup for dinner. The brandy was passed around many more times. Rock was distributing the Courvoisier to the staff, pouring it into their mugs of *chia*.

Anita objected vehemently, 'What are you doing? Don't do that.'

Medha reasoned, 'It will be wasted when mixed with the tea.'

I recall going for a stroll. The earth was pitch black but the sky was luminous. The air was very dry and I could almost feel it slicing into my lungs. I returned to the Cruiser to hear sobs. Medha instructed me, 'Give Anita a hug'. Anita was crying, shedding huge sorrowful tears, the drink having rendered her quite uninhibited.

I comforted and stroked her, but to no avail. Well after midnight, I entered my tent. My mind was absolutely clear and excited after the drive through the old channel of the Sutlej. I was very content with the findings earlier in the day. When I retired, Medha and Rock were still consoling Anita with profound words of solace.

The wind had fallen some time in the early hours and it was warm and still as we awakened to a new day. That morning the Tibetans refused to brush their teeth in the waters of the Rakas Tal. However, they found it suitable to relieve themselves in.

At dawn, Medha and I met by the shore of the lake. She complained, 'I think I have a minor hangover.'

At breakfast, Rock looked perfectly rested. Anita reported that she had retched all night and was suffering from a headache.

I had a good night's sleep, no doubt as a consequence of the soothing action of the superlatively smooth brandy. The others were inventive enough to claim that in the wee hours I had called out, 'Where is the Head (of the Sutlej)?'

For the last time on our expedition, we passed the gold mines on the isthmus between Rakas Tal and Manasarovar. The mining operations had extended very substantially in the last couple of years. There were no signs of the 'gold digging ants', but there were trucks and earthmovers. Water was still being pumped from Manasarovar to the mines.

All operations at the gold mines were in Chinese control. The administrative system that had beheaded the *dzongpa* for not stopping Mr. Drummond from taking a boat ride on the holy lake in the late 19th century, had just about tolerated Hedin's and Pranavananda's boat rides in the 20th century. It simply ignored the more invasive nature of attack on the lake's sanctity in the 21st century. Even the spirits of the lake had learnt to cope with the disturbance.

Tsering was unwell. He had a severe stomach ache and the drivers accused Rakas Tal of having cast an evil spell on him. It did not help to point out that he had not so much as sipped a drop of water from the lake. His discomfort was so obvious that I could hardly express my exasperation at Pema and the drivers for completely suspending all reasoning faculties. Rock took to the wheel of the Cruiser in place of Tsering, while we gave emergency medicines to the reluctant patient.

As in other parts of Far West Tibet, the road from Barkha to Paryang was unsurfaced. It was also dusty and often we waited for the truck with fear of it getting stuck in dry deep mud. Shortly after Hor Que, we stopped for a while by a stream full of fish. The stream was no more than a foot deep, but the current was strong and the water freezing. The fish were about a foot long. The truck arrived with the Nepalis, who were wildly excited about catching the fish. They jumped out of the truck and with great enthusiasm, waded into the stream. Actually, they were so noisy that the fish dispersed and fled in shoals.

In the meantime, the Tibetans had a little conference on the side and proclaimed that the fish could not be eaten as they were 'Kailash fish'. They pronounced the fish 'No good for Tibet Peoples'. Confidently, they claimed that the river had transported the fish there from Mount Kailash. Since that was quite possible, and we did not wish to hurt their cultural sentiments, the whole exercise was put to a halt. That quashed all our desire to eat grilled fish for dinner.

I had read somewhere that a traditional belief of the Tibetans was that the souls of the dead migrated into fish. I cannot vouch for the veracity of the statement but believe it could be the reason for most Tibetans not eating fish. I had assumed that the exclusion of fish from their diet would have changed by now, especially with the Chinese influence, but I was clearly wrong.

A couple of hours later, Tsering felt better. He smiled while he drove. An abandoned channel of the Yarlung Tsangpo was the perfect picnic spot for lunch. We relaxed by the bank, watching the Tibetans relish a dried leg of lamb. We rolled up our trousers and cooled our feet in the shallow and calm river water. Tsering said, 'Less go' (let's go), which implied that he was now well.

Medha and I were in the Cruiser. Recently relocated from New York, she said that she expected her furniture to arrive soon in Delhi.

'What do you do when you get back?'

'I'm committed to writing a paper on Male Sexuality within a week of returning to Delhi,' she said. 'And you?'

'I get back to office and work my pants off. And this time write a travel book. A personal account of our expedition.'

'I plan to begin work as a psychoanalyst shortly.'

'Are you satisfied with your holiday?'

'Very. I am very happy and satisfied.' She had been looking for adventure, large spaces, doing the *kora* . . . and she got almost all of it. The epitome of singlemindedness, Medha planned to return and undertake eleven more outer *kora* of Kailash, before another attempt at the inner *kora*. 'I have invited Ruth and Flavio, the Swiss couple I met at the Thirteen Chortens, to visit me in Delhi and plan the next trip.'

Anita wondered aloud, 'What is Manosi writing?' She asked, 'May I read your journal?'

I replied lightly, 'You can apply and I will consider your request.' I regretted being flippant as soon as I saw Anita's face. Perhaps I should have said, 'Certainly.'

For the last few days, Anita had been smoking incessantly. She worried about her longtime family retainer having a nervous breakdown and had a sense of foreboding about the death of one of her pair of old dogs. An obsessive organiser, she spent many concentrated moments packing and repackaging her personal effects.

Rock and I went over to the Saga Telephone Office to call our families and inform them we planned to arrive a couple of days early. My daughter's response was, 'Ma, can't you come a few days later? I haven't a present ready for you.'

'Irrespective, my dear, I'm coming early.'

'What are you bringing me?'

'Some fossils and pebbles!'

Rock's mother had taken ill and was admitted to hospital. He was naturally concerned for her as she was eighty-three, and felt the need to be with his father at the earliest. He made several phone calls to ensure confirmed flight bookings from Kathmandu to Pune, where his parents lived.

Rock had not been physically well on the trip. He was less resistant to the subcontinental bacteria than we three women. He had lost some weight and suffered cramps and indigestion. He admitted to being tired that day. Yet his spirits had all along been high. The state of his stomach did not deter him from tasting the dried leg of lamb that the locals ate with relish.

Medha and Anita were partaking in the ritual of '*chia*' at the camp. They were also being entertained by a group of six schoolgirls and a little boy from the neighbouring village. The children clearly watched a great deal of television and had inculcated much from Hollywood and Bollywood, besides MTV and Channel V. They had perfected dance routines and could tap, stamp and sway in unison. Their leader turned out to be an excellent dancer and the three of them gave us a praiseworthy performance accompanied by music blaring from the truck's music system, while one child stood by bashfully. We joined the girls for a few steps but gave up quickly. And now we were panting even before we got into the rhythm of the dance.

I took the opportunity to get a quick look at the textbooks the children were carrying. They were clearly cheap productions for mass distribution. The books were all illustrated with line drawings of sheep, huts, books, mountains and items of everyday use. They were written in both the Chinese and Tibetan script. These were lucky children for they lived in permanent homes and could go to school. A little while later, a messenger from the village arrived and the children were recalled. They left together, clutching their books in their hands.

Tibet lives in two completely isolated worlds. The world of the towns where modern urban amenities, like telephone services, dispensaries, schools and rows of shops impress, and the Tibet of the countryside where time has stood still for centuries.

In the country, shepherds and nomads wander over a land eking a livelihood from the grasslands just as their forefathers had done. They have been less exposed to communism or the fruits of development than the urban population. Or perhaps, distances have made the enforcing of government regulations and modernisation see limited success. So, ancient Buddhism and Bon practices are widely prevalent still. People in the countryside live their lives in a quiet natural kind of way, in empathy with the powerful environment. As I looked at the mountains, I could see why the efforts to settle shepherds into sedentary communes had failed.

There were a few shepherds and many sheep near the campsite. The sheep climbed up to near-vertical gradients on the surrounding hills and nibbled away at clumps of grass. We collected water for the kitchen from a tiny brook nearby and picked up some Chengdu Dry Red wine from Saga, which we thoroughly enjoyed.

Our last dinner in camp was under the open sky. To mark the occasion, Devi produced an inspired meal, which we ate by candlelight in the dining tent. Later, all of us sat together in the kitchen tent, while the Nepalis sang. Pradip said, 'Some of us are planning to apply to a mountaineering club in the Appalachians in the U.S. for work.' While they discussed their future plans, Kuman, member of a rock music group, entertained us with songs. I particularly liked their lilting folk songs, the ones they called their trekking songs, the haunting *'Sim sim ma, pani ma. . .'* (It rains, gently. . .).

We started early in the morning to catch the Saga ferry across the Tsangpo. For the last time on the expedition, Tsering got out his spade and dug a grave in the ground to bury the remains of the visit to the camp. The two Land Cruisers, the truck, and all of us were loaded onto the ferry. The ferry was attached to a twisted steel cable that joined the two opposite banks of the river. The operators, men and women, adjusted the cable, so the ferry magically reached the other shore. Magically, because it was difficult to comprehend how the mechanism worked against the powerful current when there were no motors involved. I admired the genius and social commitment of *bodhisattva* Thang Stong Rgyal Po and his disciples, who had first conceived of the ferry at Saga. This crossing saved us about two hundred and fifty kilometres of driving on roads riddled with potholes.

It was a wonderful drive along the picturesque southern banks of the Tsangpo, through a territory that we had not seen before. On the right bank, we passed by a camp set up for foreign tourists. Their tents were the modern spacious and collapsible kind. But after this point, we hardly saw any human life till we reached the next guesthouse, several hours later. The Himalayas with its peaks swathed in snow were on our right. On a lucky day, one could get a view of the Shisha Pangma peak, but it was engulfed in clouds on the day we went by.

Our truck and Land Cruisers on the ferry crossing the Tsangpo at Saga.

The convoy stopped at Lalung La (17,056 feet). I looked back and caught a last glimpse of the Tibetan plateau, the desiccated high plain north of the Himalayas. Lalung La is a wide-open, undulating field here. The pass, like the others, was marked by prayer flags flapping away in the breeze. The windhorses were busily carrying messages up to heaven. The approach from the northern Tibetan side was gentle and the exit was winding and steep on the southern slope. We stood together as a group and took pictures of us with the Himalayas in the background. When I later saw the last picture of us taken in Tibet, I was almost jolted into accepting the nature of our group. Medha, Rock and Anita stood close together, leaning on each other. I stood slightly apart from them. All of us were smiling and we looked happy.

No other photograph of ours represented so accurately our relationship through the journey and later. My friends and companions communicate with each other often and I with them when I can. Our worlds now seldom overlap, but when we do meet, there is complete understanding between us. It is inherent in my nature to distance myself from the present and look at life through a kaleidoscope, as one who is not a part of it, even as I play an active role in it.

For the last time, we built a small cairn of stones on the pass and recited, '*Ki ki so so lha gyalo*' ('Victory to the gods'). Then the Cruisers began a dizzy nosedive downhill that ended on the valley floor at least a couple of thousand feet below. The valley floors were now emerald green and mustard yellow with crops. Past these, we entered the Nyalam Tsangpo Valley, and stopped only briefly to see the famous Buddhist shrine on the way south and down. This shrine is famous as one where Milarepa had once meditated.

The short halt there coincided with a wait to clear the debris from a landslide that blocked the Friendship Highway at this point. We drove through the deep trough, lush with green vegetation on the valley sides, completely enveloped in cloud. At one point, Tsering and Dorji stopped under a waterfall to give the Cruisers a thorough wash while we sat inside. By the time we reached Zhangmou, we had descended almost 10,000 feet from the pass. Anita, who had been to Guilin in China, said that this valley, with its dim light-thick cloud quality, was equally

From the mountain passes, we drop to the valleys carpeted with crops of mustard.

beautiful. We felt our eardrums pop and breathing became perceptibly easier, responding to the rapid drop in altitude.

Zhangmou Hotel is adjacent to the Immigration and Customs checkpoint. Zhangmou, like many other hill towns, has organically grown along one winding high street. The top floor of the hotel opened out onto this street. It was built several floors below street level, and overlooked the valley and mountains beyond. We checked into this hotel for the night.

I will remember the hotel for many reasons, including its copious running hot water that let us luxuriate in the first hot shower in the confines of a bathroom. As I shut my eyes, even today I can visualise the mountains, partly visible through a screen of bulging clouds, framed by the enormous glass windows. The scenery could almost have been the creation of a Chinese brush painter, drawing feathery lines on a scroll. Then there was the loud Hindi music we heard through the night from the popular nightclub upstairs. The disco was absolutely empty when we visited it at eleven o'clock. In Zhangmou, at that hour, the night was very young.

The South Indian coffee at the restaurant across from the hotel, recommended by the Indian gentleman returning from Kailash, lived up to its promise. Back in the hotel room, I surfed through the TV channels, but could find nothing to see in a language I understood. So I waited to reach Kathmandu before I would get to know the state of the nations and the world.

Although I had not craved for news of the outside world in the last month, that last night in Tibet I was disappointed at not being able to find a suitable news channel. In the end, I watched a rather touching Japanese film, where four young children, who were close friends, must ultimately part. I sighed, accepting that such was the way of life. But the account of surfing channels would not be complete if I failed to mention the last channel I watched. Fred Astaire, a classical entertainment figure of the West, tap-danced his way into the Chinese hearts speaking in Chinese. Could he ever have anticipated that it would be possible one day?

Next morning, we bade farewell to our Tibetan guide and drivers. It was not so much an emotional parting as a time for our expression of gratitude for their invaluable support and superb service. Standing in a queue at the checkpoint, Customs and Immigration formalities were quickly completed. I picked up some bottles of 'Coconut' drink to carry back home. The 'Coconut' here were lychee for some odd reason, and had been one of our favourite drinks on the journey. Lhasa Beer was another popular souvenir to bring back home. Although there were officials on both sides, there was a fair amount of 'friendly' movement of Chinese and Nepali people across the border. Our papers were scrutinised by the smartly uniformed mandarins. I requested an Exit stamp on my passport and was obliged with a 'chop' and a smile.

The Nepali staff accompanying us bought many inexpensive gifts for their families at the shops at the border. The most popular items were umbrellas, soft toys and artificial flowers, besides clothes. In routine officialese, we were instructed not to photograph the bridge, which was marked 'no man's land', or more literally could have been 'no one's river'. With equal nonchalance, we ignored the warning and got ourselves photographed on it, with a roaring muddy waterfall in the background.

And thereafter, we sauntered across the Friendship Bridge into Nepal.

AFTERWORD

It may be a somewhat trite and facile thought, but it occurs to me that what goes up, must come down. We had covered a distance of over 2,500 kilometres, trekked over two hundred kilometres at high altitude, reached a height of 18,600 feet and were lost to our world for several weeks. I have photographs electronically inscribed with dates to remind me that we had been away from home for ten weeks in all.

Months later, another World Cup was on. We were reclining in the comfort of sofas and watching cricket on television. Uneventful days and nights were rapidly diluting the intensity of the Far West Tibet experience. A friend asked me, 'If going to Mecca makes you a Haji, then going to Kailash makes you what?' 'A *yatri*' should have been the answer, but I could hardly lay claim to having been on a religious pilgrimage. As before, I was escaping from the familiar and known to look for the undefined, unknown. He suggested that I should be Manosi S. Hedinus or Manosi A. Neelum (with apologies to Sven Hedin and Alexandra David-Neel!).

I told myself that the results of the exploration were destined to be lost to humanity if I did not sit down and document the facts. I should also explain to the world why I concluded that there was only one source of the Sutlej today and it lay to the west of Rakas Tal. The river was no longer connected to the alternate source at the Gunglung glacier to the southeast of Manasarovar. But to refute the explorers, whose reputations have reached exalted levels, or even to suggest that the world has changed since their explorations, required some serious writing.

Two years after my second journey to Far West Tibet and the exploration of the headwaters of the Sutlej, I was ready to propound my theory on the nature of the source of the river. In the meantime, I became increasingly aware of the significant role the rivers now play in the political psyche of any country.

Media loquacity over the 'artificial' lake formed on the Pari *chu* stream, a tributary of the Spiti in Tibet, is a case in point. A landslide blocking the stream had formed a natural lake. In 2004, knowledge of this resulted in national anxiety in anticipation of disastrous flooding in the Spiti and Sutlej valleys, in case of a breach in the blockage. In the summer of 2005, when there were flash floods in the Sutlej Valley in Kinnaur, there was renewed interest in this lake. However, there appears little concern over the truly artificial lake on the Sutlej at Toling. The construction of the barrage at the gorge forms a reservoir on the river. Potentially, the volume of water in this dam would be tremendous, for the Himalayan streams that drain into the Sutlej above this point are voluminous. The release of water by China to India and Pakistan through the Sutlej is now subject to control from Toling. In the event of a breach of this barrage, it would have a catastrophic impact in the valley downstream. And no journalist seems aware of this possibility, or of the long-term impact of this structure on the hydrography of the Sutlej.

With neither the source nor the mouth of the Sutlej in India, the middle reaches of the river pass through the state of Himachal Pradesh. It is along this valley that the chief motorable road of the area is constructed. It is in this area that the steepest valley slopes are seen and the scariest roads wind below overhanging cliffs. At the point where the Sutlej enters India, cutting transversely across the Himalayas at Shipki La, the only road precariously clings to near-perpendicular valley slopes, hundreds of metres above the river. The most dramatic landscape is at the point the tributary Spiti joins the Sutlej on its right bank. It is well worth making a special trip to Kinnaur district to get a view of the river there. The river joins the Indus (Sindhu) in Pakistan, as its most important tributary.

As I complete my journal, I confess to a certain contentment in being able to present to the world a narrative of our journey to Tibet. True, there are numerous tomes on this remote region, some embellished with stunning photographs, some focusing on geopolitics and yet others on mysticism and culture. But my narrative is about ordinary people who have undertaken an extraordinary journey; an unlikely group of middle-aged persons, who finally learnt that it was truly a test, as much of nerves and the mind, as of physical endurance.

I am humbled in acknowledging that several of my observations have been made earlier by explorers of the 19th and 20th centuries. And certainly many of them travelled under far more difficult and strenuous conditions than we ever did. In comparison, we travelled in comfort and safety. In fact, Tibetans are law-abiding citizens and thieves and brigands did not ever confront us.

What did I learn on this expedition? At one level, I could say I have learnt the nature of the Sutlej, and have lain to rest centuries of uncertainties regarding its headwaters. In today's physioclimatic reality, Lanchen Khambab, the river that spouts from the Elephant's mouth, is near Dulchu *gompa*, northwest of Rakas Tal, and not at Gunglung glacier, southeast of Lake Manasarovar.

But what I have realised is that explorations are not made to places but to ideas. The sheer excitement of finding and knowing is as powerful as making a 'discovery'. Hedin filled large gaps of *terra incognita* on the map of Tibet, but we filled in tiny gaps of information. This, I hope, may one day become a part of the enormous body of collective knowledge of the Roof of the World.

At another level, we reaffirmed our earlier belief that Tibet truly is the amateur explorer's delight: beautiful, dangerous, unexplored and isolated. The dangers are not infectious diseases, crime and preying animals, but the psychological and physical impact of the extremes of Tibet's altitude, climate and vastness. Arguably, you could get lost on a long trek or run out of food, but the greatest challenges are health related: exhaustion, cold, HAS and hallucinations relating to isolation and distance from civilization. There is always room for debate in these matters of perception, and perceptions are invariably subjective.

The quest for Lhasa is still on. This time it is a quest not only by 'foreign devils' but also by Tibetans in refuge from their homeland. There are about one-and-a-half million Tibetans who are exiles, living in foreign lands. Of these, about two-thirds live in India. Most of them have never been to their homeland. When they hear that we have travelled there, they want to know where we have been, what it was like to be in Tibet.

An elderly Tibetan woman told me in India, 'That's where my mother lives. She's eighty-six and wants to see me once before she dies. I want to go, but it's so risky. I am a refugee. If I am caught in Tibet, the Chinese would put me in prison.'

There is another group actively in quest of Tibet, and especially central Tibet, which is easily accessible and comparatively urban. They are active Christian missionaries from the West in search of their 'harvest of heathens'. The focus is on evangelising to poor and single mothers. Apparently, the numbers of conversions are more encouraging now than they were for the early Jesuits. I am told that most Christian converts in Tibet are Han Chinese.

Exactly one hundred years after Francis Younghusband's military adventure on behalf of British India into the 'buffer state', independent India reaffirmed its view that the Tibet Autonomous Region was a part of the People's Republic of China. Lhasa's defence, political system and external affairs are completely under the control of China. It is a matter of time before their impact on the everyday lives of nomadic people in remote Far West Tibet is felt as powerfully as it is today in the east. Till then, the vastness of the landscape and the emptiness of the land of the yaks will continue to captivate and beckon us.

Mandy was correct in being wary of group dynamics under extreme stress. It is true that persons tend to make unprincipled decisions under these conditions. Although we experienced some anxious moments, we never reached levels of extreme stress. So, it was not surprising that we held on as a supportive and interdependent group. On return from their aborted trip to Tibet, Mandy, Ray and Lola went on a less stressful holiday to the south of India. Ray noticed the first signs of retreat of HAS twenty minutes after the airplane took off from Lhasa.

On our arrival at Delhi, Anita gave up smoking and was quickly enveloped in family, friends and work. Medha undertook several treks to Nepal in a span of a few months and was granted an audience with His Holiness, the Dalai Lama, at Dharamsala. Rock never quite found the Tibet he had imagined on reading the philosophical work of Robert Thurman, though he saw a great deal of Tibet. He went back to London, but returned to fulfill his promise to himself: the lazy, decadent holiday in the backwaters of Kerala.

Koko and Kiyushu are jealously guarding Anita's affections, while Redd is sadly lost to irreversible terminal disease. I combat lethargy and intermittently revise my narrative of our second foray to Far West Tibet.

More than any one of us on this expedition, Anita had the greatest desire for mental peace. In a strange way, the physical act of making an extremely difficult journey to leave Vir's worldly possessions and her father-in-law's ashes at Shivathsal on Kailash, nearest to God, absolved her of earthly attachments to them. It also helped her recover from the trauma of being left behind by her close friends.

I have often thought what Anita did were actions of legendary proportions, akin to mythical characters who undertake unbelievable feats for their loved ones, long after they have died and their bodies have disintegrated, because they still live on... Is it because you seek spiritual vibrations with the ones you can no longer see and hear? Is it because you renounce them to Shiva's care? I certainly don't know the answer. But Anita came back at peace with herself, energised in body and mind.

The physical stress Rock was subject to right through the expedition was barely bearable, but he reconciled himself to it while on the plateau. Constant awareness of bodily discomfort in some ways detracted from his enjoyment of the experience of Tibet. He did not find the spiritual fulfilment that he had believed was a guaranteed part of a journey to Kailash, a view that was reinforced from reading *Circling the Sacred Mountain*.

Rock honestly admitted, 'The spiritual uplifting that I feel on a walk in the afternoon through the English Downs is more than what I have experienced on the Tibetan highlands in these several weeks.' He enjoyed the scenery, took many beautiful pictures, but does not plan to return to Tibet.

Medha is committed to returning to Tibet and completing the unfinished travel through the desolate Chung Tung. For her, a journey through Tibet is an 'awesome' spiritual experience and her love for the mountains is ever increasing. Since our trip together, Medha has successfully attempted the outer *kora* once more and also completed the inner *kora* of Kailash. She has found the spiritual sustenance of life in the world of Shiva and Buddha and is willing to undergo tremendous hardships to follow the pilgrim's trail. She would be the one amongst us to circle the sacred mountain many more times, supporting herself on her Leki sticks, to add to the magic number of thirteen *kora*. Not for her the ease of hiding behind the mathematics of one *kora* in the Year of the Horse equals thirteen in other years!

I had childishly looked upon our first travel to Tibet in the year 2000 as, for want of a more appropriate term, a 'getaway.' It turned out to be an eye-opener. It was my first visit as a tourist to an occupied territory and I came back appalled by the realisation that the civilized nations of the world can and do ignore the state of affairs within Tibet. How little the world outside knew or cared about the systematic and widespread devastation of a culture and people, which had been taking place for so many long years. I had not gone seeking knowledge or experience of this aspect of Tibetan life, but having been there, it was so obvious.

Have I finally found what I set out for on that magical second journey? I say, 'Yes.' A loud, resounding, 'Yes.' I have an answer to the geographical mystery of the source of the Sutlej and I have no fear in trekking through the circle of life and death. I no longer need to flee the face of a man coughing and searching for the correct word for the idea that is haunting him. My dreams are of the same face, now smiling, eyes twinkling and conspiratorially whispering, 'I would smoke tobacco, if I could get some here, except that Shiva only stocks *ganja*.'

When I wipe my old faded map of Tibet, bits of brittle parchment disintegrate irretrievably into dust. The Tasam Highway, long since forgotten by the descendants of the brave messengers, warriors, spies, monks and travellers who walked on it, is invisible on my map. But it had once excited my imagination enough to journey east to west across the Tibetan plateau. The little inverted 'V' of Kailash had turned out to be a monumental pyramid of awe-inspiring proportions and beauty. It taught us the meaning of determination. The stylised drawings of the two lakes now speak to me of the unlimited possibility of adventure and discovery.

Would I go back to Far West Tibet? For an unabashed lover of empty mountain spaces, where else could I find the exaggerated hump on the surface of the earth, where you can look down onto the highest ranges in the world? Where else could I see a snow swirl on the pinnacle of a rocky prism, balancing like a smoke ring around a cigar? Where could I find legends more powerful than reality that would excite my mind to solve a geographical conundrum? Where could I still find lands un-explored and dangerous to wander into, that cartographers can even today label, *Here Be Dragons*!

Our yaks.

GLOSSARY

Term	Source	Meaning
achar	Indian	pickle
Amney Machen	Tibetan	a mythical rider in a felt hat, believed to have lived on the grasslands around Mount Amney Machen in northeast Tibet
apsara	Indian	beautiful heavenly maiden
atithi	Indian	guest
barchan	English/ Russian	crescent-shaped dune
barkhor	Tibetan	circular path around temple
bhasma	Indian	ash (usually used as a verb to state 'will become ash.')
bhurel	Indian	blue mountain sheep
bodhisattva	Tibetan	an enlightened person who delays Nirvana to serve people
Brobdingnag	English	an island in Jonathan Swift's 1726 book, *Gulliver's Travels*, where people were the size of giants
cha garam	Indian	Indian hot tea
chadar	Indian	shawl

chappal	Indian	slipper
charas	Indian	marijuana
chenpo	Tibetan	'the great'
chewra	Indian	flattened rice
chhang	Tibetan	beer
chhuba	Tibetan	long dress
chia	Tibetan	Tibetan tea
choli	Indian	blouse
Chomolangma	Tibetan	Tibetan name for Mount Everest; literally, 'Mother of the Universe'
chorten	Tibetan	stupa
chos	Tibetan	black dress worn by Bons
chu	Tibetan	rivulet, small stream
chuksum	Tibetan	thirteen
Chuksum Serdung	Tibetan	thirteen stupas built on a southern ledge of Mount Kailash; literally 'thirteen yellow *chortens*' (q.v.)
dakini	Indian	in Hinduism and Buddhism, 'thousands' of old, malignant, often semi- clad, demonesses
dal-bhat	Nepali	lentils and rice
damaru	Indian	small ritual drum
degchi	Indian	pan, usually a large pan without an extended handle
Dharma	Buddhist	the teachings of the Buddha
Dharma	Hindu	the essence of character or religion

dhoti	Indian	cotton wrap-around cloth worn by men
didi	Indian	older sister
doh	Tibetan	go away
Drolma	Tibetan	another name for Tara (q.v.)
dru	Indian	river
dukpa	Tibetan	shepherd; literally 'one who dwells in a black tent'
dung	Tibetan	another term for stupa
durban	Indian	gatekeeper
dzongpa	Tibetan	government official
firinghee	Indian	foreigner
Gang Te Se	Tibetan	mountain range to which Mount Kailash belongs
ganja	Indian	mild intoxicant from marijuana
Gayatri Mantra	Indian	special prayer passed down from guru to disciple
genetic source	English	implies the origin of, or beginning of, something, e.g., the genetic source of a river
gifu	Chinese	Chinese opera
Gita	Indian	a section of the epic *Mahabharata* (q.v.); discusses the meaning of life
gompa	Tibetan	monastery
guru	Tibetan	a teacher who leads one to enlightenment

'Har Har Mahadev'	Indian	'Hail Great Divinity.' Mahadev is another name of Shiva.
havan	Indian	ritual fire
Kalidasa	Indian	a famous poet and dramatist who wrote in classical Sanskrit
Kang Rinpoche	Tibetan	Mount Kailash
kasundi	Indian	a relish made of mustard
Khamp	Tibetan	an ethnic minority within Tibet
khatak	Tibetan	a scarf made of fine gauze-like material, usually white; widely used to greet people
khenpo	Tibetan	teacher
khorsum	Tibetan	province
'Ki ki so so lha lha gyalo.'	Tibetan	'Praise to the gods.'
kora	Tibetan	circumambulation
la	Tibetan	mountain pass, col
Lanchen Kambab	Tibetan	Tibetan name of the Sulej river; literally 'the river originating from the mouth of the Elephant,' or 'Elephant river'
'Lhaghya Lo'	Tibetan	short for *'Ki ki so so lha gyalo.'* (q.v.)
lakhang	Tibetan	chapel
lhamo	Tibetan	Tibetan opera
lochan	Tibetan	translator
lungba	Tibetan	valley

Mahabharata	Indian	a sacred epic, originally recorded in Sanskrit in about 200 B.C.
mandala	Tibetan	aid to prayer
manas	Indian	mind
mani-walls and mani-steps	Tibetan	low walls and steps constructed of flat pieces of rock on which the words of the Buddhist mantra *'Om mani padme hum'* are either etched or carved in relief
Mapam	Tibetan	Lake Manasarovar
Mastermoshai	Bengali	teacher, sir
maya	Indian	illusion
Meghdoot	Indian	literally, 'cloud messenger'; title of a classic Sanskrit poem written by the poet Kalidasa in the fourth century A.D.
mela	Indian	fair
momo	Tibetan	dumplings
naag	Indian	serpent
nando	Tibetan	no
nangkor	Tibetan	inner circular path within temple
Nataraj	Indian	Shiva, in his celestial dance avatar
Ngnari Giongar	Tibetan	Mount Kailash
Nirvana	Indian	release from cycle of birth, death and rebirth
'Om mani padme hum'	Tibetan	Buddhist mantra: 'Hail the jewel in the lotus.'

'Om Namah Shivaiah'	Indian	Hindu mantra: 'I pray to thee, Shiva.'
Pali	Indian	predominant literary language at the time of early Buddhism
Pandavas	Indian	in the epic *Mahabharata*, the five honourable sons of King Pandu, the ruler of Hastinapur, banished from their kingdom by their cousins, the Kauravas
pandit	Indian	scholar
Pankhi Raj Ghora	Bengali	king of the flying horses
parikrama	Indian	circumambulation
parvat	Indian	mountain
pret	Indian	departed soul
poova	Indian	savouries, snack
puja	Indian	prayer, worship
pujari	Indian	priest
puri	Indian	settlement, habitation
Rabyung	Tibetan	the Tibetan's sixty-year calendar cycle, which is subdivided into five twelve-year cycles
rakshasas	Indian	demons
reshmi	Indian	shining like silk
rha	Tibetan	yes
roti	Indian	bread made of wheat dough
sadhu	Indian	mendicant

Saga Dawa	Tibetan	annual festival celebrating the day of enlightenment of the Buddha; celebrated on the full moon in late May or early June
Sagarmata	Nepali	literally 'Mother of the Sea (of snow)'; Nepali name for Mount Everest
sal	Indian	tropical deciduous tree with large leaves
salwar-kameez	Indian	dress, loose pants and long shirt
samagri	Indian	worshipping material
sampa	Tibetan	roasted and powdered barley, a staple of the Tibetan diet
Santhal	Indian	tribal people of Chhotanagpur plateau
sardar	Indian	leader
sari	Indian	dress for Indian women worn by winding it around the body
sarovar	Indian	lake
sata	Indian	hundred
ser	Tibetan	yellow
shikhar	Indian	peak
shlokas	Indian	religious verses
'Soh, so, so'	Tibetan	short for *'Ki ki so so lha gyalo.'* (q.v.)
Ta-lo	Tibetan	Year of the Horse, the seventh year of the Tibetan twelve-year calendar subcycle (*see also* Rabyung)
tankha	Tibetan	painted religious scroll
tantric	Indian	one who practices black magic

Tara	Tibetan	Bodhisattva Tara, also known as Drolma, is known as the Saviour of the Tibetan people. People pray to her for protection and to grant wishes. She is depicted in green (signifying night) and also in white (signifying day).
tasam	Tibetan	stage post
tashi dalek	Tibetan	greeting
tattoo	Indian	pony
Tethys	Greek	the sea that existed between Laurasia and Gondwanaland in the Mesozoic era
Tirthankara	Indian	in Jainism, a person who has reached Enlightenment and is then free of the cycle of births and deaths
tsampa	Tibetan	dried and roasted barley
tso	Tibetan	lake
thukpa	Tibetan	boiled soup made of bits of meat and *sampa* (q.v.)
Urghien	Tibetan	Padmasambhava, Guru Rinpoche
vajra	Indian	thunderbolt, symbol of destruction of evil
vanaspati	Indian	vegetable oil
vats	Indian	disciple
yakpa	Tibetan	yakherd
yatri	Indian	pilgrim, traveller

yogini	Indian	in Hinduism and Buddhism, several great and small young female deities
Yuan	Chinese	currency; 1.00 U.S. dollar equals about 7.68 Yuan as we go to press

BIBLIOGRAPHY

Note: This Bibliography includes the editions consulted by the author. Many of these works are also available in American editions.

Allen, Charles. *A Mountain in Tibet*. Andre Deutsch Ltd., 1982.

Allen, Charles. *The Search for Shangri-La, A Journey into Tibetan History*. Abacus, 2000. (First published 1926.)

Barnett, Robbie. *Saving Tibet from "Satan's Grip": Present-day Missionary Activity in Tibet*. Christian Missionaries and Tibet, Lungta, Winter 1998.

Bell, Sir Charles. *Portrait of a Dalai Lama: The Life and Times of the Great Thirteenth*. Wisdom Publications, London, 1987. (First published 1946.)

Berry, Scott. *A Stranger in Tibet, The Adventures of a Zen Monk*. Indus, an imprint of HarperCollins Publishers India Pvt. Ltd., 1992.

Bowman, W.E. *The Ascent of Rum Doodle*. Pimlico, 2001. (First published 1956.)

Burrard, Colonel S.G. and H.H. Hayden. *A Sketch of the Geography and Geology of the Himalaya Mountains and Tibet*. Geodetic Branch, Survey of India, Dehra Dun, 1933. (First published 1908.)

Chattopadhyaya, Alaka. *Atisa and Tibet: Life and Works of Depamkara Srijnana in Relation to the History and Religion of Tibet*. (Reprint) 1999.

Das, Sarat Chandra. *Journey to Lhasa and Central Tibet*. Manjushri Publishing House, New Delhi, 1970. (First published 1899.)

Das, Sarat Chandra. *Indian Pandits in the Land of Snow*. Asian Educational Services, New Delhi, Madras, 1992. (First published 1893.)

Das, Sarat Chandra. *Tibetan-English Dictionary*. (First published 1902.)

David-Neel, Alexandra. *Magic and Mystery in Tibet*. HarperCollins Publishers India Pvt. Ltd., Fifth Impression, 2002.

David-Neel, Alexandra. *My Journey to Lhasa*. HarperCollins Publishers India Pvt. Ltd. (First published 1927.)

Dorje, Gyurme. *Footprint Tibet Handbook*. Footprint Handbooks, Bath, England.

Filippi, Filipo de, ed. *An Account of Tibet: The Travels of Ippolito Desideri 1712-1727*. Asian Educational Services, New Delhi, Madras, 1995.

Francke, A. H. *A History of Western Tibet, One of the Unknown Empires*. Motilal Banarsidass, Delhi, 1998. (First published 1907.)

French, Patrick. *Tibet: A Personal History of a Lost Land*. HarperCollins Publishers India, New Delhi, 2003.

Gotami, Li. *Tibet in Pictures*, 2 Vols., Dharma Publishers, Berkeley, 1979.

Govinda, Lama Angarika. *Foundations in Tibetan Mysticism: The Way of The White Clouds*. B.I. Publishers, New Delhi. Reprint 1977.

Gyatso, Palden. *Fire Under The Snow: Testimony of a Tibetan Prisoner*. The Harvill Press, London, 1997.

Harrer, Heinrich. *Seven Years in Tibet*. (First published 1953.)

Hedin, Sven. *My Life as an Explorer*. Asian Educational Services, New Delhi, Madras, 1998. (First published 1926.)

Hedin, Sven. *Trans-Himalayas: Discoveries and Adventures in Tibet, Vol. I, II, III*. Asian Educational Services, New Delhi, Madras, 1999. (First published 1909.)

Heim, Arnold and August Gansser. *Throne of the Gods: An Account of the First Swiss Expedition to the Himalayas.* Macmillan Co., 1938.

Hopkirk, Peter. *Trespassers on the Roof of the World: The Race for Lhasa.* Oxford University Press, 1983. (First published 1982.)

Hilton, James. *Lost Horizon.* Book Faith India, Delhi, 1998. (First published 1933.)

Kashyap, S.R. *Some Geographical Observations in Western Tibet.* From the Journal and Proceedings, Asiatic Society of Bengal (New Series), Vol. XXV, No.1, 1929.

Kaul, Advaitavadini. *Buddhist Savants of Kashmir: Their Contribution Abroad.* Utpal Publications, Srinagar, Kashmir, 1987.

Kawaguchi, Ekai. *Three Years in Tibet.* (Originally published 1909.)

Knight, G.E.O. *Intimate Glimpses of Mysterious Tibet and Neighbouring Countries.* (Reprint 1992.) (First published in London in 1930.)

Landor, A. Henry Savage. *In the Forbidden Land.* Harper and Brothers, New York, 1898.

Landor, A. Henry Savage. *Everywhere: The Memoirs of an Explorer.* Frederick A. Stokes Co., New York, 1924.

Lazar, Edward, ed. *Tibet: The Issue is Independence: Tibetans-in-Exile Address the Key Tibetan Issue the World Avoids.* 1998.

MacDonald, David. *Twenty Years in Tibet.* Vintage Books. First published 1932.

Maraini, Fosco. *Secret Tibet.* The Harvill Press, London, 2000. (First published 1951.)

Markham, Clements R., ed. *Narratives of the Mission of George Bogle to Tibet and of the Journey of Thomas Manning to Lhasa.* Reprint 1999. (Originally published in London in 1876.)

Martin, Williams S. *A Bibliographic Essay on American Missionaries to the Tibetans Prior to 1950.* Christian Missionaries and Tibet, Lungta, Winter 1998.

Mayhew, Bradley, John Vincent Bellezza, Tony Wheeler, Chris Taylor. *Tibet,* 4th edition, Lonely Planet Publications, Australia, 1999. (First published 1986.)

Middleton, Ruth. *Alexandra David-Neel: Portrait of an Adventurer.* Shambhala South Asia Editions, 2004. (First published 1989.)

Moorcroft, William and Hyder Jung Hearsey. 1812.

Moorcroft, William and Hyder Jung Hearsey. *Asiatic Researches* Vol. XXII, 1818.

Norbu, Dawa. *Tibet: The Road Ahead.* HarperCollins Publishers India Pvt. Ltd, New Delhi, 1997.

Norbu, Jamyang. "The Wandering Goddess: Sustaining the Spirit of Ache Lhamo in the exile Tibetan capital" in *Lungta #15: The Singing Mask: Echoes of Tibetan Opera,* Winter 2001.

Pranavananda, Swami. *Pilgrim's Companion to the Holy Kailas and Manasarovar.* Published for The Shri Kailas-Manasarovar Kshetra Central Committee, Almora, by Rai Sahib Ram Dayal Agarwala, Allahabad, India, 1938.

Pranavananda, Swami. *Kailas-Manasarovar.* Swami Pranavananda and Surya Print Process, New Delhi, April 1983. (First published June 1949.)

Rawlings, Capt. C.G. *Chorten and Iron Chain Suspension Bridge on the River Sutlej at Toling Gorge.* Royal Geographic Society Collection, PR/073416, 1904.

Rawat, Indra Singh. *Indian Explorers of the 19th Century,* Publications Division, Ministry of Information and Broadcasting, Government of India, New Delhi, 1973.

Rennel's Map of India. 1788. Showed two lakes draining into the river Ganges.

Rockhill, W.W. *The Land of the Lamas*. Pilgrims Publishing, Varanasi, Kathmandu, 2000. (First published 1881.)

Ryder, Col. C.H.D. Exploration and Survey: "Tibet Frontier Mission." *Geographical Journal* XXVI, 1905.

Seth, Vikram. *From Heaven Lake*. Peguin Books India, 1990. (First published 1983.)

Shastri, L. "The Fire Dragon Chos 'Khor" (1076 A.D.), in H. Krasser, M.T. Much, E. Steinkellner, H. Tauscher, eds., *Tibetan Studies*, Vol. II, (7th PLATS. Gratz, 1995), Verlag der Akademie der Osterreichischen Wissenschaften, Vienna, 1997.

Sherring, Charles A. *Western Tibet and the Borderland*. E. Arnold, London, 1906.

Strachey, Lieut. H. "Note on the Construction of Map of the British Himalayan Frontier in Kumaon and Garhwal." *Journal of the Asiatic Society of Bengal*, Vol. XVII, Part II, July-December, 1848.

Strachey, Capt. H. *Physical Geography of Western Tibet*. Asian Educational Services, New Delhi, Madras, 1995. (First published 1854.)

The Dalai Lama. *Freedom in Exile*. Abacus, 2002. (First published 1990.)

Thurman, Robert and Tad Wise. *Circling the Sacred Mountain: A Spiritual Adventure Through the Himalayas*. Bantam Books, March 1999.

Tsering, Tashi. "Reflections on Thang Stong Rgyal Po as the Founder of the a lce lha mo Tradition of Tibetan Performing Arts" in *Lungta #15: The Singing Mask: Echoes of Tibetan Opera*, Winter 2001.

Tucci, Giuseppe, with E. Ghersi. *Cronaca della missione scientifica Tucci nel Tibet occidentale* (1933), Reale Accademia d'Italia, Roma 1934; published in English under the title *Secrets of Tibet*, Cosmo Publishers, New Delhi. (Reprint 1996.)

Tucci, Giuseppe. *The Religions of Tibet*. Allied Publishers. Reprint. English translation 1980. (First published as "Die religionen Tibets" in *Die Religionen Tibets und der Mongolei.* Verlag W. Kohlhammer, Stuttgart, Germany, 1970.)

Tulku, Doboom. "The Lineage of the Panchen Lamas: A Brief History and Biographical Notes" in *Lungta #10: The Lives of the Panchen Lamas,* Winter 1996. Translated from the Tibetan by Thupten T. Rikey.

Vitali, Roberto. *The Kingdoms of Gu.ge Pu.hrang* According to mNga'.ris rgyal.rabs by Gu.ge mkhan.chen Ngag.dbang grags.pa, Tho.ling gtsug. lag.khang lo.gcig.stong 'khor.ba'I rjes dran.mdzad sgo'i go.sgrig tshogs. chung publishers, Dharamsala 1996.

Vitali, Roberto. *Records of Tho.Ling: A Literary and Visual Reconstruction of the 'Mother' Monastery in Guge.* High Asia, 1999.

Young, G.M. "A Journey to Toling and Tsaparang in Western Tibet." *Journal of the Punjab Historical Society,* Vol. VII, No. 2, 1918.

Younghusband, Francis. *India and Tibet.* Book Faith India, Delhi, 1998. (First published 1910.)

ABOUT THE AUTHOR

Born in Calcutta, Manosi Lahiri studied at the Universities of Calcutta, Delhi and London and holds a doctorate in Geography from Delhi University.  A pioneer in the field of geoinformatics and a consultant of international repute, Dr. Lahiri is the founder and Chief Executive Officer of ML Infomap, New Delhi, a geographic information technology company. She has contributed to several prestigious projects of the Government of India as well as a number of UN organisations. Digital map products and IT solutions developed by her company are widely used by corporations and research institutes.

Passionate about cartography, trekking and the survey of remote destinations, Dr. Lahiri has travelled extensively in Tibet and China. She is the author of the *Understanding Geography* series of three textbooks for Indian middle-schoolers, published by Oxford University Press India. Dr. Lahiri enjoys reading maps, novels, biographies and travelogues. She has two daughters and lives in Gurgaon, near New Delhi, India.

Other Books from

The Intrepid Traveler

The Intrepid Traveler publishes money-saving, horizon-expanding travel how-to and guidebooks dedicated to helping readers make travel an integral part of their lives.

Please check with your favorite bookstore for other Intrepid Traveler titles. Or visit our website:

www.IntrepidTraveler.com

where you will also find a complete catalog, travel articles from around the world, Internet travel resources, and more.

If you are interested in becoming a home-based travel agent, visit the Home-Based Travel Agent Resource Center at:

www.HomeTravelAgency.com